50 STRATEGIES FOR ACTIVE TEACHING

ENGAGING K–12 LEARNERS IN THE CLASSROOM

Andrea M. Guillaume
California State University, Fullerton

Ruth Helen Yopp
California State University, Fullerton

Hallie Kay Yopp
California State University, Fullerton

PEARSON

Merrill
Prentice Hall

Upper Saddle River, New Jersey
Columbus, Ohio

Library of Congress Cataloging-in-Publication Data

Guillaume, Andrea M.

  50 strategies for active teaching: Engaging K–12 learners in the classroom/Andrea M. Guillaume, Ruth Helen Yopp, Hallie Kay Yopp.

    p. cm.

  Includes bibliographical references.

  ISBN 0-13-219272-1 (pbk.)

 1. Teaching. 2. Learning. 3. Motivation in education. 4. Activity programs in education. I. Yopp, Ruth Helen. II. Yopp, Hallie Kay. III. Title. IV. Title: Fifty strategies for active teaching.

LB1025.3.G85 2007

371.102—dc22

                                               2006042807

Vice President and Executive Publisher: Jeffery W. Johnston
Executive Editor: Debra A. Stollenwerk
Assistant Development Editor: Daniel J. Richcreek
Editorial Assistant: Mary Morrill
Production Editor: Alexandrina Benedicto Wolf
Production Coordination: GGS Book Services
Design Coordinator: Diane C. Lorenzo
Cover Designer: Candace Rowley
Cover Image: Super Stock
Production Manager: Susan Hannahs
Director of Marketing: David Gesell
Senior Marketing Manager: Darcy Betts Prybella
Marketing Coordinator: Brian Mounts

This book was set in New Garamond by GGS Book Services. It was printed and bound by Banta Book Group. The cover was printed by Phoenix Color Corp.

Pearson Prentice Hall™ is a trademark of Pearson Education, Inc.
Pearson® is a registered trademark of Pearson plc
Prentice Hall® is a registered trademark of Pearson Education, Inc.
Merrill® is a registered trademark of Pearson Education, Inc.

Pearson Education Ltd.
Pearson Education Singapore Pte. Ltd.
Pearson Education Canada, Ltd.
Pearson Education—Japan

Pearson Education Australia Pty. Limited
Pearson Education North Asia Ltd.
Pearson Educación de Mexico, S.A. de C.V.
Pearson Education Malaysia Pte. Ltd.

10 9 8 7 6 5 4 3 2 1
ISBN 0-13-219272-1

To our families

▰ P R E F A C E

50 Strategies for Active Teaching: Engaging K–12 Learners in the Classroom is a practical text designed to help you, the classroom teacher, engage your students actively in their own learning. It presents powerful principles of active teaching, helps you select active teaching strategies and implement them across the curriculum, and provides advice on tailoring your teaching to your particular learners. As a result, students' motivation to learn increases, their learning is enhanced, and the teaching and learning process is more rewarding for all.

How Can This Book Help Me?

Current demands for increased student achievement—such as those fueled by the No Child Left Behind Act—place pressure on teachers and students alike as learners are expected to master *more* content *more* quickly and at *higher levels* than ever before. The effective teaching research of the 1980s and subsequent research make it clear that when students are *engaged* in the lesson, they are working toward lesson objectives and are more likely to learn. Fortunately, student engagement is in the teacher's hands. Each of us is responsible for providing lessons that ensure every student gets—and stays—actively involved in important learning. By implementing active teaching and learning strategies, we increase the participation rates in our lessons and heighten the probability that students will learn.

How Is This Book Organized?

50 Strategies for Active Teaching: Engaging K–12 Learners in the Classroom is organized in two parts. Part I, A Foundation for Active Teaching and Learning, presents principles for active teaching and gives advice for selecting and embedding strategies within the lessons you already teach. Part II, Strategies for Active Teaching and Learning, presents in plain language 50 strategies that can help you boost student engagement. The strategies are organized in five chapters based on the major purposes each strategy serves. Chapters include Strategies for Activating Prior Knowledge and Building a Purpose for Learning, Strategies for Encouraging Student Interaction, Strategies for Generating and Testing Hypotheses, Strategies for Organizing Information and Making Connections, and Strategies for Facilitating Rehearsal and Consolidation of Content. The text concludes with Teacher Resources Templates, which are also available on the accompanying CD.

How Are the Strategies Structured?

We love teaching. As classroom teachers in the public schools and as teacher educators, we are dedicated to the pursuit of lively, focused instruction. We have implemented many active teaching strategies (some of which we have developed ourselves) in a wide variety of classrooms and across a broad range of topics. As a result of our experience, we present each of the 50 strategies in brief, clear, and accessible language to help you implement each strategy smoothly and successfully. Each strategy is structured as follows:

1. **Brief description:** We describe the strategy and the purposes it serves. We include support from major theories and research.

2. **Preparation:** We list the steps you will need to follow before implementing the strategy.

3. **Implementation:** We give step-by-step directions for using the strategy in your classroom.

4. **Alternatives:** We give concrete suggestions for using the strategy in different ways, including ways to accommodate different learning needs.

5. **Time allotment:** We give estimates of how long the strategy will take, as well as factors that can affect timing.

6. **Examples:** For each strategy we give more than one sample use of the strategy. Samples span K–12 grade levels and include many that we have used or observed ourselves.

7. **Troubleshooting:** We give tips for implementing the strategy smoothly and avoiding potential pitfalls.

ACKNOWLEDGMENTS

We give our sincere thanks to the continuing enthusiasm and insights provided by our editors, Debbie Stollenwerk and Alex Wolf, at Merrill/Prentice Hall. We also appreciate input from Ben Stephen, also at Merrill, on the initial development of the text. The production team at Merrill/Prentice Hall deserves our appreciation, as does the team at GGS Book Services, led by Trish Finley. Finally, we are grateful for the input of numerous reviewers who added to the quality of the text. They include Sue R. Abegglen, Culver-Stockton College; Suellen Alfred, Tennessee Technological University; Debra Ambrosetti, California State University, Fullerton; Ronald J. Anderson, Texas A&M International University; Karen A. Bosch, Virginia Wesleyan College; Jioanna Carjuzaa, Linfield University; Wade A. Carpenter, Berry College; Grace Cho Choi, California State University, Fullerton; Sara Delano Moore; Amy P. Dietrich, The University of Memphis; Michele Wilson Kamens, Rider University; Cynthia G. Kruger, University of Massachusetts Dartmouth; Andrea McLoughlin, Long Island University; Gwen L. Rudney, University of Minnesota, Morris; and Marsha Savage, Santa Clara University.

Andrea M. Guillaume
Ruth Helen Yopp
Hallie Kay Yopp

◼ T E A C H E R   R E S O U R C E S   C D

The Teacher Resources CD contains 32 printable templates designed to help you implement selected strategies found in the text. These templates are also found at the end of this book. Templates are included for the following strategies:

CHAPTER 1

Appointment Clock and Log

CHAPTER 2

Figure 2.6   Sand Dollars

CHAPTER 3

Strategy 1   Quick Scans
Strategy 4   Idea Share
Strategy 5   Partner Share
Strategy 6   Group Graphs
Strategy 7   Overheard Quotes
Strategy 9   Important Words

CHAPTER 4

Strategy 11   Think-Pair-Share
Strategy 14   Make the Point
Strategy 19   Four Corners

CHAPTER 5

Strategy 23   Question Only
Strategy 25   Object-based Inquiry
Strategy 26   Problem-based Learning
Strategy 28   Photo Analysis
Photo 28.1   Family with Baby
Photo 28.2   Two Fire Workers
Strategy 29   Structured Decision Making

CHAPTER 6

Strategy 37   Give One, Get One
Strategy 38   Sticker Selection
Strategy 39   Treasure Hunts

CHAPTER 7

Strategy 43   Q & A Match
Strategy 46   Word Journal
Strategy 49   Found Poems

ABOUT THE AUTHORS

Andrea M. Guillaume (pictured left below) is Professor in the Department of Elementary and Bilingual Education at California State University, Fullerton. She began her active teaching journey as a public school teacher and continues that journey by working with preservice and practicing teachers at the university and in local schools. She writes numerous articles and books for teachers, exploring her professional interests in pedagogy, content area instruction, and teacher development.

Ruth Helen Yopp (pictured right below) is Professor in the Department of Elementary and Bilingual Education at California State University, Fullerton. She teaches preservice and graduate students, writes on topics of literacy and classroom teaching, and works closely with beginning and experienced teachers in the field through an induction program. She taught in the public schools for 10 years and was recipient of the Orange County (California) Teacher of the Year Award.

Hallie Kay Yopp (pictured center below) is Professor in the Department of Elementary and Bilingual Education at California State University, Fullerton, where she was named Outstanding Professor. She has written several texts for teachers, actively conducts research, and spends many hours in classrooms. She was a public school teacher in a bilingual setting before joining the university. Hallie and her coauthors engage in many collaborative adventures.

Teacher Preparation Classroom

TEACHER PREP

MERRILL PRENTICE HALL

See a demo at
www.prenhall.com/teacherprep/demo

Your Class. Their Careers. Our Future. Will Your Students Be Prepared?

We invite you to explore our new, innovative and engaging website and all that it has to offer you, your course, and tomorrow's educators! Organized around the major courses pre-service teachers take, the Teacher Preparation site provides media, student/teacher artifacts, strategies, research articles, and other resources to equip your students with the quality tools needed to excel in their courses and prepare them for their first classroom.

This ultimate on-line education resource is available at no cost, when packaged with a Merrill text, and will provide you and your students access to:

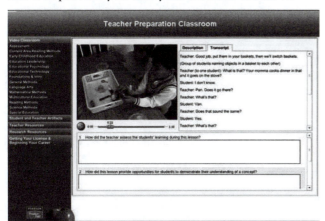

Online Video Library. More than 150 video clips—each tied to a course topic and framed by learning goals and Praxis-type questions—capture real teachers and students working in real classrooms, as well as in-depth interviews with both students and educators.

Student and Teacher Artifacts. More than 200 student and teacher classroom artifacts—each tied to a course topic and framed by learning goals and application questions—provide a wealth of materials and experiences to help make your study to become a professional teacher more concrete and hands-on.

Research Articles. Over 500 articles from ASCD's renowned journal *Educational Leadership*. The site also includes *Research Navigator*, a searchable database of additional educational journals.

Teaching Strategies. Over 500 strategies and lesson plans for you to use when you become a practicing professional.

Licensure and Career Tools. Resources devoted to helping you pass your licensure exam; learn standards, law, and public policies; plan a teaching portfolio; and succeed in your first year of teaching.

How to ORDER *Teacher Prep* for you and your students:

For students to receive a *Teacher Prep* Access Code with this text, instructors **must** provide a special value pack ISBN number on their textbook order form. To receive this special ISBN, please email: **Merrill.marketing@pearsoned.com** and provide the following information:

- Name and Affiliation
- Author/Title/Edition of Merrill text

Upon ordering *Teacher Prep* for their students, instructors will be given a lifetime *Teacher Prep* Access Code.

BRIEF CONTENTS

CONTENTS

I

A FOUNDATION FOR ACTIVE TEACHING AND LEARNING

SETTING THE CONTEXT FOR ACTIVE TEACHING STRATEGIES

This book provides a wealth of strategies that can enhance teaching and learning in your classroom. You have the highest probability of success with active teaching strategies if you understand the rationale behind them and can fit them into the bigger, more colorful, and highly textured picture of classroom teaching and learning as a complex endeavor. Decisions about active teaching strategies are rarely made in isolation; very rarely do teachers simply pick up a strategy and plop it into place. Instead, teachers select and implement active teaching strategies equipped with rich understandings of the classroom context where people, place, and purpose all matter very much; they select and use active teaching strategies as one important part of their professional knowledge and skills. Therefore, Chapter 1 provides step-by-step instructions that you can use to situate active teaching strategies within an ever richer repertoire of professional knowledge and skills.

ACTIVE TEACHING STEP BY STEP

Teacher effects research indicates that active teachers elicit larger achievement gains than do others by providing instruction with plenty of purposeful, content-centered interaction among teacher and students (Brophy & Good, 1986). What is active teaching? In our definition, **active teaching** *is an approach to instruction vigorously pursued by the teacher with full intention to improve student learning and student control over that learning. Active teaching is characterized by clear purposes and is based on what the teacher knows about her particular students and about human learning and motivation. Active teachers modify instruction based on learners' reactions and mastery of new information and manage their classrooms to maximize student success.* This far-reaching definition makes it clear that active teaching involves decisions made throughout each minute of the teaching day and year—long before the students enter the room and long after they head home. Step-by-step advice can assist you in building this context for active teaching:

Step 1   Answer the Question, "Why Am I Here?"

Step 2   Answer the Question, "What Are My Goals?"

Step 3   Answer the Question, "Who Are My Students?"

Step 4   Answer the Question, "How Can I Manage My Environment to Ensure Success?"

Step 5   Answer the Question, "How Can I Teach in Ways that Enhance Motivation and Learning?"

Step 6   Answer the Question, "Based on Feedback, What Shall I Do Next?"

Step 1: Answer the Question, "Why Am I Here?"

Every teacher has a particular philosophy, or vision, of teaching at its best. Some teachers see education predominantly as the transfer of discrete skills that are likely to apply directly in the workplace. Some teachers view it mainly as the development of powerful ways of thinking. Some see it chiefly as the exploration and attainment of the human potential inherent in each of us. Some view it principally as the mechanism for transforming society. Active teaching begins with an examination of your own philosophy, or vision, of teaching. Next, you can breathe life into your own vision of education by making conscious, thoughtful selections of instructional strategies. Although most strategies can be modified to meet a variety of visions, Figure 1.1 suggests some strategies from Part II that might be useful in realizing a few different visions of education.

In addition to overarching visions of education, teachers' personal preferences related to factors such as classroom noise level, messiness, and student movement also play a role in their teaching decisions. These personal preferences can serve as a starting point in selecting active teaching strategies that feel natural. However, it is also important to remember the potent role that every teacher plays as a filter. Based on his own preferences, a teacher screens learning activities so that students will have some experiences and will not have others. For example, if a teacher does not count himself as a dramatic type, he might steer clear from using Dramatizations and Tableaux (p. 212) and stick with strategies that more closely match his own perceived strengths or comfort areas. That choice, although safe, could have two unfortunate consequences. First, *students'* preferences are not necessarily their *teachers'* preferences, so students may be robbed of an opportunity to engage in a strategy that they would find enjoyable and meaningful. Second, avoiding the strategy limits students' opportunities to develop competence in a powerful manner of communicating ideas: dramatization.

Despite individual variation in style, active teachers are guided by a nearly single-minded pursuit: the pursuit of student learning. They know and act on the knowledge that they carry a heavy (and exciting!) burden of responsibility to ensure that learning

Vision of Education	Sample Strategies	
Skills (or Factual) Attainment	True-False Sorts Content Structures Note Checking Pairs Q & A Match	Jigsaw Geniuses and Super Inteligentes
Development of Thought Processes	Concept Attainment Inquiry Training List-Group-Label	Photo Analysis Overheard Quotes Structured Decision Making
Personal Exploration	Graffiti Board Four Corners Magnetic Quotes	Interactive Journals Snowballs Sticker Selection
Social Problem Solving	Object-based Inquiry Problem-based Learning Self-directed Learning	Up and Out

Figure 1.1   Sample Strategies Consistent with Various Visions of Education

occurs in their rooms. They are deeply committed to preparing and implementing lessons that allow every student to learn. They assume the onus of responsibility for assessing learning and modifying their instruction based on student performance. They realize that when students fail to learn, the teacher can almost always do something better. Long before you select strategies for any particular lesson, we suggest that you examine the guiding purpose you hold for the work you do. Why are you here? What is the one thing you must accomplish with your students?

As part of their vision of learning as the goal for teaching, active teachers are aware of their duty to help students recognize and fulfill their own responsibilities to learn. *Active teachers* view students as *active learners* and help students take responsibility for what and how they learn. They help students mature into assuming increasingly greater responsibility for their learning. Active teachers understand that, although they play an undeniable role in student learning, ultimately, learning resides in the students' control.

Teachers support students' growth into independent, active learners by helping them develop an appropriate locus of control. Research suggests that students with an internal locus of control tend to spend more time on homework and studying and receive better grades (Findley & Cooper, 1983). Although none of us can control all of the things that happen in our lives, active teachers help students to take ownership of the learning factors that they *can* control. An internal locus of control—the belief that our actions make a difference in outcomes—helps us to persist, even in the face of failure.

Active teaching strategies can support you in your efforts to help students realize that learning is caused by their efforts. When students know what they are expected to learn, see the purpose for learning it (Chapter 3), generate and test hypotheses (Chapter 5), and get feedback on their thinking and performance (Chapters 4 through 7), they can take ownership of their learning, redefining it as an active process that is under their control rather than as something that just happens. Figure 1.2 shares some specific factors and techniques that active teachers can employ to help students take control of their learning.

To take control of their learning, students need . . .	Active teachers can . . .
To know what they are expected to learn.	• Tell participants what they will learn and be able to do in the next 15 minutes, hour, today, or this year. • Display the agenda; number the items.
To see a purpose for what they are expected to learn.	• Surface students' own purposes for learning. • Allow student input into what they will learn. • Create buy-in and a sense of purpose by building a sense of importance of the topic. • Start a lesson with a real-life problem that showcases the content.
To build, test, and revise ideas related to the content at hand.	• Ask students to make early conjectures. • Allow students to revise their thinking when they receive more information. • Use inductive (or discovery learning) strategies.
To receive timely and accurate feedback on their learning and performance.	• Use frequent checks for understanding. • Use overt participation strategies where every student responds. • Use a variety of assessment techniques, such as observation, that allow for quick feedback. • Give specific (not just global) feedback on student performance. • Teach and use peer-assessment strategies. • Teach and use student self-assessment techniques.

Figure 1.2 Helping Students Take Control of Their Learning

Step 2: Answer the Question, "What Are My Goals?"

Active teachers hold a clear notion of what they want learners to learn, and they work diligently to help students learn it. Rather than planning lessons by thinking solely about *activities*, or things students will do throughout the lesson, active teachers are guided by a clear sense of what they expect students to learn. Active teachers think first about the *target*, not the *activity*. They start with the intended outcome, and they plan instruction that is likely to bring about that outcome.

To select goals for what students are to learn, teachers tap into two levels of content knowledge; the first is knowledge of the content domain. Students who work with teachers who possess higher levels of content expertise typically demonstrate higher levels of achievement (see, for example, Goldhaber & Brewer, 2000; National Center for Education Statistics, 2001a, 2001b). This is not surprising because teachers with content expertise are more likely to focus on relevant aspects of the content, anticipate possible areas of misunderstanding, and help students build relevant connections.

Next, active teachers translate their knowledge of the content into specific learning outcomes. This requires a shift in teachers' thinking *away* from the content they will address and *toward* the outcomes they want students to master. Active teachers ask, "What do I want students to know and be able to do as a result of instruction? And, how will I know that students have met these objectives?"

Today's teachers are guided in their search of discrete learning targets by state standards. Under the No Child Left Behind Act (2001), all states are required to implement rigorous content standards in reading, mathematics, and science. Many states also adopt content standards in other content areas such as social studies, physical education, and the visual and performing arts. The regulations of No Child Left Behind require that standards describe what students will know and be able to do. Written in terms of measurable student outcomes, content standards provide the targets for mandated yearly assessments. A sample mathematics standard for fifth graders in Florida is: "The learner will be able to compute the probability of a specific event occurring from a set of all possible outcomes" (Florida Grade Level Expectations, 1999). A sample reading standard for first graders in California is that learners will: "Retell the central ideas of simple expository or narrative passages" (California Department of Education, 1999).

Many active teachers begin their instruction with careful planning that involves building a deep understanding of student content expectations not only for their grade level but for the grade levels (and subject areas) that articulate with theirs. Careful study is required so that instruction can focus on true priorities and can maximize learning across subject areas and grade levels. Additionally, teachers who understand their standards are better able to plan lessons that address complementary goals simultaneously. Figure 1.3 gives suggestions for selecting active teaching strategies that can meet two or more standards within the same lesson.

Active teachers, however, think beyond lists of state standards when they think about what their students should be expected to master. Focusing only on state standards can serve the unfortunate purpose of narrowing the curriculum to those things that can be tested through standardized tests (Valencia & Villarreal, 2003). Thinking about other outcomes as well, such as social or developmental ones, can ensure that we as an educational team are working toward the most important targets for our nation's youth. Active teachers think broadly and deeply about what students are expected to learn and use that vision to guide their instruction.

Step 3: Answer the Question, "Who Are My Students?"

Your students' success is largely in your hands. Reviews of research (e.g., U.S. Department of Education, 2003) indicate that the teacher is a critical—perhaps *the* critical—factor in student success. Thus, active teachers *must* be experts on students. As you select active teaching strategies, you will need to rely on your knowledge of student development in

Meeting Multiple Standards at the Same Time	Examples of Active Teaching Strategies That Can Help
Addressing a standard in *written language* with a content standard	Found Poems Interactive Journals Invented Dialogs Quick Writes Snowballs Sticker Selection
Addressing an *oral language* standard with a content standard	Content Links Four Corners Idea Share Magnetic Quotes Q & A Match Share the Wealth Think-Pair-Share
Addressing an *English language development* standard with a content standard	Give One, Get One "I Didn't Know That …" Response Frames Partner Share Picture Sorts Geniuses and Super Inteligentes
Addressing a *process* standard (such as sorting, drawing conclusions, or testing hypotheses) with a content standard	Concept Attainment Inquiry Training Object-based Inquiry Mystery Bags Content Structures List-Group-Label Picture Sorts Sequencing Cards
Addressing a *visual or performing arts* standard with another content standard	Quick Draws Photo Analysis Dramatizations and Tableaux Picture Sorts
Addressing a *social development* outcome with a content standard	Problem-based Learning Self-directed Learning Jigsaw Note Checking Pairs

Figure 1.3 Using Active Teaching Strategies to Meet Multiple Learning Outcomes at the Same Time

four different dimensions: cognitive (including linguistic), physical, emotional, and social. Young students, for example, are just developing the ability to use abstract language, and they will probably do better with strategies that offer structured language use than ones that require extended use of abstract language. Figure 1.4 serves as a general reminder of the kinds of needs students at certain ages may be expected to exhibit. However, teachers witness daily huge developmental differences for students of the same chronological age; each student's developmental path is unique. Only careful assessment allows an understanding of each student.

Active teachers embrace the diversity of students within a single classroom, and they are knowledgeable about the needs of exceptional learners. They recognize that the education of those with special needs—those with learning disabilities, communicative

Age Group	Cognitive	Physical	Social	Emotional
Primary Grades (Ages 5–7)	• Concrete experiences with direct sensory input • Frequent breaks or changes in activity • Meaningful context and other strategies to facilitate memory • Opportunities to build and use language • Humor through riddles, nonsense words, and practical jokes	• Plentiful physical activity • Opportunities to use tools to develop eye–hand and small muscle coordination • Opportunities to develop physical skills	• Teacher affection and approval • Assistance in managing conflicts • Opportunities to take turns and play organized games • Opportunities to develop empathy	• Teacher reassurance of worth and capability • Help inhibiting aggression • Help expressing emotions appropriately • Help understanding the reasons behind rules • Help delaying gratification • Opportunities to be independent with physical tasks
Middle Grades (Ages 8–10)	• Hobbies • Extended projects that include planning • Opportunities to use cause-and-effect and logical reasoning • Opportunities to build and use abstract language • Opportunities to exchange ideas	• Physical game playing • Development of physical skills	• Teacher approval, with increasing attention to peer approval • Support in addressing perceived competition • Opportunities to test, refine, and confirm values • Belonging	• Warm, accepting relationships with adults • Increased opportunities for personal and social responsibility • Withholding of criticism and ridicule • Help in building and maintaining positive self-esteem
Upper Grades, Junior High (Ages 11–13)	• Opportunities for formal problem solving • Opportunities for critical thinking and inductive reasoning • Opportunities to build and use abstract language • Opportunities to refine use of language	• Tolerance of physical changes and the stress and changes in self-concept they may bring	• Opportunities to make decisions • Support in accepting differences at a time when conformity matters • Support in asserting own values, despite peer influence • Opportunities to discuss social issues and understand ethical abstractions such as justice	• Adult support in quiet yet warm ways • Opportunities to explore own emotions • Opportunities to build self-identity and self-confidence

Figure 1.4   Typical Needs and Interests by Age Group and Developmental Dimension

Sources: Based in part on information found in Tyler, Marcus, Flatter, and Hunt (1975) and Charles and Senter (1995).

Age Group	Cognitive	Physical	Social	Emotional
High School (Ages 14–18)	• Continued use of refined, formal language • Continued opportunities for abstract reasoning and logical thought	• Support during period of physical development, sexual identity formation, and self-consciousness • Support during time of behavioral exploration (e.g., substance use and sexual activity)	• Peer group acceptance, positive peer influence • High value placed on friendships • Consideration of the importance of relationships and the consequences of one's actions on others • Exploration of the inherent value of particular rules	• Continued kind, unobtrusive guidance by teachers • Opportunities to be independent, within safe settings • Opportunities to affirm self as separate from family while maintaining family cohesiveness

Figure 1.4 *Continued*

disorders, attention deficit disorder, giftedness, or other special needs—is as much their responsibility as the education of other students. Active teachers know their students and work closely with specialists to offer all students instruction that optimizes their success.

Assessment of students' actual interests, needs, and abilities can be conducted by pursuing several kinds of evidence. Inventories and informal class discussions can provide insights into students' interests. So can activities such as student-created bulletin boards. Additional potentially useful information sources for ongoing assessment in the cognitive, physical, social, and emotional domains are found in Figure 1.5.

Additionally, active teachers take time to learn what their students know about specific topics, and they begin instruction there. The strategies presented in Chapter 3 can help

Performance Area, Developmental Domain	Assessment Strategy
Cognitive Performance	• Examination of previous test scores • Paper-and-pencil tests • Portfolios • Writings • Read alouds • Clinical interviews • Class discussions
Physical Performance	• Review of existing scores or assessment results • Observation during spontaneous periods such as recess • Observation on assigned physical tasks (e.g., cutting with scissors, skipping, throwing a ball) • Reports of out-of-school physical activity
Social and Emotional Development	• Observation of peer interactions • Writings • Interviews • Class discussions

Figure 1.5 *Assessing Needs and Abilities*

teachers determine, as well as build and activate, students' background knowledge. Active teachers also use a variety of quick "everyone responds" techniques to discover their students' current level of expertise. To know their audience, active teachers might

- Ask students to rate their current knowledge level for a topic (The Civil War? Dividing fractions?) by holding a number of fingers (1 = little knowledge; 5 = great knowledge) in front of their chests at the teacher's command.

- Ask students to place two colored dots on a class chart of topics: the green dot near the topic they know the best, the red one near the topic they know the least well. The teacher can scan the two rows (green and red) to prioritize points in her lesson.

- Ask students to indicate whether their existing knowledge of a topic would fill a self-adhesive note, a paper, or a book by holding up the appropriate item.

These and other strategies for learning about students' existing knowledge are found in Quick Scans (p. 43).

What may have been disastrous with last year's (or last period's) class may be a rousing success with this year's (or next period's) students. You dramatically increase the probability that strategies will be met with enthusiasm and will foster student success by employing your solid understanding of students and their interests, abilities, and needs as you select and—when necessary—modify active teaching strategies. For example, Ron is a junior high school teacher who is considering using Snowballs (p. 96), which requires students to throw a crumpled piece of paper, because of how it will enhance the closure portion of an upcoming lesson. He feels fairly certain that periods 2 through 6 will do well with the strategy, but period 1 . . . Ah, period 1! Period 1 has many students who need assistance in behaving appropriately. The initial thought of them throwing paper causes Ron to shudder. He might skip Snowballs entirely and replace it with another strategy for period 1. Or, because Ron knows his students well, he can structure their success by carefully wording his directions, modeling expected behavior, checking for understanding on those directions, providing feedback on their actions during Snowballs, and perhaps having planned consequences at the ready. Knowledge of students is a powerful tool in selecting and using active teaching strategies in ways that maximize student success.

Step 4: Answer the Question, "How Can I Manage My Environment to Ensure Success?"

Literature reviewed by Brophy (1997) and others (e.g., Stronge, 2002) suggests that teachers who manage classrooms effectively produce higher achievement gains. Effective classroom managers maximize learning time by minimizing time spent on gathering materials, organizing students, addressing behavior issues, and switching activities. Effective teachers maximize the degree to which students are engaged in ongoing academic activities. To use active teaching strategies as part of a well-managed class, you will need to make decisions about creating a positive atmosphere, managing space and time, and using student groups effectively.

Creating a positive atmosphere. Work by Maslow (1954) and, later, Alderfer (1972) suggests that human drives, at the most basic level, are similar to the needs of all animals; the needs for physical survival include food and safety, for instance. Levels are dynamic, can change quickly, and affect the kinds of information people seek at any one time. Unfulfilled needs at the basic level can interfere with the drive to fill higher human motivations such as the need to belong and be accepted, the need to achieve, and the need to learn and grow as a person. When students are concerned about their physical or emotional safety, for example, they are less likely to attend to your lesson.

Active teachers use this information by first doing what they can to ensure that students' basic needs are met. Then they support student motivation by creating safe learning environments where students perceive the level of threat to be low (Brophy, 1987).

Choices to Be Made	Level of Risk Associated with the Choice	
	Low Risk	**High Risk**
Physical Movement	No movement	Lots of movement, or skilled movement
Social Interaction	No interaction, or interaction with one partner who is perceived as safe	Interaction with many people, or interaction with people considered threatening
Self-disclosure	No disclosure, or disclosure in topics that are not perceived as threatening (for instance, information that is public knowledge or noncontroversial)	High disclosure (disclosure in topics perceived as threatening, such as controversial issues, illegal behaviors, or issues perceived as linked to a person's worth or competence), or disclosure to greater numbers of people or to people who are not considered safe
Creative Self-expression	No creative self-expression	High degrees of creativity and self-disclosure; expression to greater numbers of people

Figure 1.6   Teacher Choices for Instructional Strategies and Levels of Risk

A supportive environment, one that students perceive as pleasant with positive rapport among teacher and students, encourages students to feel safe and take learning risks. As you select instructional strategies, consider potential risks to students and keep the level of threat low enough that students can focus on learning. Although there are many, four factors that vary in the risks they present for students are physical movement, social interaction, self-disclosure, and creative self-expression. Figure 1.6 identifies the teacher choices to be made in considering the risk of each of these factors.

Structuring the physical environment. Active teachers work to use the physical environment to their fullest advantage. They use their surroundings to support student understanding of the content, creating, for instance, print-rich environments that support their literacy goals and democratic arrangements that support their social science goals. Active teachers organize student seats to maximize student interaction, to allow for visual contact with the teacher and the presentation, and to provide effective paths for themselves to travel their classrooms. They devise physical arrangements that allow them to support students' behavior and foster engagement in learning.

Active teachers also attend to students' motivation as they structure the physical environment. They use tools that appeal to students' sense of novelty and that heighten students' understanding of the content. Examples include visuals such as artifacts, student work, photographs, posters, overhead transparencies, and multimedia presentations. They draw students' attention to relevant information using frames or pointers. They may use music to enhance the lesson and to signal transitions between activities.

Maximizing learning time. Good classroom managers teach with a sense of urgency, conveying the notion that time is limited and that every moment is precious. They realize that it is not enough to allocate a certain amount of time to a subject in their plan book. Active teachers ensure not only that students are engaging in content-related activities during allocated times, but also that students are successfully mastering lesson objectives during every possible minute. To use time carefully, active teachers set and enforce time limits for activities,

- *Save time by planning for materials*: On your lesson plan, write the necessary materials for the entire lesson (or day?) in a prominent spot; we like the upper-right corner. Or write them all on an index card. Build in 5 to 10 minutes before instruction begins to collect materials and put them within easy reach.

- *Save time by planning, teaching, and reinforcing procedures (certain steps) for routine distribution and collection of materials*: Will you use student helpers? What is their job? Where is the paper kept? When may students get it? Such routines are especially helpful for students who have emotional, behavioral, or learning disabilities.

- *Save time by creating permanent places for materials*: Make a permanent place for students to submit work without handing it to you. How about a set of folders with a check-off list clipped to the front cover?

- *Save time by using efficient procedures*: If students are seated in rows, pick up papers by having students pass papers across rows rather than up columns. That way students can see the face of the person taking their paper. In table groups, have one student collect and neatly arrange the papers for the group. Then have all groups' papers travel to a single desk for your collection.

- *Save time by avoiding traffic jams*: Place materials for distribution, such as science trays, in a low-traffic area and have just one student per group go to that area. Minimize the number of students out of seat by using a system to send them to materials ("If you are number 2 in your group, please go get the rulers for your group.").

- *Save time by using student numbers*: Number students and have them write their numbers on their assignments. Ask one student to place papers in numeric order when they are collected. Collect materials by student number too (Morris, 2000).

- *Save time by dividing the work*: Arrange blank papers in stacks and distribute them to just one student at the table. In returning student work, place stacks (Student names A–K? Student numbers 1–10?) on different tables and allow students to quickly go to the appropriate tables to pick up their work.

- *Save time by building in student choice*: When students have choices in the materials they select, such as in art, place art materials on a long table or counter and have students form a long, quickly moving line to collect one item on the first pass, and one (or more) on subsequent passes. That way each student has a chance of getting preferred items.

- *Save time by avoiding distractions*: If materials tend to be highly interesting to students, distribute them just before students need them, and collect them (or have a plan to put them out of sight) as soon as students are finished with them.

Figure 1.7 Time-savers for Distributing and Collecting Materials

monitoring students' progress and encouraging students to self-monitor. They may use reminders such as egg timers, overhead timers, and stopwatches. Active teachers distribute and collect materials in ways that minimize lost time. Figure 1.7 gives some tips for getting materials out to students and back again quickly. Realizing that the human ability to pay attention is limited, wise teachers provide for regular physical breaks, and they vary their activities.

Organizing groups. Classroom teachers typically manage learners in groups. For that reason, active teachers must use a variety of skills to manage groups of learners so that time is used effectively and learning is maximized. With apparent ease, active teachers group and regroup students to serve the lesson's purpose. They use flexible groups that are based on a variety of criteria such as student need, student interest, and the need to provide students with opportunities to interact with a variety of peers. Figure 1.8 gives 10 ideas for grouping students quickly within a lesson. Active teachers, additionally, are able to pull groups back together when their tasks are completed. Techniques such as the use of noisemakers, visual signals, and well-taught procedures allow active teachers to regain students' attention so that the lesson can continue.

To help you manage the classroom for success, the descriptions of strategies in Part II include tips for grouping students and give troubleshooting tips for managing groups effectively. The descriptions also include information about how long activities typically take, managing paper and other materials, and other factors that will help you maximize the learning of all your students.

- Have students count off up to a predetermined number and then begin again (1, 2, 3, 4, 1, 2, 3, 4 . . .). Those students with the same number work together.

- Have students gather by the month of their birth so that those born during the same month become group mates. Adjust groupings so that each group is about the same size, if you wish.

- Ask students to record several clock hours that you provide on a piece of paper (e.g., 3:00, 6:00, 9:00, and 12:00). Students circulate to make appointments at those times with one or more class-mates, with each member recording the name of the other(s) with whom he or she is making the appointment. When you are ready for students to meet in pairs or small groups, have them check their appointment log and tell them to meet with their 3:00 appointment. Later, when you wish students to work with different partners, have them check their logs and meet with their 6:00 appointment. See Teacher Resources CD for two sample templates that can be used by students to make appointments.

  > You can find these templates on the accompanying Teacher Resources CD and at the back of the book.

- Distribute playing cards. Have students form groups if they hold the same suit (if you wish large groups), the same number (if you wish smaller groups), or the same number and color (if you wish pairs).

- Randomly distribute index cards, each of which has written on it the name of a book character that is familiar to your students (e.g., Charlotte, Wilbur, and Templeton from *Charlotte's Web*). Students find classmates who have characters from the same book.

- Instead of book characters, use the names of individuals you have studied. Students find partners who have the names of individuals who are somehow related (e.g., George Washington and Abraham Lincoln).

- Give each student a colored index card, using as many colors as you wish groups. When you are ready for students to meet in groups, have them meet by color. Later they may meet in mixed groups, that is, in groups in which no two students have the same color.

- Ask students to find a partner who has the same number of siblings.

- Distribute picture postcards that have been cut in half. Give each student one half of the card. Students partner with the student who has the other half.

- Put stickers on cards. If you wish groups of three, have three cards that have the same sticker. Shuffle the cards and distribute them. Students holding the same sticker form groups.

Figure 1.8   *Quick Ideas for Grouping Students Within a Lesson*

Step 5: Answer the Question, "How Can I Teach in Ways That Enhance Motivation and Learning?"

Active teachers take hold of the large body of knowledge that explains why—and how—people learn. They keep this knowledge front and center as they make their instructional decisions.

How can I enhance motivation? Active teachers recognize that, despite the fact that learning belongs to the student, there are many ways to positively influence students' motivation. Theorists have been writing about motivation in various settings and from various perspectives for many years. From their work, active teachers can draw a number of useful conclusions. Here are two.

Everyone is motivated by something. An exasperated teacher who claims, "These kids just aren't motivated!" is forgetting the important fact that everyone is motivated *to do something* and to do it *for some reason*. Part of a teacher's responsibility is to discover which actions and incentives are motivating to students. Some helpful theorists provide hints at the needs that exist in all of us . . . all the time. Glasser (1986) suggests that humans are in a constant search to fill five needs:

- The need to be safe
- The need to belong
- The need to acquire power

- The need to be free
- The need to have fun

Wise teachers meet these needs through subtle tweaks to their instruction. For instance, teachers create an atmosphere of acceptance so that all students feel included in the classroom culture. They help their students understand and respect the differences among them. To meet students' need to belong, teachers may build class spirit and teach students to work in groups. Groups may develop a team name, logo, or handshake. To meet their needs for power and freedom, teachers may allow students to make choices for some assignments, and they may use community learning projects such as service learning. To meet their need for fun, teachers may incorporate the use of humor, music, color, and novel materials.

Expectancy theory (Vroom, 1964) gives us clues for discovering and influencing individual motivations. According to expectancy theory, people will be motivated to act in a particular way based on two things: the expectation that their action will be followed by a certain outcome, and the attractiveness of the outcome. Teachers can affect students' motivation toward particular actions by considering students' implicit questions such as, "What is the reward?" "How likely is it that I will succeed?" and "How hard will I need to work to achieve it?" By carefully attending to rewards (both explicit and implicit), by providing students with accurate and immediate knowledge of results, and by ensuring high levels of student success, teachers can affect students' motivations toward particular tasks (Hunter, 1969). Based on students' needs and abilities, teachers vary students' success levels by presenting tasks at appropriate levels of difficulty; raising the level of success typically raises student motivation.

Teachers can also enhance student motivation by discovering their students' tendencies to be motivated by different things. For instance, McClelland (1987) finds differences in people's motivations at work: Some people are motivated more by the need for affiliation (the need to be liked and to have positive relationships with others), some are driven by the need for power and authority, and some by the need to achieve. Additionally, some people tend to be motivated more by extrinsic rewards than intrinsic ones. Extrinsic rewards in the classroom include teacher approval, tangible rewards for performance, and competition. Intrinsic rewards relate instead to students' interests, choice, and autonomy. Although each of us is motivated by extrinsic and intrinsic rewards and by different needs at different times of our lives (or of the hour?), students' tendencies to be motivated by particular incentives can provide teachers with useful information for how to structure their classrooms to address students' varying needs. As a caution, although extrinsic rewards can be effective, many educators (e.g., Kohn, 1993) are concerned that their use (or overuse) can decrease intrinsic motivation in the long run.

"Motivation to learn" deserves special attention. A subset of their general motivation, students' motivation to learn is their tendency "to find academic activities meaningful and worthwhile and to try to get the intended learning benefits from them" (Brophy, 2004, p. 249). Ames (1990) defines it as students' long-term, quality involvement in learning and commitment to the process of learning. Although motivation to learn appears high in virtually all preschoolers as they actively explore their worlds, it seems to fade away for a number of students as the years progress. It may be that students increasingly see instruction as irrelevant to the things they want to know. Effective teachers attend to students' interests by utilizing a variety of strategies for eliciting students' questions. Figure 1.9 suggests some techniques for gathering student questions.

Brophy (1987, 2004) emphatically reminds us that our students' motivation to learn is largely in our hands. We encourage motivation to learn by modeling it ourselves. By projecting enthusiasm, a sense of intensity, and a keen interest in the content and its importance, we show students what it means to be motivated to learn. Next, we encourage motivation to learn by providing direct instruction in it when students need support.

- Build a questioning attitude by stressing the tentative nature of knowledge: Begin a lesson by sharing the major or unanswered questions pertaining to the topic.
- Begin a lesson by asking what students want to know about a topic. Model your own question(s) first.
- Allow partners or small groups to discuss, and perhaps record, questions at one or more points throughout the lesson.
- Plant a few questions in the audience before a lesson begins. On cue, student plants ask the questions you have distributed. Allow other questions to follow.
- Distribute index cards before a lesson and ask students to list their questions as they occur. Collect questions at one or more points during the lesson.
- Post a "parking lot" poster near the door for students to "park" questions or other ideas that occur to them.
- Use strategies found in Part II, such as Snowballs and Interactive Journals, that are effective for eliciting questions.

Figure 1.9 Techniques for Eliciting Student Questions

Finally, by providing powerful instruction, each of us can enhance students' motivation to learn. Figure 1.10 gives specific suggestions from the literature (e.g., Brophy, 1987; Keller, 1987) for enhancing students' motivation to learn. Although teachers must be conscious of motivating all their students to learn, students with emotional or learning disabilities often need teachers who are particularly skilled at and attentive to motivational aspects of instruction.

Part II's strategies are designed to address motivational factors such as interest, novelty, level of concern, and knowledge of results. Part II contains many strategies that our students have found enjoyable and engaging. We are all motivated by different things, though, so you will need to select strategies that appeal to your learners and that contribute to their success. We give tips throughout Part II to help you continue thinking about motivational factors such as the risks your students may perceive.

Factor of Motivation to Learn	Technique
Expectation of Success	• Communicate high expectations for all students. • Share specific criteria for each assignment or lesson. • State objectives and provide previews or advance organizers. • Work to help students meet high expectations.
Accurate Attribution	• Help students explain their success as a factor of their ability and their effort. • Help students link their effort with achieved outcomes. • Acknowledge students' progress toward a goal.
Student Interest in the Content	• Use novelty. • Produce incongruence; encourage exploration by presenting challenges that are puzzling to students and using instructional strategies that encourage discovery. • Establish relevance for the content. • Capitalize on students' interests and expertise. • Help students link content to their current values and interests. • Contextualize the content within real-world events or daily significance.

Figure 1.10 Techniques for Enhancing Students' Motivation to Learn

How can I enhance learning? Active teachers use strategies that are supported by what we know about human learning. Several theoretical approaches provide insights into how people learn. Some teachers, for example, are highly influenced by brain-based approaches (e.g., Hart, 1983) to how people learn. The two theoretical approaches to learning that most directly influence the strategies presented in Part II include information processing theory and constructivism.

Information processing theory (Gagne, 1965; Miller, 1956; Miller, Galanter, & Pribram, 1960) tells us that humans take in sensory information from the environment and put it through a series of filters before storing some of it in long-term memory. The task of efficiently storing and then retrieving information at will is an active process that is facilitated when teachers, first, ensure that learners are attending. When they present information, they "chunk" it into bits that can be handled effectively. Thus, teachers must make hierarchical structures of knowledge (e.g., major ideas and related subpoints) clear. They must also highlight the connections between new information and existing information. By facilitating students' engagement with the content, teachers can foster meaningful and lasting learning. Rather than addressing content briefly so that students think about it solely at the surface level, teachers facilitate learning when they encourage students to process information deeply. Finally, teachers foster lasting learning and minimize chances for students to forget important information by providing regular, effective opportunities to rehearse, or practice, information.

Constructivism emphasizes the idea that no knowledge can be handed intact from one person to another. Instead, knowledge is built as a person integrates new information with existing information, or background knowledge (Bruner, Goodnow, & Austin, 1956). Interaction with the physical environment (Piaget, 1929) and with peers and others (Vygotsky, 1978) factor prominently in the construction of knowledge. We all build understandings that are limited in their accuracy, so constructivism addresses the need for teachers to help students resolve their current explanations with more sophisticated or accurate explanations. In attending to constructivist learning theory, active teachers facilitate learning by providing a rich physical environment. They surface and address students' background knowledge and theories. They present problems or tasks that force students to confront their thinking. Furthermore, they structure lessons to include social interaction.

Together, the theoretical approaches of information processing theory and constructivism, along with what we know about helping students take control of their learning, provide powerful instructional advice. This advice is, in fact, so powerful that we structured Part II of this text, and we selected the strategies within it, according to the advice. Teachers can enhance learning by

- Helping students to *activate prior knowledge* and *build a purpose* for learning.
- Encouraging *student interaction*.
- Allowing students to *generate and test hypotheses*.
- Fostering students' ability to *organize information* and *make connections*.
- Facilitating *rehearsal and consolidation* of content.

You can use the chapters of Part II and their strategies as you build instruction that enhances learning.

Step 6: Answer the Question, "Based on Feedback, What Shall I Do Next?"

Teaching and learning are interactive processes; the teacher's next move is in part determined by the students' actions, and students act in response to the teacher's instruction. Brophy and Good's (1986) review of the teacher effects research finds that teachers who produce higher levels of student achievement establish their classrooms as effective learning environments. Effective teachers gain the cooperation of their students and maximize the degree to which their students are engaged in academic activities. Doing so

When the students . . .	It may mean . . .	As an active teacher, you might . . .
Remain silent when asked to volunteer . . .	• Students do not understand your question. • Students do not know the answer. • Students know the answer but choose not to share it for a number of reasons (e.g., they perceive sharing as risky; they do not think you care about the answer; the social norms are against them sharing; they think if they are quiet, the lesson will progress more quickly).	• Comment on the lack of volunteers. ("I don't see many hands up.") • Suggest that it is your fault. ("I don't think my question was clear.") • If you think you are likely to get honest responses, seek—in a nonconfrontational way—an explanation for the lack of participation. ("It may be that you haven't thought about this before, or it may be that you are tired. Knowing the reason will help me teach you better. Take a second to think about that, and then I'll call on three people for their insights.") • Use a lower-risk response strategy. ("Let's do a Quick Write on this." Or, "Sometimes people prefer to talk about this to a partner. Take 30 seconds to tell the person next to you . . .")
Wiggle or shift during the lesson . . .	• The content agitates the students. • Something else is agitating the students. • The students need a change in activity.	• Recognize the behavior. ("I see some wiggling.") • Give your inference for the behavior. ("I think something happened that I missed." Or, "I think you've been sitting for a while.") • If appropriate, get feedback on your inference. ("Did I call that right?") • Make and enact a plan to address the behavior. ("I'm tired, too. Let's stand and stretch a minute.")
Chatter during the lesson . . .	• What you said was so provocative that students simply must talk about it to each other. • Students did not understand you and need to clarify with their peers. • Some other topic of conversation is, at the moment, more important than your content. • Students need a break.	• Comment on the behavior. ("Wow! That got a response!") • Use your attention signal to regain students' attention. • Make and enact a plan for addressing the behavior. ("I think you didn't understand my directions. Let's try again." Or, "You all seem to have a story to share about this topic! Tell your partner, and then a few of you can share with the class.")

Figure 1.11   Active Responses to Student Behavioral Cues

requires active teachers to read and respond—to monitor and adjust—to both behavioral and performance cues from students.

Active teachers are careful observers of their students' behavior during a lesson. To maintain a productive pace during their lessons and to maximize student success, active teachers watch and listen to ensure that students are engaging in the content at hand. Figure 1.11 gives sample student behaviors and active teacher responses to those behaviors. Notice that the active teacher explicitly recognizes a behavior, seeks to interpret it, may check the quality of the interpretation, and uses an immediate plan to address it. The sample teacher responses seek to maintain students' cooperation and value their perspectives while at the same time allowing the teacher to stay on track.

Active teachers also seek ongoing feedback on students' understanding of the content. Asking such questions as, "Does everyone understand?" or "Are there any questions?" are not enough for the active teacher. Instead, active teachers use a variety of strategies to elicit students' current understanding of the topic. Typical classroom interactions follow a pattern (Dillon, 1988a):

- The teacher asks a question.
- One student responds.
- The teacher evaluates the response and asks another question.

Unfortunately, this pattern limits the classroom discourse and the teacher's understanding of all students' progress. Productive discourse, instead, encourages extended, in-depth conversations about open-ended and higher-level avenues of the content (Brophy, 2004).

Effective teachers pursue strategies that allow all students to respond in meaningful ways. Examples include strategies that facilitate student-to-student interaction as well as more immediate overt participation strategies. Instead of calling on a single student for a response, active teachers use strategies such as unison response, colored flashcards, and partner talk (more to come in Part II!) to provide all students with a chance to share their progress and to seek feedback on what—and how—students are understanding. Once active teachers have obtained feedback on what, whether, and which students are understanding, they do something with that feedback. They may decide that their pace is appropriate and continue with their lesson as planned. They may, instead, need to "skip ahead" several steps based on student mastery. They may need to stop, go back, and fill in missing pieces of prerequisite knowledge for the entire group or for a smaller group or a single student at a later time. Or, active teachers may shift their discussion after discovering that a side topic has emerged as essential and deserving of the class's attention.

SUMMARY

This chapter attempted to help you build or enrich your understanding of the context in which you will select and implement active teaching strategies. It argued that instructional decisions such as which active teaching strategies to employ are best made when teachers have a firm sense of their purposes, of the content, of the students, and of professional knowledge related to teaching and learning. With this foundation in place, Chapter 2 offers more specific advice on how to choose and use active teaching strategies.

CHOOSING AND USING ACTIVE TEACHING STRATEGIES

Part II of this text includes 50 strategies designed to enhance your repertoire with approaches that actively engage K–12 students in learning. This chapter helps you choose and use Part II's strategies in your own classroom. It is organized in the three major sections of Choosing Active Teaching Strategies, Targeting Diverse Learning Needs, and Using Active Teaching Strategies in Your Lessons.

CHOOSING ACTIVE TEACHING STRATEGIES

Before *you* choose active teaching strategies, please let us present the choices *we* made in selecting the 50 particular active teaching strategies found in this text. If you flip ahead to Part II and thumb through the descriptions of strategies, you will see strategy after strategy that encourage students to engage deeply in their learning. What you will *not* see in the descriptions is a denotation of any particular content area or content standard; nor will you see a specification of grade level. That is because we selected strategies for inclusion in Part II for their flexibility and wide applicability across subject areas and grade levels. Many strategies work as effectively in mathematics lessons as they do in medieval history lessons. Many work as well with 5-year-olds as they do with 15-year-olds.

In addition to flexibility, we also used a number of other criteria for selecting the strategies in Part II. We selected strategies in Part II to meet the notions of active teaching explored in Chapter 1. The strategies help both teachers and students take responsibility for student learning, they capitalize on what is known about human learning, they foster student motivation, and they provide ongoing feedback on student performance. We also selected strategies that can be used often rather than just once or twice for highly specific content. Finally, we selected strategies that can be easily implemented, usually with a minimum of preparation and follow-up. Although all the strategies in Part II are flexible, have wide applicability, model good teaching, and can be easily implemented, some will work better than others for particular purposes and settings.

Now it is your turn. Choosing active teaching strategies that will maximize success in your classroom is enhanced by three kinds of knowledge from you: knowledge of yourself, knowledge of your content, and knowledge of your students. As suggested in Chapter 1, choosing appropriate active teaching strategies begins with a clear vision of your big picture of education—your answer to the question, "Why am I here?" What are you hoping to accomplish with your students? Read through the chapter headings and skim the strategy descriptions to make an initial determination about the strategies that will serve as starting points to help you bring about your vision of teaching. Too, at least initially, you will probably choose active teaching strategies that feel comfortable to you because they are similar to the kinds of strategies you already use. As you gain comfort, you can stretch by selecting less familiar strategies.

In thinking about the content your students need to master, begin with your learning goal and choose active teaching strategies that have good potential to maximize both the time spent and the opportunities presented for students to master that goal. You may very well begin by thinking about the standards students need to master and how those standards fit into the puzzle of the larger domain. As you examine your standards, consider the kinds of thinking that they require. For instance, do they require students to compare different perspectives? To state connections among diverse ideas? Perusing the chapter headings of Part II can help you choose strategies that will work toward your content outcomes and the thinking demands they make. Skimming the introduction of likely strategies can provide additional information. Also, remember that choosing active teaching strategies with foresight can help you to meet multiple learning outcomes at once (review Chapter 1, Figure 1.3, p. 7). And the strategies will provide useful formative, progress monitoring, or summative assessment information. (See the chart on the inside cover of this text.)

Your knowledge of your students also should figure prominently in your selection of active teaching strategies. What do they find interesting? What do they like doing? What do they need help doing? Familiarizing yourself with Part II's strategies can help you select those that will be enjoyable for your students; that will help them engage in the learning process and take control of it; and that will push them to develop as thoughtful, literate people. In addition to thinking about your students as a group, you also need to think about them as individuals: What distinct learning challenges do your students present? What special needs do they have? The following section provides information that can help you choose and use active teaching strategies in ways that support students in learning, whatever their needs.

TARGETING DIVERSE LEARNING NEEDS

Most teachers today work with at least a few students who struggle in reading and writing, who are acquiring English, or who have specifically identified learning challenges. Fortunately, there are many tactics for targeting learning needs so that all students can achieve. We address a number of general ideas and approaches, below, for addressing particular learning issues. Additionally, as you read over the strategies in Part II, you will see that each includes sections entitled "Alternatives" and "Troubleshooting." These sections offer suggestions to build student success when a variety of learning issues arise.

Helping Students When They Need Support in Reading or Writing

A number of options exist for helping students who are not independent readers or writers. One option is to use active teaching strategies that require little or no independent interaction with the written word. This option is viable when the teacher wishes students to have access to content knowledge made available in the lesson despite students' lower reading performance. The chart inside this text's cover lists the level of readers for whom each strategy is appropriate. Figure 2.1 lists strategies with limited reading demands. Strategies in Figure 2.1 can also be effective with younger students who are just learning to read.

To help you locate active teaching strategies with appropriate reading demands, strategy descriptions in Part II contain a box that states the appropriateness of the strategy for readers at different levels. Here is a sample:

> **LITERACY DEMANDS**
>
> Appropriate for:
>
> Emerging Readers/Writers
>
> ✔ Intermediate Readers/Writers
>
> ✔ Proficient Readers/Writers

A second option for working with students who struggle in reading is to use active teaching strategies that have higher reading demands, but to lower those demands through instructional modifications. To lower reading demands, students who are independent readers can be paired with those who need reading assistance. For example, in Give One, Get One (p. 176), students can record and share their ideas in pairs rather than individually. Similarly, small groups can be formed so that each has at least one independent reader. A teacher who uses True-False Sorts (p. 66) in a class with some struggling readers, for instance, can arrange small groups to contain students with a mix of reading levels. Those who have difficulty reading the true-false statements can listen and follow

Strategies for Activating Prior Knowledge and Building a Purpose for Learning (Chapter 3)	Quick Scans Quick Draws Group Graphs Important Words
Strategies for Encouraging Student Interaction (Chapter 4)	Share the Wealth Think-Pair-Share Graffiti Board Make the Point Stand and Share Up and Out
Strategies for Generating and Testing Hypotheses (Chapter 5)	Concept Attainment Mystery Bags Question Only Inquiry Training Object-based Inquiry Problem-based Learning Revealing Information Photo Analysis Structured Decision Making
Strategies for Organizing Information and Making Connections (Chapter 6)	Sequencing Cards Concept Maps Picture Sorts Treasure Hunts
Strategies for Facilitating Rehearsal and Consolidation of Content (Chapter 7)	Geniuses and Super Inteligentes Q & A Match Graphic Organizers Dramatizations and Tableaux "I Didn't Know That . . ." Response Frames

Figure 2.1   Active Teaching Strategies with Limited Reading Demands

along as their peers read the statements aloud. Placing an adult such as a parent, aide, volunteer, or student teacher in each group serves this purpose, too. Reading demands can also be lowered by replacing the written word with alternatives. Directions can be presented orally and as pictures or diagrams rather than as a written list. Text can be presented as the spoken word through media such as CDs, videotapes, and audiocassettes. A teacher using this modification, for example, might have read the content for Jigsaw experts (p. 193) onto an audiotape and allowed students needing assistance to listen to the tape as they read along.

A third important option for working with students when reading performance is an issue is to address students' reading needs while simultaneously addressing the content of the lesson. This option provides students with the critical opportunity to develop in an area where they need significant support: reading. Note that many active teaching strategies from Part II can provide assistance in helping students develop as competent readers. In fact, each chapter of Part II contributes to components that are associated with helping students develop as readers: activating prior knowledge and building a purpose for learning (see Chapter 3), increasing student interaction including talk (see Chapter 4), generating and testing hypotheses (see Chapter 5), organizing information and making connections (see Chapter 6), and rehearsing and consolidating content (see Chapter 7). Thoughtful use of active teaching strategies at different points of a lesson can support reading growth in areas such as vocabulary development and comprehension.

Some active teaching strategies in Part II place literacy demands on students because they ask students to write. Examples include Interactive Journals (p. 201) and Note Checking Pairs (p. 196). When they struggle with writing, students can be assisted through practices such as

- Building an atmosphere of trust and of peer acceptance of students' ideas and works.
- Focusing on the content of a piece of writing until the editing phase.
- Encouraging classwide acceptance of temporary spellings for informal or early works.
- Encouraging the use of computers for composition.
- Allowing partner groups, with one partner serving as the scribe.
- Using dictation.
- Using shared writing experiences.
- Accepting the use of single-word responses, bulleted phrases, or other abbreviated responses.
- Allowing the use of diagrams or other visually supported writings.
- Focusing on growth over time.

Helping Students While They Acquire English

More than one-quarter of U.S. students are acquiring English while they simultaneously work to master the rigorous content required by a K–12 education. English learners need careful support from their teachers as they work toward the demanding twin goals of English acquisition and content mastery. How can teachers help? The literature (e.g., Cummins, 1981; Krashen, 1981; Swain, 1985; Thomas & Collier, 2002) offers five big suggestions for teachers who work with English learners.

1. **Foster a supportive environment.** Students need to feel free to take risks with language. Teachers can help by fostering environments that help students feel safe and motivated to learn and to talk.

2. **Provide comprehensible input.** Students need to receive content and language input that is within their reach. Support in the primary language and the use of context-embedded language are two ways that input can be rendered comprehensible.

3. **Foster comprehensible output.** Students need opportunities to talk and to write that are appropriate for their level of language proficiency. They need meaningful opportunities to interact with each other and with their teacher in order to practice and build their language skills and in order to build their understanding of the content.

4. **Scaffold.** Teachers need to provide just enough support so that students can succeed at tasks that would have been impossible to complete independently. Scaffolding includes support that is carefully planned and well timed.

5. **Work toward higher-level thinking.** All students need to be given opportunities to think at the higher levels, but as students progress in their ability to use English, teachers need to make special efforts to require language learners to use English in ways that require elaborate and complex thought.

Figure 2.2 lists some specific tips (and strategies from Part II) that can take these five big pieces of advice into the classroom every day.

As Figure 2.2 suggests, active teaching strategies can provide tremendous support for English learners by making input comprehensible, by fostering student interaction for meaningful communication, and by encouraging students to think deeply about the content and to use their language to represent their thoughts. You can select strategies from Part II with these particular goals in mind. Also, to select active teaching strategies appropriate for your students' English proficiency, you can check the "language demands" box that accompanies the description of each strategy in Part II. Here is an example from a strategy that can work well with all levels of English learners:

LANGUAGE DEMANDS

Appropriate for:
- ✔ Early English Learners
- ✔ Intermediate English Learners
- ✔ Advanced English Learners

In implementing any particular active teaching strategy in a class with English learners, we offer the following advice.

1. **Ensure that students understand what they are expected to do.** Provide your instructions in a number of different formats, such as in writing and in pictures. Demonstrate the activity first, perhaps in a fishbowl. In a fishbowl, you teach a few students the directions as the rest look on. Check for understanding to ensure that students are ready to proceed.

2. **Build appropriate student groupings.** Use pairings or groupings that will assist English learners in getting comprehensible input and that will allow them to use language. Small groups with both English speakers and same-language students may be appropriate, for example.

3. **Ensure that students have access to the information they need.** Use primary language text, adapted texts, or video- or computer-based input to ensure that English learners have access to the content.

Big Advice	**Tips and Active Teaching Strategies**
1. Foster a supportive environment.	• Maintain classroom routines. • Use multicultural content and culturally relevant examples. • Draw from and value students' diverse experiences (see Chapter 3). • Focus on students' meaning rather than the form of their language. (Refrain from overcorrecting errors.) • Encourage questions and talk about language. • Teach students to support each other.
2. Provide comprehensible input.	• Use primary language support when available and appropriate. • Focus on developing a few key concepts well. • Connect new content to existing knowledge and experience (see Chapters 3 and 6). • State the day's objective or activities. • Preview key vocabulary terms and concepts. • Simplify speech by speaking slower, using fewer figures of speech, using repetition, and using body language (such as gestures) to support the message. • Print. • Use visual aids and real artifacts. Try Photo Analysis (p. 134), Picture Sorts (p. 163), and Object-based Inquiry (p. 124). • Model and demonstrate. • Use Graphic Organizers (p. 204). • Review frequently. Use internal summaries.
3. Foster comprehensible output.	• Provide meaningful contexts for student communication. • Compose student groups with a focus on language acquisition. Including native English speakers can provide language models, and same-language peers can provide support in comprehension. • Use cooperative learning strategies. • Plan for a variety of student responses and for a range of levels of English usage. Try Share the Wealth (p. 72). • Use strategies that encourage student talk (see Chapter 4). • Use strategies that let students talk about what they learned (see Chapter 7).
4. Scaffold.	• Ensure that directions are clear by providing them in different formats (in writing, in speech, in pictures, and in demonstrations, for example). • Provide intermediate support to foster student independence. Examples include providing students with partially completed lecture notes and doing shared writings before requiring independent writings. • Try Make the Point (p. 84), Revealing Information (p. 130), and Response Frames (p. 218) to scaffold success.
5. Work toward higher-level thinking.	• Require critical and creative thinking. Try strategies for making and testing hypotheses (Chapter 5) and for making connections (Chapter 6). • As they progress into the advanced stages of English acquisition, require elaborated use of academic English. Try strategies like Content Structures (p. 154) and Invented Dialogs (p. 210).

Figure 2.2   Tips for Working with English Learners

4. **Repair misunderstandings.** Teach students to negotiate meanings as they communicate in English. Monitor students carefully. Reteach when you see that students did not understand the directions, when students convey inaccurate information about the content, or when they need assistance to get communication going again.

5. **Allow students to use English in interactions that are appropriate for their level of language proficiency.** Students who are early English learners, for example, should be allowed to draw pictures, to point at correct responses, to manipulate materials physically, or to give single-word answers rather than to speak in complete English sentences to describe their thoughts. More advanced speakers should be encouraged to use not just basic communication skills but academic English (including content specific vocabulary and modes of expression) as well.

Helping Students with Specifically Identified Learning Challenges

Each learner presents a unique set of strengths and areas for growth based on the interesting and infinitely varied ways that humans are put together. For this reason, addressing students' exceptional needs, as argued both in Chapter 1 and earlier in this chapter, begins with building solid knowledge of each student. It also requires professional knowledge of general approaches and specific tactics for tackling particular learning requirements. As a foundation, teachers can foster active teaching in classrooms where many specific learning challenges are present by

- Modeling, teaching, and reinforcing a culture of acceptance.
- Incorporating students' strengths (such as good listening skills) into the quest for learning new information.
- Providing opportunities to develop in areas of difficulty.
- Finding ways to provide access to the core curriculum, regardless of the learning challenges present.
- Teaching social skills in addition to content mastery.
- Working closely with specialized personnel to maximize student growth.

Although in-depth treatment of precise techniques for addressing special needs is beyond the scope of this book, Figure 2.3 includes some suggestions for boosting success when using active teaching strategies to meet the special needs found in many K–12 general education classrooms: learning disabilities, communication disorders, attention deficit hyperactivity disorder, emotional or behavioral difficulties, and giftedness.

Special Learning Need	Suggestions for Using Active Teaching Strategies
Learning Disabilities	• Use strategies to help students gauge their own learning, including ones that provide quick feedback on performance. Try strategies like Revealing Information (p. 130), Concept Attainment (p. 107), and Note Checking Pairs (p. 196). • Use learning aids that help compensate for the area of difficulty and still provide the student with access to the lesson content. • Control the level of difficulty of instructional tasks and adjust workload or time allotments to fit students' abilities. • Teach students in small, flexible groups. • Be sure students know where the lesson is headed by using techniques such as previewing major concepts and lesson activities.

Figure 2.3 Addressing Specially Identified Learning Needs through Active Teaching Strategies
Source: Based in part on information found in Vaughn, Bos, and Schumm (2003).

Special Learning Need	Suggestions for Using Active Teaching Strategies
Communication Disorders	• Teach language in purposeful contexts, and encourage conversation rather than overuse of formal question-and-answer drills. Strategies like Magnetic Quotes (p. 90), Up and Out (p. 101), and Structured Decision Making (p. 141) can help. • Lower the perceived risks associated with communication by adjusting relevant factors such as the size of the audience (try Partner Share, p. 56) and the form of the communication (try Dramatizations and Tableaux, p. 212). • Allow students with production difficulties time to process information and prepare responses. Strategies like Share the Wealth (p. 72) can help. • Provide opportunities to practice speech or to use it more than once. Try Think-Pair-Share (p. 76), Give One, Get One (p. 176), and Up and Out (p. 101) for this purpose. • Make sure that lessons provide support and opportunities for both language comprehension and language production. • Use a full range of communication options, including visual and auditory techniques as well as assistive devices to provide input (activity directions and content information) and to allow for student output. • Adjust the pace of language in the classroom, in part by providing wait time.
Attention Deficit Hyperactivity Disorder	• Allow for student movement, and optimize stimulation based on student need. Strategies like Give One, Get One (p. 176), Stand and Share (p. 93), and Content Links (p. 173) allow for physical movement. • Help students remain organized, both in terms of materials and in terms of organizing ideas. Strategies like Content Structures (p.154), Concept Mapping (p. 158), and Graphic Organizers (p. 204) can help. • Maintain classroom schedules and routines. • Use color, frames, or other devices to highlight important information. • Teach directions explicitly; check for understanding. Monitor behavior carefully while students follow directions, and provide feedback on behavior. • Be clear with time limits, perhaps using timers to help students keep track. • Be especially vigilant in planning and monitoring transitions between activities.
Emotional or Behavioral Difficulties	• Use highly structured activities with low physical movement requirements to encourage student success initially. Strategies to try include Revealing Information (p. 130), Response Frames (p. 218), and Picture Sorts (p. 163). • Provide opportunities for students to explore and share their own perspectives in positive ways. Try strategies like Magnetic Quotes (p. 90), Stand and Share (p. 93), Sticker Selection (p. 179), and Found Poems (p. 215). • Maintain an orderly physical environment. • Be clear with expectations for behavior: Select rules carefully, state them clearly, provide information about consequences, and follow through consistently. • Give special consideration to planning logical behavior consequences to serve as alternatives to active teaching strategies if students choose not to follow directions. Alternatives should maintain time spent mastering the content. • Teach conflict resolution skills. • Build social skills such as turn taking when interactive opportunities arise with active teaching strategies.

Figure 2.3   *Continued*

Special Learning Need	Suggestions for Using Active Teaching Strategies
Giftedness	• Use preassessment data to adjust learning goals to avoid focusing on previously mastered material. See Chapter 3 for ideas for accessing prior knowledge. • Provide plenty of opportunities for abstract thinking; try strategies such as Invented Dialogs (p. 210) and Word Journal (p. 207). • Provide opportunities to explore curiosities; try strategies such as Object-based Inquiry (p. 124), Self-directed Learning (p. 145), and Problem-based Learning (p. 127). • Allow students to create materials to be used in active teaching strategies such as True-False Sorts (p. 66), Q & A Match (p. 198), and Content Links (p. 173). • Focus on social development goals (including leadership) during interactive strategies such as Jigsaw (p. 193), Important Words (p. 69), Content Structures (p. 154), and Treasure Hunts (p. 183). • Provide a wide variety of resources to accommodate students' quicker learning pace; increased depth of understanding; and multiple, wide-ranging interests. • Vary grouping formats to require both individual pursuits and success within the larger group. • Adjust expectations (typically upward) for both content and format of students' responses.

Figure 2.3 *Continued*

USING ACTIVE TEACHING STRATEGIES IN YOUR LESSONS

Although active teaching strategies can be used as brief stand-alone activities, like sponges, to soak up spare moments of the day, they are most typically embedded within larger lessons. Many of the active teaching strategies found in Part II are flexible enough not only to be used with students up and down the grade levels and across the curriculum, but also to be embedded within any type of lesson. They can be used, for instance, in two prevalent lesson designs: direct instruction and the learning cycle (a prominent version of inquiry, or discovery learning). Figure 2.4 provides general guidelines of where to find strategies to embed into each phase of the lesson design. As an important caveat, however, note that, **although we have grouped strategies within particular chapters for meeting certain purposes, we have every expectation that you will use them inventively to meet your own purposes**. For instance, Important Words (p. 69) can be used to facilitate consolidation of content (Yopp & Yopp, 2002) in addition to activating prior knowledge (Stephens & Brown, 2000). Strategy descriptions in Part II sometimes give suggestions for different uses of the strategies, but you can also rely on your own expertise to use them in a variety of ways.

Suggestions for Embedding Strategies

The number of active teaching strategies you use in any one lesson, your choice of specific active teaching strategies, and their placement within the lesson all depend on your understanding of the big picture of teaching and learning. Chapter 1 presented a step-by-step

A. Direct Instruction Model
Anticipatory Set (*Teacher gains students' attention, states the objective, and states a purpose for learning.*) Chapter 3: Strategies for Activating Prior Knowledge and Building a Purpose for Learning Chapter 5: Strategies for Generating and Testing Hypotheses
Input (*Teacher gives explicit instruction and checks for understanding.*) Chapter 4: Strategies for Encouraging Student Interaction Chapter 6: Strategies for Organizing Information and Making Connections
Guided Practice (*Students practice objective under teacher's direction.*) Chapter 4: Strategies for Encouraging Student Interaction Chapter 5: Strategies for Generating and Testing Hypotheses Chapter 6: Strategies for Organizing Information and Making Connections Chapter 7: Strategies for Facilitating Rehearsal and Consolidation of Content
Closure (*Teacher conducts final check on mastery of the objective.*) Chapter 4: Strategies for Encouraging Student Interaction Chapter 6: Strategies for Organizing Information and Making Connections Chapter 7: Strategies for Facilitating Rehearsal and Consolidation of Content
Independent Practice (*Students use the content independently.*) Chapter 7: Strategies for Facilitating Rehearsal and Consolidation of Content
B. Learning Cycle Model
Engage (*Teacher presents interesting real-world problem or phenomenon.*) Chapter 3: Strategies for Activating Prior Knowledge and Building a Purpose for Learning Chapter 5: Strategies for Generating and Testing Hypotheses
Explore (*Students explore the real-world problem or phenomenon.*) Chapter 5: Strategies for Generating and Testing Hypotheses
Develop (*Teacher helps students consolidate content through explicit instruction.*) Chapter 4: Strategies for Encouraging Student Interaction Chapter 6: Strategies for Organizing Information and Making Connections Chapter 7: Strategies for Facilitating Rehearsal and Consolidation of Content
Apply (*Students use content in a new real-world context.*) Chapter 3: Strategies for Activating Prior Knowledge and Building a Purpose for Learning Chapter 5: Strategies for Generating and Testing Hypotheses Chapter 7: Strategies for Facilitating Rehearsal and Consolidation of Content

Figure 2.4 Some Ideas for Which Strategies Fit Where

series of questions for you to consider as you look at that big picture and think about embedding active teaching strategies within your lessons. Thus far, Chapter 2 has asked you to revisit the first three steps in that process:

Step 1   Answer the Question, "Why Am I Here?"

Step 2   Answer the Question, "What Are My Goals?"

Step 3   Answer the Question, "Who Are My Students?"

To embed active teaching strategies in your lessons, you will consider for each particular lesson the other questions:

Step 4   Answer the Question, "How Can I Manage My Environment to Ensure Success?"

Step 5   Answer the Question, "How Can I Teach in Ways that Enhance Motivation and Learning?"

Step 6   Answer the Question, "Based on Feedback, What Shall I Do Next?"

As you consider classroom management (Step 4), think about how to arrange the social and physical environments, how to use time effectively, and how to group students in order to maximize students' opportunity to engage in the content, to master objectives, and to develop as thoughtful people. What special materials do you need? Where will you place them? How will you support students who challenge your rules? How will you tell students how much time they have? What will you do if students take longer than you expect? How will you give directions to ensure smooth transitions between activities? Careful thinking about management questions such as these contributes greatly to the time students spend engaging in important learning—and to your own sanity.

Step 5 asks you to use, for every lesson you teach, what you know about human motivation and learning to embed active teaching strategies within your lessons. In terms of motivation, think about how your choice of active teaching strategies helps meet students' basic needs such as the needs to be safe and to be accepted. Remember students need both structure and certainty *as well as* novelty. Varying the type of involvement required by learners within a lesson can help meet this need. Ask yourself how you can help students see the purpose in the lesson and how you can gauge their performance. These factors enhance motivation to learn *and* contribute to your single-minded pursuit of student learning.

Use what you know about how people learn when you select and sequence activities. (Remember, this text draws from information processing theory and constructivism.) The sequencing of the chapters in Part II can help. Although strategies can be used flexibly, the chapters are sequenced, in a general way, from early lesson strategies to later lesson strategies (review Figures 2.4A and 2.4B). For instance, you need—early in a lesson—to discover what students know so that you can build on it. Chapter 3 (Strategies for Activating Prior Knowledge and Building a Purpose for Learning) can help here. Then you need to provide access to new information in interesting, meaningful ways. Try Chapters 5 and 6. Throughout your instruction, students need opportunities to talk in order to share what they know, deepen their understanding, and practice what they are learning. Chapter 4 (Strategies for Encouraging Student Interaction) can be of assistance for this purpose. Lessons typically close with students building connections among ideas (Chapter 6) or in some other way reflecting on or practicing what they learned (Chapter 7).

Finally, as you embed active teaching strategies within your lessons, Step 6 asks you to answer, for each lesson you teach, the question, "Based on Feedback, What Shall I Do Next?" Insert active teaching strategies into your lessons that will allow you to get information about how students are interacting with the content and what they are learning. Then consider how you will respond to the range of feedback that you are likely to obtain regarding students' behavior and performance. Monitoring and adjusting will allow you to maximize student learning—and everyone's satisfaction with the teaching and learning process.

How do all of these pieces fit together as teachers choose and use active teaching strategies within their lessons? The next section presents three lessons that demonstrate a wide range of objectives, lesson designs, learning needs, and active teaching strategies as they follow the step-by-step process for active teaching.

Three Sample Lesson Descriptions with Active Teaching Strategies

Here are descriptions of three lessons that demonstrate the use of strategies in different grade levels and content areas:

- Kindergarten language arts lesson (distinguishing reality and fantasy) (Figure 2.5)
- Fifth-grade science lesson (investigating sand dollars) (Figure 2.6)
- Eleventh-grade U.S. history lesson (exploring the road to World War II) (Figure 2.7)

Each lesson addresses objectives derived from state content standards. The lessons use two prevalent lesson designs (direct instruction and inquiry) as well as a third more generic format (open-body-close) to show that active teaching strategies can be embedded into any lesson format. Lesson descriptions also demonstrate that the number of active teaching strategies can vary; the lessons contain one, two, or three strategies. Other lessons may contain even more! Finally, the lessons list instructional supports for a sampling of specific learning needs.

Housekeeping Information

Time Estimate:
  20 minutes
Active Teaching Strategy:
  Concept Attainment (p. 107)
State Standard:

- The learner will be able to distinguish between reality and fantasy, between fictional and nonfictional accounts.

Additional State Standard (Science):

- The learner will be able to verbally communicate observations.

Materials:

Picture set of real animals and fictional animals (approximately 10 of each)

Drawing materials

Class library books

Objectives:

1. Students will state whether an animal is real or fictional.
2. Students will describe observations of animals that lead them to their conclusion of whether the animal is real or fictional.

Supporting English Learners:

1. Find primary language translations for terms such as *real* and *make believe*. Use as appropriate during instruction.
2. Pair same-language students for informal conversations during lesson.
3. Point to key words in pictures, repeat them, and use unison response to practice terms that may indicate whether animals are real or fictional. (Examples: clothes, wings, fire.)
4. Allow students to point to picture cards or use one-word responses rather than require longer responses.

Figure 2.5 Kindergarten Language Arts Lesson: Reality and Fantasy

Open

1. (Teacher and students sit at rug in front of magnetic board.) The teacher leads brief game: "I'm going to call some students up. I will only call a few. They all have something in common that makes them part of a group. See if you can guess what they all have." He calls up only students wearing pants (or shoes with laces, or shirts with stripes, or some other visible similarity). He leads students to guess the group by giving names of students who are not part of the group and gives hints to focus. Optional: They play again, this time with another observable characteristic.

2. The teacher describes the lesson and gives its purpose: "Today during language time, we're going to play a game like the one we just played. The game will help us understand the books we read."

Body

1. Active Teaching Strategy: Concept Attainment (p. 107)
   a. The teacher presents, one at a time, pictures that depict either a real animal or a fictional animal.
   b. He places them, one at a time, into one of two areas on the board (real and fantasy) without telling students his rule. Students make initial guesses about the commonality of the items in each group and refine their guesses as the teacher presents more pictures.
   c. Students guess the rule after seven pictures for each group have been presented: "Animals on this side are real, and animals over there are not!"
   d. Students confirm the rule with the remaining pictures. The teacher asks, "Okay, Smarties, where would this creature go then?"

2. The teacher asks, "How do we know what is real and what is not?" and draws students' attention to observable aspects of the animals that give clues to whether they are real or fantasy. He also points out that we need to know about our world to determine that.

3. Troubleshooting: The teacher prepares to address possible questions that may arise from students about two kinds of creatures: (1) ones that are associated with holidays or cultural traditions encouraged by families, and (2) contested creatures—such as a space alien, Chupacabra (a creature rumored to suck blood from goats), or the Loch Ness monster (a creature rumored to inhabit Scotland's Loch Ness)—who are believed to be real by some. If questions arise, he will deflect discussion of holiday creatures to the family. For contested creatures, he will say, "Sometimes people disagree about whether a creature is real. Scientists would tell us that those creatures belong over here with the 'not real' creatures until we have plenty of evidence that they exist."

Close

1. The teacher draws the lesson to a close by summarizing: "Excellent job, you detectives, of guessing my rule: 'Things that are real and things that are not.' " (He gestures to the board, emphasizes the word *real*, and asks students to repeat it.) "Knowing what is real and what is not helps us understand the books we read, and it helps us make decisions in the real world, too."

2. For assessment purposes and to extend the learning, the teacher directs the students to, individually, draw one animal of their choice: one that is real or one that is not real. Early finishers and advanced learners are instructed to visit the class library and find examples of "real and not real" in familiar or new books.

3. While they work, the teacher calls individuals to him and asks them to tell whether their animal is real or not real. He requires them to use evidence in their drawings or from their background knowledge to support their conclusion of real or not real. For new English speakers, the teacher asks students to use the words "real" and "not real" as they point to real and not real animals.

Figure 2.5 *Continued*

Housekeeping Information

Time Estimate:
60 minutes, with writing occurring in subsequent lessons

Active Teaching Strategies:
Object-based Inquiry (p. 124)
"I Didn't Know That..." Response Frames (p. 218)
Graphic Organizers (p. 204)

State Standards:

- The learner will be able to relate the structures of an animal to their functions (e.g., transport, digestion, waste removal).
- The learner will be able to describe adaptations that allow an animal to survive in its environment.
- The learner will be able to pursue questions through data collection and interpretation.

Additional State Standard (Language Arts):

- The learner will be able to write descriptive, narrative, expository, and persuasive texts (500 words).

> **Materials:**
> Sand dollars (can be purchased online)
> Overhead transparencies and charts
> Hand lenses
> Measurement devices such as rulers and scales
> Computers with Internet access (or printed information on sand dollars)
> Writing and drawing paper (including paper or electronic journals if desired)
> Glue, construction paper, and markers

Objectives:

1. Students will pursue empirical questions of their choosing through observation and research.
2. Students will explain the sand dollar's structures and adaptations.
3. Students will compose 500-word expository texts to describe their findings.

Supporting Gifted Learners:

1. Allow another avenue for students to record extensive numbers of questions if they arise (e.g., journals or wall charts).
2. If students' experience with sand dollars is well developed, provide another animal (perhaps of students' choice) for investigation.
3. Provide extensive resources for research, such as contact information for marine scientists.

Supporting Learners with Behavioral Difficulties:

1. Provide leadership roles for students needing support.
2. Review expectations for handling materials appropriately.
3. Check for understanding and obtain students' agreement with behavior guidelines.
4. Be prepared with alternative learning experiences if students make inappropriate choices. Follow through.
5. Use physical proximity for behavior support.

Engage (*Teacher presents interesting real-world problem or phenomenon.*)

Active Teaching Strategy: Object-based Inquiry (p. 124)

1. The teacher describes her experience in searching for the perfect sand dollar on the beach. It begins, "For one of my recent birthdays, my family and I spent some time at the beach. For my birthday, I wanted just one perfect sand dollar. We hunted and hunted until my son reached down into the glistening sand and grasped it! A flawless sand dollar!" She holds up the sand dollar and smiles. She continues with her story, telling in detail of finding not just one, but many, many unbroken sand dollars. She posts an overhead transparency depicting her finds (below). (Note: She also points out that she checked the legality of collecting shells before her search and encourages students to do the same, as some coastal areas are protected.)
2. The teacher presents her questions, working hard to create an air of intrigue: "I began to worry that some sand dollars were very small." (She pauses.) "That made me ask myself some questions: Why are some smaller than others? How did they die? Did something in the water kill them? These are just the hard remains (shells) of the animals. What did they look like when they were alive? Were they huge? What color were they?"

Figure 2.6 Fifth-grade Science Lesson: Sand Dollars

3. The teacher distributes just one sand dollar to each group of students to pique their interests and to fuel questions. She asks for their questions and records them in a list on the overhead (chart created on paper or projected computer chart may be used instead). She models by listing her questions first. Students' questions come easily: "What are the petals on top?" "Do all sand dollars have a flat side?" "What's making that noise when I shake it?" "Were they animals?" The teacher uses facial expressions and verbal signals to convey her appreciation of students' questions and to encourage more: "Oh!" she tells one student, "Great question! I bet other people wonder that, too!" Students fill two overhead transparencies with questions. The teacher tells students that more questions will no doubt arise during the lesson and that students should continue to state them so that they can be added to the question overheads.

4. Troubleshooting: If students' questions are slow in coming, the teacher plans to let students talk in pairs before asking them to contribute questions to the class chart.

Explore (*Students explore the real-world problem or phenomenon.*)

1. The teacher leaves students' questions posted and invites students to begin their investigations: "You have asked such interesting questions! We have so much to learn about these creatures! Now is the time to begin finding the answers to our questions. Let's start with some more careful observation."

2. The teacher instructs students on and demonstrates appropriate behavior and use of materials during the lesson. Sand dollars are fragile, and measurement tools need to be used correctly. She gives special, though low-key, attention to ensure that students who need behavior support understand expectations and are ready to proceed.

3. She distributes more sand dollars—at least one for each pair. She asks students to carefully observe and sketch their sand dollars on the drawing paper. "Draw your sand dollar in such good detail that each of us could pick your sand dollar out of a pile just by looking at your drawing." The teacher invites students to use words in addition to their drawings, and she suggests that students use measuring tools to increase the specificity of their observations. "We can answer our questions more easily if we have very precise information. Try finding the mass of your sand dollar. Try measuring its diameter. How about its height?"

4. She invites students to list observations in their own journals (optionally). Students also continue to add questions to the list begun earlier in the lesson.

Develop (*Teacher helps students consolidate content through explicit instruction.*)

1. After 15 minutes of excited class exploration, the teacher leads a discussion to help students find patterns across their observations: "Let's see what we can conclude about sand dollars at this point. Are there things that all sand dollars in the room have in common? That only *some* have in common? How do they range in mass? In diameter?" To prepare students for the discussion, she invites them to, briefly, visit other student groups, observe their sand dollars, and discuss their observations.

2. Active Teaching Strategy: Graphic Organizers (p. 204) (The teacher uses one form of Graphic Organizer, a semantic map, and builds it with the students throughout the lesson.) The teacher draws the semantic map (below) on the board and uses it to record information about sand dollars during the students' discussion here and throughout the develop phase of the learning cycle. (Note that the semantic map depicted below includes a few of the students' thoughts.) At this point in the lesson, most observations will pertain to just one category on the map: structures. Many students create their own semantic maps for note taking, which can enhance their later writings. The teacher leaves in view the overhead transparency depicting questions and focuses students on determining which of their questions now have some tentative answers.

3. When students note that many of their questions are unanswered, the teacher reminds them of the importance of research. They use the Internet and printed resources to conduct further research on their sand dollar questions. The teacher ensures that two questions are included in the research: "What adaptations do the sand dollars have that help them survive?" and "What structures do they have to carry out basic functions?" (These two questions are from the state standards and from the lesson objectives.)

4. Students record results of their inquiries both on the class semantic map and, as desired, in their journals.

5. The teacher concludes the discussion by ensuring that all students in the class have done three things:
   • Sought answers to their own sand dollar questions.
   • Discovered a number of structures that allow the sand dollar to carry out basic functions such as digestion and waste removal. (Examples include the mouth, breathing tube feet, and the anus.)

Figure 2.6 *Continued*

- Discovered behavioral and structural adaptations that enhance sand dollars' survival. (Examples include the limited size, the flattened disk shape, and the swallowing of sand for ballast.)

Apply (*Students use content in a new real-world context.*)

Active Teaching Strategy: "I Didn't Know That . . ." Response Frames (p. 218)

1. Later, during writing time, students compose expository text to share the results of their sand dollar explorations. They create sand dollar books using "I Didn't Know That . . ." Response Frames (p. 218) with multiple pages. As one possible format, each left-hand page may complete the structured prompt, "I didn't know that . . ." and the right-hand page may contain extended text to support that statement. Students may be asked to write one paragraph of text for each of the four major sections of the semantic map, ensuring that they address the sand dollar's structures and its adaptations. They use construction paper as a backing, and for illustrations, they use their earlier sketches and new ones created in markers. (This phase may take several days of instruction, depending on students' need for support during the writing process.)

2. The class examines the sand dollar questions that are unanswered and lists any new questions that have since arisen. Students discuss possible avenues for discovering their answers in a discussion on what they would like to learn next. Examples include questions about animals that live in interaction with the sand dollar and how scientists have learned about humans by studying sand dollars.

3. Extension: Some students (including a group of gifted students) become so interested in sand dollars that the teacher creates a "beach center" in one corner of her room where students bring in and investigate other legally collected specimens. She invites two parents, one a marine biologist and one a beach crew worker, to visit the class to provide additional insights.

You can find a color version of this photo on the accompanying Teacher Resources CD.

Figure 2.6   *Continued*

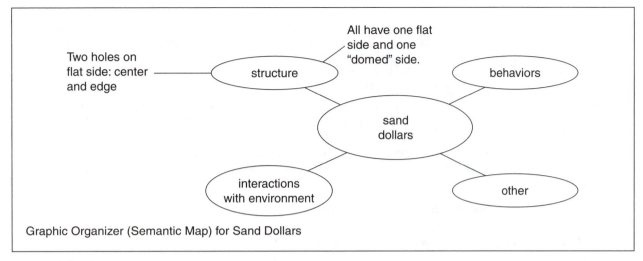

Graphic Organizer (Semantic Map) for Sand Dollars

Figure 2.6   *Continued*

Housekeeping Information

Time Estimate:
    1 or 2 class periods

Active Teaching Strategies:
    Mystery Bags (p. 110)
    Geniuses and Super Inteligentes (p. 190)

State Standard:

- The learner will explore the origins of U.S. involvement in World War II, with a focus on the events leading up to Pearl Harbor.

Objective:

- Students will explain events precipitating the attack on Pearl Harbor.

Supporting Students with Learning Difficulties:

1. Students who need support in processing information can be paired with other students.
2. This lesson provides good support for independent reading. Additionally, students with reading difficulties can read text that has been highlighted or that has marginal notes added.
3. The independent writing activity (homework) can be adjusted to meet students' individual needs.

Materials:

Paper bags (1 per group) filled with pictures and objects related to WWII events (following this plan)

Teacher computer station with projection capabilities

Overhead or other projection of major points (following this plan)

Student textbooks

Brief quiz

Timer

Anticipatory Set (*The teacher sets the stage for the lesson.*)

1. Focus: Active Teaching Strategy: Mystery Bags (p. 110)
    a. The teacher distributes one bag to each group and tells them that clues for the day's lesson are found within the bags. Students are to act as detectives in piecing together those clues.
    b. He reminds them of how to handle materials and ideas with respect.
    c. Within each group, students pass the bag from person to person, each drawing out one item and hypothesizing on the lesson's content based on that item. The teacher circulates and listens to ideas, and he responds without evaluating the ideas.

Figure 2.7   Eleventh-grade U.S. History Lesson: The Road to World War II

d. After all items have been discussed within the groups, the teacher holds up one or two of the items that provoked interesting responses from the students (perhaps the plastic tiger and the coin) and summarizes what he heard from the class. He concludes by saying, "As we move through today's lesson, test your ideas and see how your initial hypotheses match our discussion. You have some good ideas, and I think you may be in for a few surprises!"

2. The teacher states the objective: "By the time you leave for next period, you will not only be able to describe the significance of each of those items from your bag, but also be able to recount the major events that led up to U.S. involvement in World War II."

3. The teacher states the purpose of the lesson: "This lesson will shed light on how Americans learned to think globally as a result of World War II, a lesson we seem to continue to value as our modern world continues to shrink."

Input and Guided Practice (*The teacher provides information and checks for understanding. Students practice information under the teacher's direction.*)

Active Teaching Strategy: Geniuses and Super Inteligentes (p. 190)

1. The teacher provides input on events leading up to U.S. involvement in World War II, using key points found in the chart below to structure his input.

2. He begins by putting students in partner groups, with one partner labeled the "Genius" and one the "Super Inteligente." Threesomes allow students who need support to work with two partners. Together two people fill the role of Genius or Super Inteligente.

3. For the odd-numbered items, he speaks only to the Geniuses: "Geniuses, this is for you. You are the ones with the skills to master this important information. You also have the skills to teach it to your Super Inteligente friend. When I've finished talking, it's your turn to teach. Super Inteligentes: You sleep for a few minutes." He speaks for no more than 2 minutes, using materials such as Internet sites and maps from the students' texts to support his points. When he concludes, he invites questions from the Geniuses and then times them for 3 minutes as they teach the same information to the Super Inteligentes.

4. For the even-numbered items, the teacher speaks only to the Super Inteligentes: "This information is just for you. Only you can make it clear to those Geniuses." After 2 minutes of teaching time, he fields questions from the Super Inteligentes and then asks them to instruct their Genius partners.

5. The teacher finishes this section of the lesson by asking recall questions related to each major point.

Closure (*The teacher draws the lesson to a close and does a final check on student mastery of objectives.*)

1. As a final check on their mastery of the lesson's objectives, the teacher distributes a brief true-false quiz that can be quickly checked. Or, he flashes it on the board or overhead projector. After a couple minutes, they correct the quiz, with students calling out answers using unison response. The teacher quickly addresses any troublesome items.

2. For an emotional close, the teacher plays President Franklin Delano Roosevelt's "The Day Which Will Live in Infamy" radio address, wherein he addresses Congress to request a declaration of war (found at http://www.archives.gov/digital_classroom/lessons/day_of_infamy/day_of_infamy.html). Congress nearly unanimously supported the request, and the United States was swept officially into the second world war.

Independent Practice (*Students practice information without the teacher's guidance.*)

1. As homework, students read their textbook's account of the events preceding Pearl Harbor and the attack itself. They write one paragraph to answer the question, "What caused the United States to enter World War II?"

2. Students are also invited to read on the Internet compelling information on Pearl Harbor, including numerous firsthand accounts. One such site is http://plasma.nationalgeographic.com/pearlharbor/

Figure 2.7 *Continued*

Mystery Bag Items for the Road to World War II Lesson

Object	Significance (Background for Teacher)
Internet-retrieved photograph of the Lugouqiao (translated as "The Moon over the Lugou Bridge at Dawn," known also as the Marco Polo Bridge) in Beijing	Japan's attacks on China brought China into the war and roused countries such as the United States and Britain against Japan, though none was willing to use force to halt Japan's expansion efforts. The Incident at Lugou Bridge at Dawn marked the beginning of the Sino-Japanese War (1937–1945).
Small sealed container of bath or baby oil (or photo of oil barrel), or a piece of iron or steel	In 1940 and 1941, the United States and other countries (Britain and the Netherlands) imposed economic sanctions on Japan in response to Japan's continued efforts to expand into regions such as China and French Indochina. First, the United States instituted an embargo on fuel, steel, and scrap iron. Next, an oil embargo was instituted. Japan, seeing the embargo as a threat to its national security, prepared for war even as it continued to search for ways to obtain its desired territories.
U.S. coin (the older the better)	The Lend-Lease Act (1941) authorized the president to aid any nation whose defense was deemed vital to the United States. The United States provided aid to the Allies even before officially declaring war.
Small plastic tiger (or drawing of tiger)	Two referents are possible: 1. The Flying Tigers were a group of U.S. volunteer pilots who flew during the Japanese attacks on Burma, 1941. 2. Some Japanese pilots mistakenly read Japanese Commander Mitsuo Fuchida's telegraph message ("to ra, to ra . . .") as "tora," the Japanese word for tiger. Actually, the message meant, "Attack, surprise successful."
Chart of Pearl Harbor, captured from Japanese mini-subs after the attack	(Available at Department of the Navy, Naval Historical Center: http://www.history.navy.mil/photos/events/wwii-pac/pearlhbr/ph-ja5.htm) Accurate intelligence contributed to a successful attack.

Major Points for Geniuses and Super Inteligentes Lesson Input

1. Acts of Aggression: Germany and Italy
2. U.S. Policy of Neutrality
3. Japanese Aggression
4. U.S. Economic Response to Japanese Aggression

Figure 2.7 *Continued*

◤ PARTING WORDS: MASTERING ACTIVE TEACHING STRATEGIES

Active teaching strategies can infuse incredible excitement and meaningful learning into the classroom by encouraging interaction, language use, and personal connections with the content. But mastering any strategy can provide challenges; using active teaching strategies virtually always involves at least some degree of risk for the teacher. Some tips for implementing and mastering active teaching strategies include the following:

1. Start with strategies that feel low risk.

2. Take small steps. Try just one or two strategies at a time.

3. If a strategy seems particularly difficult or foreign, try watching a colleague model it first.

4. Try a strategy several times before evaluating its place in your repertoire. Staff development experts (Showers, Joyce, & Bennett, 1987) suggest that a complex teaching strategy may not become a fully comfortable part of a teacher's repertoire until after two dozen uses!

5. Sometimes active teaching strategies work, and sometimes they do not. The trick is to learn from mistakes, so get and analyze feedback. Discover students' reactions to a strategy and the degree to which it helped them learn. (As a side note: Expect a mixed review, at least initially, from students. People have different preferences.) Ask a colleague to observe. Reflect on your own observations. What, specifically, went well? What could be improved for next time?

Welcome, now, to Part II: Strategies for Active Teaching and Learning. Bon Voyage!

P A R T

II

STRATEGIES FOR ACTIVE TEACHING AND LEARNING

STRATEGIES FOR ACTIVATING PRIOR KNOWLEDGE AND BUILDING A PURPOSE FOR LEARNING

Active teachers help students think about what they already know about a topic and support them in building purposes for learning. Because prior knowledge is essential for making sense of new information, prompting students to think about what they already know helps students establish connections between new and existing knowledge. Additionally, when teachers activate students' background knowledge, they discover what students know about the topic and can then incorporate that knowledge into their instruction, further supporting linkages between the new and the known. When students generate their own purposes for learning, they are more likely to take control of that learning. The strategies in Chapter 3 have two goals in common: to activate students' relevant background knowledge, making that knowledge accessible to students and visible to teachers, and to help students set purposes for learning. Although the strategies can be used at any point in a lesson, they are particularly effective at the beginning of the lesson or unit of study.

Chapter 3's strategies ask students to reflect on what they know using a variety of structures. Students write, they draw and build, they share ideas with peers, articulating what they know and gaining additional knowledge or insights from others. Students analyze information they have generated related to the topic. They sort it and combine it. They make generalizations and draw conclusions. As students think about what they know and what they want to know, they ready themselves for learning.

When students participate in strategies that activate prior knowledge and build purposes for learning, they

- ✔ Attend to the information.
- ✔ Increase their engagement with the content.
- ✔ Make varied connections with the information.
- ✔ Put language to their ideas as they share with peers.
- ✔ Learn from the experiences and ideas of their peers.
- ✔ Take ownership for their learning.
- ✔ Establish relevance for the lesson.

You may wish to review Chapter 2, especially Figures 2.1 through 2.3, for suggestions on using active teaching strategies with students who are not independent readers and writers, students who are learning English, and students who have specific learning needs. You may also wish to review Figure 1.4 for typical cognitive, physical, social, and emotional needs and interests of students of various ages.

STRATEGY 1 Quick Scans

LANGUAGE DEMANDS	LITERACY DEMANDS
Appropriate for:	Appropriate for:
✔ Early English Learners	✔ Emerging Readers/Writers
✔ Intermediate English Learners	✔ Intermediate Readers/Writers
✔ Advanced English Learners	✔ Proficient Readers/Writers

Quick Scans serve many purposes in the classroom. First, they can be used as informal formative assessments of students' knowledge of the content, thus providing the teacher with important information that will guide planning. Quick Scans provide tentative insights into whether the students have considerable background knowledge on the topic, some knowledge, or little knowledge. Quick Scans also are useful for activating students' background knowledge and for prompting students to make connections with the content, both of which contribute to learning new content (Pressley, 2002). They facilitate an active approach to the content, promote a reflective frame of mind and an appreciation of students' existing knowledge, and may pique students' interest in the subject matter. Furthermore, the practice of thinking about what we know before engaging in new learning is a form of self-assessment, and the ability to engage in self-assessment is central to reading success (Afflerbach, 2002) and likely to success in all learning. Quick Scans are typically conducted before the onset of a unit of study or lesson.

PREPARATION

1. Determine when you will conduct a Quick Scan and select a Quick Scan strategy from among the alternatives below. Note that some rely on self-report of students' understanding, and others take a small sampling of that understanding. Determine, also, the nature of the question you will ask. Will it be a general question, such as what they know about a broad topic? Or will it be a more specific question, such as what they know about a particular term (or terms) or a specific content standard?

You can find this template on the accompanying Teacher Resources CD and at the back of the book.

2. Collect items needed for the alternative you select. Some alternatives call for no materials. See the Teacher Resources CD for a blank target that can be duplicated for On Target (Alternative 4, below).

IMPLEMENTATION

The strategies that follow offer students a relatively anonymous means for indicating familiarity with the content. Once you have collected student data, share it with your students and talk about what it means. Is the class as a whole rather knowledgeable on the topic? What does their background knowledge (or lack of background knowledge) mean for them as they study this topic? What does it mean for you, their teacher? After the unit of study or lesson, you may wish to encourage students to reexamine the ratings they gave earlier in the lesson. You may even ask students to give themselves a postlesson rating. How has their knowledge base changed? Do they wish to know more? How might they pursue further information?

Select from among the following Quick Scan alternatives. Scans 1 through 5 rely on self-report. Scans 6 through 8 sample students' knowledge directly.

ALTERNATIVES

1. Colored Dots:

a. Determine several items for student consideration. For instance, if your high schoolers soon will be studying Mao's influence on China, you might include the following: Chinese dynasties, communism, Little Red Book, Let a Hundred Flowers Bloom, Great Leap Forward, agriculture, capitalism, Chinese birth rate, Taiwan, and communes. If your third graders will be learning about computer technology, you might include these terms: flash drive, cursor, software, memory, disk drive, hard drive, CD, keyboard, monitor, and mouse.

b. Write each of your items in a column on a chart, and share the chart with your students. Indicate that these are some of the topics you will be studying.

c. Provide each student with two red and two green dot stickers (1/2-inch in diameter because this size can be easily seen across a classroom but does not take up too much space on a chart).

d. Tell your students to consider each item and identify the two they know the least about and the two they know the most about. Advise them that the red dot represents little knowledge and the green dot represents a great deal of knowledge.

e. Allow one row, table, or group at a time to affix their dots next to the two items they think they know least and most about. Encourage students to have mentally made their selections before approaching the chart; you do not want excessive time taken because students are standing at the chart pondering their choices. Have students place their dots in a row next to the item so that a bar graph is developed. Because the same item may have both red and green dots, have your students place different colored dots in separate rows so that a single row does not have a mix of colors. At a glance, you and your students will be able to see how the class as a whole rates its knowledge of the items listed on the chart.

  You may choose to require that students use all of the dots you gave them, but if some students feel they know very little about all of the topics and so do not wish to affix their green dots, that should be acceptable.

  Illustrations, rather than words or phrases, may be used at all grade levels, as in the example provided in Figure S1.1.

  You will need to teach your students how to place their dots on the chart so that a bar graph is constructed. It helps students if you draw a line at the starting point and then tell students to have their dots equidistant from one another. Demonstrate for all ages. Provide practice for younger students.

2. Finger Ratings:

a. Announce to students the upcoming topic of study. Ask students to think about what they already know about the topic and to rate their knowledge using a scale of zero to five. Ratings of zero are represented with a fist and indicate that the student believes she knows virtually nothing about the topic as you stated it. Ratings of one, indicated by one finger, indicate that the student knows very little. Ratings of two, three, and four indicate increasingly more knowledge, and a rating of five suggests that the student considers herself extremely well versed in the topic.

b. Give students about 30 seconds to determine a rating and then, upon your signal, to hold their rating in front of their chests for you to see. Discourage students from raising their hands high in the air because that makes their ratings more public and may cause some self-consciousness. Scan the room quickly to get an impression of students' self-perceptions of their knowledge of the topic.

c. As an alternative, announce the topic and then allow students 1 or 2 minutes to talk with peers. This may spark their thinking, and students may realize they know more about the topic than they initially thought. Then ask for students' ratings.

3. Class Continuum:
   a. Write the topic on the board or chart paper and place a horizontal line below it. Label one end "Completely Unfamiliar" and the other end "Very Familiar." Tell students to place a slash or tally mark at a point on the continuum that reflects their level of familiarity with the topic. Have several markers available and have students move in groups to the board to record their ratings. Alternatively, you may have the continuum on an overhead transparency that quickly gets passed around the classroom with an overhead transparency pen. After each student has made a mark, place the transparency on the overhead projector to share the findings with your students. To speed up the process, you can use several transparencies, say one for each row of students, and then stack them so the continua overlap.
   b. View the completed continuum and note the range of familiarity with the topic.

   Rather than a continuum, you may create discrete categories. Blachowicz (1986), for instance, suggests having students rate their knowledge of vocabulary by marking one of three categories: can define, have seen/heard, or ? ("?" indicates "no knowledge"). Others use categories of a Self-adhesive Note, Sheet of Paper, Small Book, and Large Book and ask students to indicate which of these they could fill given the amount of knowledge they currently have on the topic.

4. On Target:
   a. Distribute paper and have students sketch a target with a bull's eye and two outer rings.
   b. Provide a brief list of terms. Ask individuals to write the terms on their targets. The more they know about a term, the closer that term goes to the bull's eye.
   c. Alternatively, create a class target and allow small groups to determine where to place the terms, based on group consensus.

5. Yes or No (Gregory & Chapman, 2002):
   a. Have students write "Yes" on one side of an index card and "No" on the other. Or, write "Got it!" and "No clue!" or "Way!" and "No Way!" or two other contrasting terms your students might find amusing.
   b. Display—one item at a time—a brief list of terms, pictures, diagrams, or concepts.
   c. Ask students whether they understand the meaning or significance of the item you display. Allow brief partner or group discussion time first, if desired.
   d. Give the students a signal ("Show me!") and ask students to display their cards.
   e. Alternatively, use three cards (one for "Somewhat"). Modify your cards based on the nature of the content. Blank colored flash cards are good for this purpose.

6. Book Look:
   a. Ask students to scan the chapter or lesson in the textbook. Focus their attention on chapter objectives, photos, headings, and the questions at the close of the chapter.
   b. Ask students what they know about a sampling of these items.

7. Sample Problem:
   a. Begin the lesson by displaying an item on the overhead projector, projected computer screen, or white board that addresses the heart of the lesson's content. Examples include math problems, key vocabulary terms, or central questions.
   b. Ask students individually or in pairs or groups to discuss what they know about solving the problem or answering the question. Remind them that you do not expect them to solve it completely at this point; you are determining where to focus your instruction.

8. Quick Quiz:
   a. Review your lesson objectives and use them to develop a Quick Quiz (a brief pretest). Quick Quizzes have three to five items that vary in difficulty. The first item is the easiest.

b. Read the items aloud or display them and give students no more than 5 minutes to complete the quiz. Students may work individually, in pairs, or in groups.

c. Score the quizzes on the spot. One technique is to have students pass their papers (no names, please) continuously until you say stop. Students grade the quiz they are holding. To analyze results, ask students to raise a hand if the paper they are holding has the item number you call out correct.

d. At the lesson's close, ask one or more of the Quick Quiz questions again.

TIME ALLOTMENT

Keep the Quick Scans to less than 5 minutes. Subsequent conversations, however, may take longer.

EXAMPLES

Figure S1.1 displays a colored dot chart developed by first graders prior to learning about weather instruments. Figure S1.2 shows a continuum on which high school students made a slash mark indicating their familiarity with Homer's *Odyssey* when told that it is an epic poem that relays the story of a man trying to get home after the Trojan War.

TROUBLESHOOTING

1. If students look completely blank when you announce the topic, you might give a few brief highlights of the content before asking for their ratings. For instance, in Figure S1.2, simply hearing "Homer's *Odyssey*" might not activate any knowledge; however, once told that the literature includes the Cyclops and Sirens and a 20-year journey after the Trojan War, students may realize they do indeed have some background on the topic.

2. Students who have background knowledge may express enthusiasm about their knowledge and wish to share their expertise. You will need to decide whether to allow this discussion. We think it is likely to stimulate other students' interest, and we appreciate it when students want to share information. Nevertheless, it may reroute your plan, so be prepared.

3. Many Quick Scans are based on self-report. Encourage students to be honest with themselves, neither shying away from indicating that they know a great deal about the subject matter nor suggesting that they know more than they do because they think that is a desirable response. Assure students that there is no value judgment placed on their ratings and that, in fact, you are not paying attention to individual ratings. Tell students the value for you in learning whether they have background on the topic and the value for them in considering their existing knowledge on the topic.

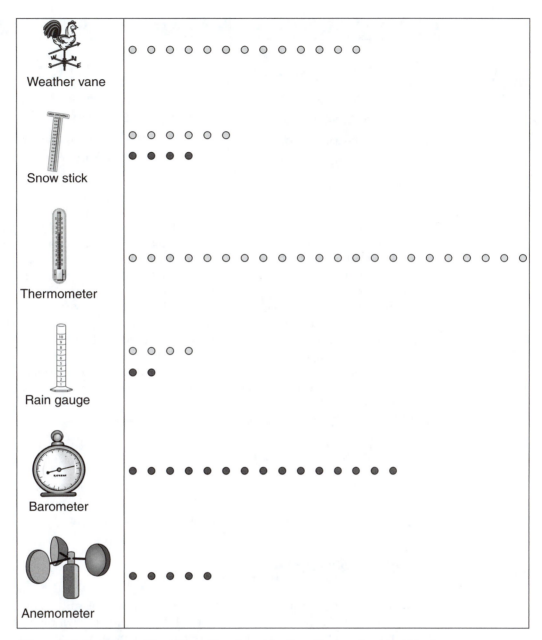

Figure S1.1   Colored Dot Chart Developed by First Graders Studying Weather Instruments

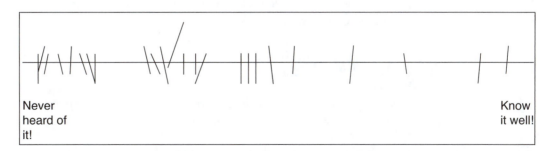

Figure S1.2   Continuum Completed by High School English Students Before Studying Homer's *Odyssey*

STRATEGY 2 Quick Writes

LANGUAGE DEMANDS	LITERACY DEMANDS
Appropriate for:	Appropriate for:
Early English Learners	Emerging Readers/Writers
✔ Intermediate English Learners	✔ Intermediate Readers/Writers
✔ Advanced English Learners	✔ Proficient Readers/Writers

Quick Writes (Elbow, 1973) may be used to activate students' relevant experiences or background knowledge on a topic, thus facilitating connections between new and existing knowledge. As the name suggests, students quickly write about a topic. Because this is a quickly written piece, students should not be concerned with the form of their writing (i.e., spelling, grammar, organization of ideas) at this time. The point is to get ideas on paper. Students may be given a more or less open prompt. An example of an open prompt is "Quickly write what you know about the respiratory system." Some open prompts require simple listings, as in brainstorming, such as "Write as many real-life uses of percentages as you can think of in 1 minute." A less open prompt asks student to complete a sentence and then elaborate. For example, middle schoolers might be asked to complete the following statement: "Many Japanese-Americans were placed in internment camps when . . ."

PREPARATION

1. Develop a prompt that will draw on students' knowledge or experiences with the content.
2. Plan whether and how students will share their writing.

IMPLEMENTATION

1. Tell students about the topic of the upcoming unit of study. For example, you might inform students that you are about to begin a study of civil rights. Alerting students to the upcoming unit of study, however, is optional; you may wish to have students engage in the Quick Write prior to informing them of the context of the prompt.
2. Ask students to quickly write in response to the prompt you provide.
3. Allow students to share their writing with one another. Encourage volunteers to share with the entire class.

ALTERNATIVES

1. To increase fluency in students' writing, which can be especially helpful for students acquiring English, try these suggestions in isolation or in a combination that suits your purposes:
   a. Require students to think for a specified amount of time (30 seconds?) before they pick up their pencils to write.
   b. Allow students to talk with a peer for a brief amount of time (30 seconds?) before they write. Talking first can help students access their memories.

    c. Allow partners to compose joint Quick Writes. One partner might hold the pen, or they may trade off.

  2. Consider writing again after partner or class discussion.

TIME ALLOTMENT

Although Quick Writes can take as few as 5 minutes, plan on about 15 minutes for this strategy if you include time for sharing and discussion.

EXAMPLES

See Figure S2.1 for examples of Quick Write prompts.

TROUBLESHOOTING

  1. Tell students they must write. No blank pages are permitted! If they are having difficulty expressing complete thoughts, they may write words or phrases. Over time, they are likely to be more comfortable with rapidly writing elaborated ideas, particularly once they realize that their writing is not evaluated in this strategy.

  2. The time pressure may make some students uncomfortable. You need to assure them that your intent is to give them a few moments to consider a subject before you begin your lesson. Do not grade Quick Writes. Use them to encourage students to think about what they know about a topic or what experiences they have had relevant to a topic. By writing, they are giving language to their knowledge and experiences. Students who otherwise might have sat passively in your classroom are more engaged through participation in this strategy.

  3. This strategy is useful with students who are able to record their thoughts in writing. However, be aware that even some older students struggle with written language. Be sure to tell students that you will not be looking for spelling, punctuation, or other elements of form.

  4. Allow students to tell one another what they wrote rather than read it verbatim if you believe they may be self-conscious about their writing.

First-grade Science:	Quickly write some information about the ocean.
Third-grade Science:	Quickly write about an experience with rain.
Fifth-grade Language Arts:	Quickly write what you know about dictionaries.
Junior High Physical Education:	Quickly write what you know about the importance of physical activity.
High School Social Studies:	You have 2 minutes to list as many African nations as you can.

Figure S2.1   Sample Quick Write Prompts

STRATEGY 3 Quick Draws

LANGUAGE DEMANDS	LITERACY DEMANDS
Appropriate for:	Appropriate for:
✔ Early English Learners	✔ Emerging Readers/Writers
✔ Intermediate English Learners	✔ Intermediate Readers/Writers
✔ Advanced English Learners	✔ Proficient Readers/Writers

Before studying a topic, students quickly draw in response to a prompt. Drawing provides a nonlinguistic means of representing knowledge (Marzano, Pickering, & Pollock, 2001; Short, Harste, & Burke, 1996) and so is particularly useful with students who are new to the language or who do not have sufficient command over written language to write in response to a prompt. Students access their prior experiences and background knowledge as they develop their drawings, and drawings can reveal much to the teacher about students' readiness to engage in the unit of study or lesson.

PREPARATION

1. Decide on the prompt.
2. Although generally students use drawing instruments of their choice, on some occasions they may need particular media. For instance, students may need access to colored pencils or markers if they are to draw the visible spectrum. On the other hand, a pencil is sufficient if students are asked to draw radio waves of different frequencies.
3. Ensure that students have access to drawing paper.

IMPLEMENTATION

1. Tell students that you are about to begin a unit of study on whatever topic you will be teaching. (This is optional; it may be that you do not want students to know the upcoming topic.)
2. Provide a prompt related to the topic. For example, as you begin a unit on mammals with first graders, you might ask students to draw two animals: one that is a mammal and one that is not. Or, as you begin a unit on the human body with fifth graders, you might ask students to quickly sketch an outline of the human body and then to draw the major organs, paying attention to their location, size, and shape.
3. Assure students that your purpose is to learn about their experiences and that you will not judge the artistic quality of their work. If some students seem hesitant to draw, try the second suggestion in Troubleshooting, 2.
4. As students work, look at their drawings to gain a sense of their background knowledge. You may wish to make a few supportive statements about their work in general. For instance, you might say, "I can tell already that you know quite a bit about snails' bodies!" Be sure to monitor your responses to drawings. If you react negatively (e.g., "You don't know all the parts of an insect?!" or "This is a pretty simplistic rendering of a basketball court.") to a student's sincere attempt to respond to the prompt, you are likely to inhibit further participation.
5. Let students talk about their drawings with one another. You may wish to ask students what their drawings have in common. For instance, if kindergarteners are given the prompt, "Take a few minutes to sketch a bird; include as many features as you

can think of and have time for," many students may include wings and beaks. Ask students to look at one another's drawings and identify the commonalities. This discussion may be referred to later as you share features of birds. You may also wish to ask about differences in the drawings: "All of the birds in your sketches have wings and beaks, but not all are colored blue. How else are the pictures different? What does that tell us about birds?"

6. You may wish to collect the drawings for further analysis.

7. Think about displaying students' work, being sure to identify them as "Quick Draws" so students are not too focused on their artistic skills. Warn students in advance if you plan to display their drawings.

ALTERNATIVES

1. Develop a prompt that elicits students' personal experiences rather than their knowledge base. For example, as you begin a lesson on the moods that music can evoke, you might ask students to recall some of their favorite music and draw what it makes them feel. Or, as you begin to study the needs of animals, ask students to draw a pet they have (or wish they had) and something that they are doing (or would do) to care for the pet.

2. Rather than drawing, have students construct three-dimensional representations of their understandings (i.e., Quick Builds). For instance, fourth graders may use buttons to represent their understanding of a division problem. High school students may use pipe cleaners to show the double helix structure of DNA.

3. Consider using Quick Draws both before and after students have completed a lesson or unit of study. Ideally, they—and you—will see a change, refinement, or elaboration of their initial understandings. Using a folded paper, with one half for the "before" Quick Draw and one for the "after" Quick Draw, can portray this growth vividly.

4. Use white boards for the Quick Draws and allow students to modify their drawings throughout the lesson or unit of study.

TIME ALLOTMENT

Quick Draws may take 1 to 5 minutes, depending on the age of the students, the demands of the prompt, and the time available. More time is needed if students are going to share with one another.

EXAMPLES

See Figure S3.1 for examples of Quick Draw prompts.

Kindergarten Science:	Draw something that tastes sweet.
Second-grade Mathematics:	Draw what you think of when you hear the word *shapes*.
Fourth-grade Social Studies:	Draw something related to our state.
Junior High Science:	Draw pollution.
High School Social Studies:	Use the tan piece of yarn at your desk to shape an outline of the continent of Africa. Use the blue yarn pieces to add major rivers (a Quick Build prompt).

Figure S3.1   Sample Quick Draw Prompts

TROUBLESHOOTING

1. Use Quick Draws when students have at least some knowledge of the topic so that they can participate. If students have little background knowledge on the topic of the prompt, they will be unable to generate a drawing. Asking students to draw what they know about molecules when they have no knowledge of molecules places them in a frustrating situation.

2. Some students may be concerned about the accuracy of their drawings or feel uncomfortable with their ability to draw. Try one or more of these suggestions to put them at ease.
   a. Remind them that you *hope* that their drawings show they do not know everything about the topic because you hope they will learn a few things in the upcoming unit of study.
   b. Remind older students that they probably viewed themselves as great artists in kindergarten.
   c. Gently reinforce high expectations that developing the willingness and skills to represent thoughts, objects, and events through images are part of becoming well educated; the more ways we have to express ourselves, the more powerful we are as communicators. List a few appealing jobs that may require some drawing. Some examples include artist, auto mechanic, physician, draftsperson, videogame designer, scientist, and cartographer.
   d. Interject a little humor. Allow students to say, in unison, "I can't draw!" one time, and then ban the statement. We know a sixth-grade teacher who, with her class, held a funeral for the phrase "I can't" and then buried it in the schoolyard.
   e. Provide students with a choice regarding sharing with peers by indicating that if students wish, they may show one another their drawings.
   f. Use the strategy frequently. Hesitant students tend to become more comfortable with sketching as it becomes a normal or typical part of classroom instruction.

3. Prepare students to respond to each other's work in caring ways. Ban negative comments or criticisms, and teach students to give their peers neutral feedback ("You used so many colors.") or specific positive feedback ("The way you drew the tail looks so realistic!").

4. Drawings can reveal students' misconceptions or stereotypes. Information about misconceptions can be highly valuable for planning future instruction. Avoid making judgments about students' knowledge based solely on their drawings, however. Students' knowledge may far exceed what they choose to represent. Likewise, they may by luck render a drawing that captures a sophisticated understanding.

STRATEGY 4 Idea Share

LANGUAGE DEMANDS	LITERACY DEMANDS
Appropriate for:	Appropriate for:
Early English Learners	Emerging Readers/Writers
✔ Intermediate English Learners	✔ Intermediate Readers/Writers
✔ Advanced English Learners	✔ Proficient Readers/Writers

Idea Share asks students to generate and share an idea related to a topic based on their experiences. Students might share an observation, an activity, or one example from a category. Idea Share requires students to tap their background knowledge by considering something they already know or have experienced. Strategies that prompt students to activate background knowledge related to a topic under study promote understanding of new material (Anderson, 1984). In addition, Idea Share builds students' background knowledge by exposing them to peers' ideas and provides them with the opportunity to learn about the interests or experiences of peers. It may also allow students to see how much they have in common with classmates and therefore build a sense of community in the classroom.

In Idea Share, each student writes an idea related to a topic on a small piece of paper or index card and circulates through the room sharing and explaining his idea to others. When a student hears an idea he likes, and if the other student agrees to a trade, they trade ideas.

PREPARATION

1. Develop the prompt for the Idea Share. As you decide what you want students to share, consider the ability of the students to answer the prompt in a fairly short time as well as the potential for the prompt to elicit diverse, but brief, responses. Students' experiences should be considered when developing the prompt.

You can find this template on the accompanying Teacher Resources CD and at the back of the book.

2. Make a choice about the type of paper you will use. Self-adhesive notes, index cards, or notebook paper cut into fourths are appropriate for this strategy. See the Teacher Resources CD for a template that can be duplicated and used for recording ideas and trades.

IMPLEMENTATION

1. Provide each student with the blank paper.

2. Provide the prompt to the students. The prompt will ask the students to record one idea about the topic onto the paper.

3. Ask students to circulate through the room, sharing their idea with peers. Tell students that after listening to several ideas, their task is to find an idea they are willing to exchange for their own—because they think it is interesting, because they agree or disagree with it, because they want to try it, because they have seen it or tried it before, or for whatever reason. Have students trade papers.

4. Inform the students that they are to return to their seats once they have exchanged papers. If you are using the template, students may record the ideas and the reason for the trade now.

5. Ask for volunteers to share the idea they are now holding and to provide a brief explanation of why they selected this new idea.

6. If appropriate, comment that many of the ideas the students generated and shared will be discussed in the lesson or unit. Throughout the lesson or unit, highlight ideas that were shared with the group as they connect to the content.

ALTERNATIVE

1. Emerging readers and writers might be given a prompt that asks them to draw a picture related to the topic and then explain it to their classmates.

TIME ALLOTMENT

This strategy takes about 10 minutes.

EXAMPLE

Figure S4.1 presents Idea Share prompts for several grade levels on a variety of topics.

TROUBLESHOOTING

1. Occasionally a student may have difficulty generating an idea that he feels is worthy of recording and sharing. To ensure that all students participate, circulate around the room while the students are writing and chat with individuals. When you come across a student who has written nothing, ask a few probing questions about the topic and use your knowledge of the student to support him in developing an idea.

2. If you are concerned that students may share erroneous information, devise a plan for confirming the accuracy of their ideas before they share. For instance, you may quickly check students' written ideas prior to giving the signal for them to circulate.

3. You do not need an even number of students in your class to use this strategy. Modify the directions to allow—or encourage—students to trade ideas more than once. Or, explain that trades do not need to be among pairs only. Three students might agree to exchange ideas in a small cluster. However, do not allow or encourage students to gather in small groups and share their idea in round-robin fashion. One of the benefits of this strategy is that students have the opportunity to share their idea many times. The opportunity to talk about their idea supports their understanding of their idea as they modify their explanations and provide elaborations with each sharing. It also provides English learners with a good opportunity to practice speaking about a meaningful experience in a relatively low-risk setting.

First-grade Science:	Draw a picture of your favorite animal.
Third-grade Mathematics:	Write one way fractions played a role in your life yesterday.
Fifth-grade Social Studies:	Write the name of a state that you would like to visit.
Sixth-grade Science:	Write one example of erosion you saw on your way to school this morning.
High School Social Studies:	Write an interesting word related to geography.
High School Literature:	Write the name of your favorite author.

Figure S4.1   Sample Prompts for Idea Share

4. State at the beginning that all students must get up and circulate around the room to share with peers. Engagement is generally higher when all students are moving and talking. Unless there is a good reason to do so, no student should be permitted to sit and let others come to him.

5. If your students need support in terms of behavior, be sure to provide explicit directions, model, and reinforce appropriate behavior.

6. Once in a great while you will encounter a student who does not wish to exchange her idea because she likes it better than the ideas shared by her peers. Although you might state at the beginning that students cannot be seated until they have exchanged their idea, we usually are tolerant of a student who wants to hold on to her idea, although we do ensure that she participates in the sharing.

7. Be ready with a timer or signal to draw students back to their seats if their enthusiasm prolongs the sharing session.

STRATEGY 5 Partner Share

LANGUAGE DEMANDS	LITERACY DEMANDS
Appropriate for:	Appropriate for:
Early English Learners	✔ Emerging Readers/Writers
✔ Intermediate English Learners	✔ Intermediate Readers/Writers
✔ Advanced English Learners	✔ Proficient Readers/Writers

What students know about a topic dramatically influences their future learning (Dochy, Segers, & Buehl, 1999) and other important outcomes like reading comprehension (Johnson & Pearson, 1984; Pressley, Johnson, Symons, McGoldrick, & Kurita, 1989). Reviews of research (Strangman & Hall, 2004) point to the effectiveness of activating students' prior knowledge as an active teaching strategy. Partner Share provides a quick way for students to remind themselves, and their friends, what they already know about a topic prior to instruction. In pairs, students share information related to the topic. Partner Share helps set a purpose for learning by allowing students to share what they already know and anticipate new additions to what they know. It can also be used to help students review class information and solidify learning through verbalization of the content.

You can find these templates on the accompanying Teacher Resources CD and at the back of the book.

PREPARATION

1. Generate prompts that ask for a number of responses.
2. See the Teacher Resources CD for two templates that can be duplicated if you elect to have students record their Partner Share.

IMPLEMENTATION

1. Organize students into pairs, with one trio if necessary, and ask pairs to sit facing each other.
2. Explain that students are to orally list everything they know about a topic, but that they must take turns and that each partner may share only one idea at a time. First, partner A shares one idea, then partner B shares one idea, then partner A shares another idea, and partner B shares another idea. This back-and-forth sharing continues until time is called or until both students run out of things to say.
3. Call time, comment on the interesting things you heard, and resume the class. Or, conduct a quick Whip around the room and ask each student to share one idea with the entire group. In a Whip, every student makes a brief comment in response to a prompt. Students proceed in order, up and down rows or from table to table, with no interjection from the teacher or other students. Students are encouraged to share their response even if it matches one that was already shared. Some teachers allow students to say "pass" if they do not wish to contribute.

ALTERNATIVES

1. Instead of having students share with their partner orally, ask them to share in writing. Each pair uses a single piece of paper, which is passed back and forth between them. You may wish to collect the papers at the end of the activity and review them to get a sense of what the students know or have learned.

2. If you have students who are quite new to the English language, you may give them the choice to share ideas through drawing, or you may ask all students to share this way. For instance, students may pass a paper back and forth on which they quickly sketch a variety of sea life (science) or different land forms (geography). Students may name their drawings (in any language) to the extent that they are comfortable doing so as they interact. Or, they may engage in the sharing-through-drawing silently.

3. Rather than requiring a back-and-forth exchange, occasionally use Partner Share as an opportunity for low-structured sharing of a single idea or experience: "Tell your partner about a time when you should have 'looked before you leaped'" or, "Tell your partner about one of the amendments to the U.S. Constitution."

TIME ALLOTMENT

We usually limit the Partner Share to 2 or 3 minutes if sharing orally. Written sharing takes longer, and so 3 or 4 minutes may be more appropriate. The entire activity, including giving directions and conducting a Whip, takes approximately 15 minutes, depending on the size of the class.

EXAMPLES

Figure S5.1 lists possible Partner Share prompts for a variety of settings.

TROUBLESHOOTING

1. Some people have difficulty generating ideas without a bit of "think time." For example, many students might have difficulty with quickly identifying an instance of "looking before leaping" in their own lives (as above) without some time for reflection. You may wish to let students silently and independently ponder the prompt and/or record ideas before participating in the Partner Share. They may use any written notes during the Partner Share.

2. Take care in pairing students so that they are likely to be fairly balanced in the amount of information they have to share about a topic.

First-grade Social Studies:	Tell each other about different types of transportation.
Second-grade Fine Arts:	Tell each other what comes to mind when you hear the word *art*.
Third-grade Social Studies:	Tell each other what you know about the history of our city.
Fourth-grade Science:	Tell each other what you know about the water cycle.
Fifth-grade Mathematics:	Tell each other all the places you might see a decimal.
Middle School Language Arts:	Tell each other the parts of speech.
High School Biology:	Tell each other what you know about the structure of the cell.

Figure S5.1   Sample Partner Share Prompts

STRATEGY 6 Group Graphs

LANGUAGE DEMANDS	LITERACY DEMANDS
Appropriate for:	Appropriate for:
✔ Early English Learners	✔ Emerging Readers/Writers
✔ Intermediate English Learners	✔ Intermediate Readers/Writers
✔ Advanced English Learners	✔ Proficient Readers/Writers

Group Graphs provide an opportunity for students to combine their own individual data with data shared by classmates. Students identify or gather information about a topic they will soon be studying and construct a graph representing the collective data from the class. This strategy invites students to contribute to the learning experience by providing their own information and to observe how their information fits within a bigger picture. By providing data, students become a part of the unit of study and may feel more personally connected to the topic. Additionally, this strategy allows students to be physically active as they move around the classroom to construct Group Graphs or as they provide objects or representations to build those graphs. Physical activity increases the likelihood of active engagement with the lesson (Apel, 1995; Middendorf & Kalish, 1996).

PREPARATION

1. Decide what you wish to depict with the graph. For example, as can be seen in Figure S6.1, kindergarten students might be asked to graph their birth months or the kinds of shoes they brought. Junior high students might be asked to graph their eye color.

2. Next, determine the type of graph the students will construct. Histograms and circle graphs are easily constructed as Group Graphs. See Figure S6.1 for examples.

3. Ensure that you have adequate space in your classroom to build a Group Graph. You may need to push aside some desks. Or, you may choose to construct your Group Graph outdoors.

4. Determine whether any materials will be needed. Histograms may require labels for each of the bars. Circle graphs will require string or yarn and scissors for cutting it. If the data you will collect are measurements, gather appropriate instruments. If you elect to have students transfer their Group Graph to paper later, you may wish to use one of the templates available in the Teacher Resources CD.

You can find these templates on the accompanying Teacher Resources CD and at the back of the book.

IMPLEMENTATION

1. Have the students gather their individual data.

2. Share the graph format with the students and explain that they will construct a Group Graph displaying their collective data.

3. To construct a histogram, identify for the students the areas of the room where their bars will be formed. If appropriate, mark these areas on the floor or

somehow label each bar. To make human graphs, invite the students to form bars by standing in the appropriate position. Asking students to line up in order first and then move into columns can help. If using objects or representations, have the students place them in the appropriate positions. Consider using a grid laid out on the floor.

4. To construct a human circle graph, first have the students line up based on their data such that all those with the same response stand next to each other, followed by those with a different response. For example, if students are sharing geographic features they most recently visited, responses may include deserts, mountains, lakes, oceans, and valleys. Those who visited deserts are followed in line by those who visited mountains and so on. Give the first person in each category a long piece of yarn (approximately 10 feet). Maintaining the order they established in line, have the students form a circle around you. Each student holding yarn brings you one end of the yarn and then returns to the circle. The pieces of yarn mark the divisions between the areas on the circle graph.

5. Discuss what you observe about the students' data as shared in these Group Graphs. Determine the median and mode(s) for data depicted on a histogram. If appropriate, discuss how data can be represented in different ways.

ALTERNATIVES

1. Have the students transfer their data to a spreadsheet and generate electronic graphs that can be revisited later in the lesson or unit.

2. Use Quick Scan techniques (p. 43) such as Colored Dots or Class Continuum to generate information to be graphed as a lead-in to the lesson.

TIME ALLOTMENT

This strategy generally takes from 10 to 20 minutes.

EXAMPLES

Figure S6.1 shares suggestions for group graphs for several grade levels.

Kindergarten Social Studies: Prior to learning about putting events in temporal order using a calendar, students build a histogram showing the month of their birthday. Be prepared to provide students with information if you think they may not know the month of their birth. Next door, where two students do not celebrate birthdays, the class builds a graph of favorite seasons.

Kindergarten Science: Warned the day before, students wear (or bring) one shoe to toss into the center of a circle. Students practice sorting the shoes in different ways. To convey their results, they line up members of groups ("These have laces, these have Velcro, and these have no laces or Velcro.") on a grid, marked with tape on a plastic table cloth, to build a histogram of groups of shoes, as shown on page 60.

Figure S6.1 Sample Group Graphs

Fourth-grade Mathematics: As an introduction to probability, students roll dice and construct a histogram depicting the number of students who rolled a one, the number of students who rolled a two, and so forth, up to the number who rolled a six. Students roll the dice again and build a new histogram. Then the students roll the dice twice, add their rolls together, and develop a histogram that depicts the number of students whose rolls added to two, the number whose rolls added to three, four, five, and so on, up to twelve. They repeat. What do the students notice about their histograms? What might explain their observations?

Middle School Social Studies: At the beginning of a lesson on push–pull forces in immigration, students have interviewed an adult in the community (a parent, family member, or other adult) to determine two things: (1) the decade that person's family came to the United States and (2) the major reason that person's family came to the United States. For question 1, students arrange themselves in a timeline and then "stack" the timeline into categories, building a histogram to represent time periods of immigration to the United States.

Figure S6.1 *Continued*

Junior High Science: At the beginning of a unit on heredity, students develop a human histogram showing the number of students who have blue eyes, brown eyes, or green eyes. An "other" category includes students who have two different eye colors. Students construct a human histogram for hair color or for curly and straight hair. Using the same data, students develop human circle graphs to look at the data another way. Students discuss the findings.

Green Eyes

Blue Eyes

Brown Eyes

High School Mathematics: Prior to instruction on normal distribution, students develop histograms that will likely depict a normal curve. For example, students build human histograms based on the measurements of the length of their finger spread or their arm span. Students graph the amount of time they can balance a ball on their fingertip. If the teacher thinks any of this information might be embarrassing to students or result in teasing, she provides fictional data on cards and has students build graphs based on the cards that are handed to them.

Figure S6.1 *Continued*

TROUBLESHOOTING

1. Anticipate the amount of support students will need developing their graphs and provide appropriate assistance. The first several times you develop Group Graphs, you may need to orchestrate student movement to the appropriate spots in the graph.

2. Think about your questions carefully and mentally walk through what a graph might look like, given your questions. Have you accounted for all possible responses?

STRATEGY 7 Overheard Quotes

LANGUAGE DEMANDS	LITERACY DEMANDS
Appropriate for:	Appropriate for:
Early English Learners	Emerging Readers/Writers
✔ Intermediate English Learners	✔ Intermediate Readers/Writers
✔ Advanced English Learners	✔ Proficient Readers/Writers

Years ago John Dewey (1909) argued for the importance of critical thinking to sustain a healthy democracy, and critical thinking skills are just as important in today's complex, information-driven world (McKendree, Small, Stenning, & Conlon, 2002). Fortunately, reviews of research (e.g., Cotton, 1991) indicate that teachers can enhance students' abilities to think critically by focusing on skills such as analyzing the accuracy of information and using evidence to support conclusions. During Overheard Quotes, students circulate to hear a variety of quotes related to the topic under study and then analyze and identify patterns in the quotes. Each student receives a piece of paper with an "overheard quote" written on it. Students read and independently consider the quote and then circulate around the room reading it to peers. Next they return to their table groups to discuss what they heard. Analyzing what people say, or might say, related to the content helps students generate questions and tentative ideas that can be explored or challenged through instruction. The patterns students find and the analyses they conduct during Overheard Quotes set a purpose for the learning that follows in the remainder of the lesson.

PREPARATION

1. Prior to the lesson, develop statements related to your topic. Statements may be actual or hypothetical. For example, second graders may be given comments overheard on the playground (see Figure S7.1). Sixth graders studying statistics may be given statements heard on the radio, on television or the movies, or in conversation. High school civics students may be given comments overheard in a restaurant as people talked about the role of women in today's military. To achieve the richest conversations, generate as many quotes as you have students. If that is not possible, duplicate some of the quotes so that each person has one. You may want to generate some quotes that are a bit controversial or that represent views that need to be addressed.

2. Write or print each quote onto a separate strip of paper or index card.

3. Have blank index cards ready, one per student, if you use Alternative 1.

4. See the Teacher Resources CD for a template that can be duplicated and used to structure students' participation in Overheard Quotes.

 You can find this template on the accompanying Teacher Resources CD and at the back of the book.

IMPLEMENTATION

1. Distribute the quotes face down and ask students not to read them until directions are provided. (This will help prevent them from discussing the quotes at their tables.)

2. Ask students to read the Overheard Quote they received and quickly write a brief response to it on a piece of scratch paper or on the template provided on the Teacher Resources CD.

3. After the students have responded to their Overheard Quote, ask them to circulate and read their quote to several peers, one at a time. Request that they not discuss the quotes at this time; they are merely to read them aloud to each other in pairs.

4. Observe the students. After they have had the opportunity to share their quote several times and hear several quotes, ask them to return to their table and complete a second brief writing based on the other quotes they heard, either on scratch paper or on the template provided on the Teacher Resources CD.

5. Ask students to read their quotes to those at their table and to paraphrase quotes they heard around the room. Then ask them to find patterns in the quotes by asking questions such as the following:
   • What did we hear often?
   • How accurate were the quotes? How do we know?
   • What did we not hear?
   • What issues seem to be emerging?
   • What are some implications of what we heard and did not hear?
   • What conclusions can we draw?
   • How can we work with those who hold these attitudes, or how can we deepen their thinking related to the issues?
   • How can we get more information about this topic?

   Patterns may be recorded in writing, perhaps on the template found on the Teacher Resources CD.

6. Lead a whole-group discussion about the information or issues raised in the groups. Tie students' tentative conclusions or current questions into the upcoming lesson.

ALTERNATIVES

1. Instead of generating quotes and distributing them, ask students to think about recent comments they heard related to the subject. For example, before students write their own works of fiction, you might say, "Over the year, I have heard you talk to each other about what makes a good story. Write down one of the things you have heard someone say about what makes a story good." Be prepared to share a couple of examples so students understand what you are asking of them. Ensure that your examples are quite different from each other so that students do not limit their quotes to match your examples. Then complete steps 3 through 6 above. (The writing in number 4 will be their first and only writing.) This alternative works best with older students.

2. Even if you have students generate their own Overheard Quotes, you can supply some quotes of your own to ensure that students face certain information or experience a diversity of ideas.

3. If you are working with very young students or are short on time, delete the writings and instead focus on analysis through discussion.

TIME ALLOTMENT

Depending on the nature of the quotes and the attitudes and experiences of the students, this strategy takes about 20 minutes.

EXAMPLES

Figure S7.1 lists some of the quotes that might be heard in a second-grade class where students have difficulty working together. Figure S7.2 presents some quotes from a sixth-grade class beginning their study of statistics. Figure S7.3 provides some quotes that a high school civics class could consider in thinking about the role of women in the military.

TROUBLESHOOTING

1. If your selection of quotes lacks variety, conversations may be limited. Make an effort to have a different quote for each student and to have the quotes represent varying viewpoints or experiences. When the table sharing occurs, each member of the group should be able to share something he or she heard that others did not hear. Depending on the number of people in the room and at each table, you will want to allow more or less partner sharing at the beginning of this activity. With a group of about 30, sharing quotes with 4 to 6 others is about right. We do not, however, set a limit for the students. We merely observe their interactions and call time.

2. If students develop their own quotes, you may want to read them before students share to ensure that the quotes are appropriate for the classroom setting.

3. If the quotes are sensitive in nature, as some of those in our examples are, tell students that it is important to practice wait time and be a good listener during the whole-group discussion. Students may have much to say about the quotes, and some—having perhaps heard themselves in the quotes—may be defensive. Allow the students to support controversial quotes, and rest assured that their peers will respond to them with different viewpoints. You will not be the only "voice of reason" in the room. Depending on your audience and purposes, be prepared to share some strategies for working with individuals who have negative attitudes.

4. If some of the quotes provide negative statements or inaccurate information, stress that just *saying something* does not make it right or true. Remind students that, as critical thinkers, they always need to keep in mind the possibility that the information they hear is inaccurate or biased. Be certain your discussion of quotes addresses issues such as accuracy, truth, and bias.

"He looks so funny."

"Leave us alone!"

"What a stupid idea."

"I always get picked last."

"Nobody will be my partner."

"I don't want to work with him."

"She won't be my friend."

"You can't play."

"I'm telling on you."

"You always ruin it."

Figure S7.1   Sample Overheard Quotes Used in a Second-grade Class to Help Students Learn to Work Together

"Thirty-five percent of U.S. fourth graders read for fun every day."

"The human head weighs 8 pounds."

"Ninety-eight percent of all the world's crayfish live in Louisiana."

"The average American wastes 3 pounds of food each day."

"Approximately 97% of all water on earth is salt water."

"The median age of people in the United States is 36.7 years."

"People blink more than 10,000,000 times each year."

"One type of snake, the Red Bellied Black Snake, gives birth to up to 40 live snakes at one time."

"Alaska has the country's longest coastline. It is 6,640 miles, which is greater than that of all other states put together."

"The current population of the world is 6,446,131,400."

Figure S7.2   Sample Overheard Quotes Used in a Sixth-grade Class Studying Statistics

"Women can do anything men can do."

"Women are just as smart as men, and they should be allowed to serve in the military, just not in combat. There are *some* differences between men and women!"

"In combat, men will be too worried about women to fight well."

"No one should be able to tell women how they are able to serve their country."

"It's wrong to address our problems through force. Neither men nor women should be allowed to kill other people."

"Women need to provide loving role models for our society, not physically aggressive ones."

"Women won't be able to pull their weight in a combat unit, and men will have to make up for their weakness."

"Women are allowed in combat units in other countries."

"Limiting women's participation in the military in any way because of their gender is sexist."

"The United States is a democracy. People should be allowed to vote on women's involvement in the military."

Figure S7.3   Sample Overheard Quotes Used in a High School Civics Class Considering the Role of Women in Today's Military

STRATEGY 8 True-False Sorts

LANGUAGE DEMANDS	LITERACY DEMANDS
Appropriate for:	Appropriate for:
Early English Learners	Emerging Readers/Writers
✔ Intermediate English Learners	✔ Intermediate Readers/Writers
✔ Advanced English Learners	✔ Proficient Readers/Writers

In True-False Sorts (Silberman, 1996), students work in small groups to sort statements into two stacks: statements that are true and those that are false. This strategy serves several purposes, especially when used at the beginning of a lesson. First, it prompts students to begin thinking about the topics to be discussed. Second, it helps students identify what they already know about the topics, raises curiosity about statements of which they are unsure, and increases their motivation to learn. Third, it engages students in meaningful conversations with their peers and encourages them to learn from each other. Fourth, it provides the teacher with a quick assessment of the knowledge base of the group. The strategy is useful when students have some background knowledge or experiences related to the topic. This is not the strategy to use if the content is so specific or technical that students are unlikely to have encountered it in previous school or life experiences. This may be the case, for instance, for highly specific content such as "Kreb's Cycle" or "Alexander Hamilton."

PREPARATION

1. Compose a list of statements about the topic, half of which are true and half of which are false.
2. Order the statements on the list so the true and false statements are randomly distributed.
3. Number the statements.
4. Print enough copies of the statements for each small group of students to have a copy.
5. Cut each copy into strips, with one statement on each strip.
6. Scramble and put each set of strips into an envelope.

IMPLEMENTATION

1. Give each small group an envelope containing the strips.
2. Tell the students to remove the strips and sort them into two groups based on the truthfulness of the statement. Inform them that exactly half of the statements are true and half are false.
3. When they have finished sorting the statements, ask the students to order them numerically and lay them out in columns: true and false. This will allow students to check the accuracy of their sort and follow the subsequent discussion with ease.
4. Read aloud or invite a student to read aloud statement 1. Ask all students to indicate with a thumbs up (true) or thumbs down (false) signal the truthfulness of the statement.
5. Provide the correct answer and elaborate as appropriate. Encourage students to move the statement to the correct column if it was placed incorrectly. Allow time for comments.
6. Repeat steps 4 and 5 for each statement in order.

Note: For some topics, you will need to strategically order the statements so the discussion that follows the sorting supports understanding of the topic. For example, if the sentences include references to historical events, a sequence, or cause and effect, you will want to order the sentences historically, sequentially, or causally. Similarly, if the statements contain information that can be chunked in meaningful ways, the statements should be ordered to reflect the chunks.

ALTERNATIVES

1. Instead of written statements, some content may lend itself to accurate and inaccurate drawings or diagrams. For example, you might provide five diagrams of circuits that will light a bulb and five diagrams of circuits that will not.

2. Use an enlarged set of the statements, handing each statement to a student at the front of the room. As a class, arrange the students into true and false groups.

TIME ALLOTMENT

Depending on the number of items, the level of detail you wish to provide for each item as you discuss them in turn, and the extent of whole-group discussion you wish to allow, this strategy generally takes from 20 to 30 minutes.

EXAMPLES

Figure S8.1 is a list of the statements for a fourth-grade lesson on squid. Figure S8.2 presents statements for use with ninth graders prior to their discussion on the cause of seasons. In each of these examples, students are likely to approach the topic with some knowledge—and some misconceptions—thus leading to lively conversations.

TROUBLESHOOTING

1. Too many statements can make this a long strategy and also a frustrating one for learners who are trying to juggle too many pieces of paper on their tables. Too few statements limit the opportunities for discussion that arise at the tables. We have found that 10 to 20 statements is a good number. The older the learner, the greater the number of strips.

---

1. Squid have a backbone to give their body a rigid shape. (F)
2. Squid are like other lower animals: They can't see. (F)
3. Squid can change colors. (T)
4. Squid move by jet propulsion. (T)
5. A giant squid's eye is the size of a beach ball; a giant squid can be 60 feet long. (T)
6. Squid are like octopus in that they have 3 appendages. (F)
7. Squid protect themselves by shooting ink. (T)
8. Squid have one very well developed heart. (F)
9. Squid are mostly used as bait; scientists aren't really interested in them. (F)
10. Squid eat other animals. (T)

Figure S8.1   True-False Sort Used in a Fourth-grade Science Lesson on Squid

1. Our planet is farther from the sun in winter months than summer months. (F)
2. Some places on earth experience 24 hours a day of sun during certain times of the year. (T)
3. A massive earthquake can affect the earth's rotation on its axis. (T)
4. The hottest days of summer occur during the longest days of the year. (F)
5. Areas near the equator are not affected much by the tilt of the earth on its axis. (T)
6. Like the earth, most of the planets in our solar system have a tilted axis relative to their orbit around the sun. (F)
7. If the earth were not tilted on its axis, we would have no seasons. (T)
8. Our year is equally divided into four seasons. (F)
9. The coldest days of the year occur well after the winter solstice. (T)
10. All planets in our solar system rotate in the same direction. (F)

Figure S8.2   True-False Sort Used in a High School Geography Class

2. Students may give up if you do not include several obviously true or false statements. Be sure to develop a few easy, but important, statements to ensure some degree of success. Conversely, include several items that are less obvious and will require discussion and debate among group members as they work toward consensus.

3. Often groups are so invested in this strategy that once they learn that they have incorrectly identified a statement, they scramble to resort their statements. (After all, because exactly half are true and half are false, one incorrect answer means there must be another one.) Be tolerant of this buzzing in the room, but do not schedule time for resorting after each item. Proceed with the next statement, and you should find that learners quickly look up because they do not want to miss the next statement.

4. Be prepared to limit the discussion that takes place about each item. Your goal is to get through the statements as an overview of your lesson or as a review of foundational information, and that purpose can get derailed if you let learners ask too many questions about each item. Assure them that the item will be discussed more thoroughly in your lesson (if it will) and express pleasure that they are so interested. If the item will not be discussed in greater depth later, provide a brief answer while also validating the students' interests.

5. Have an answer key. It is easy to get confused when you are standing in front of a group, and the students have devoted enough time and thought to sorting the ideas that they have a real need to know. They, and you, will be frustrated if you cannot provide the correct answers.

STRATEGY 9 Important Words

LANGUAGE DEMANDS	LITERACY DEMANDS
Appropriate for:	Appropriate for:
Early English Learners	✔ Emerging Readers/Writers
✔ Intermediate English Learners	✔ Intermediate Readers/Writers
✔ Advanced English Learners	✔ Proficient Readers/Writers

Similar to Taba's (1967) List-Group-Label technique (p. 168), Important Words requires students to generate a list of words related to the topic of the lesson or unit of study. This strategy differs in that students must select 10 words that they consider the most important. Thus, as students think about and articulate what they already know about a topic, they identify the "big ideas" related to the content, summarize and clarify what they know as they talk with others, and discriminate between important and less important information (Yopp & Yopp, 2002). The strategy provides the teacher with insights into the understandings of the group.

PREPARATION

You can find these templates on the accompanying Teacher Resources CD and at the back of the book.

1. Determine the topic of the Important Words strategy (e.g., will it be the overall unit of study or a subtopic?).
2. Have paper available for groups to collaboratively develop lists of important words. You may choose to use one of the two templates provided in the Teacher Resources CD for this purpose.

IMPLEMENTATION

1. Organize the students into small groups. Existing table groups work well.
2. Ask students to work in their small groups to develop a list of 10 important words related to the topic. You may want the students to first work alone and then meet in groups. This helps ensure that everyone is thinking and is prepared to make a contribution to the group.
3. Ask the groups to set their lists aside.
4. Provide information related to the topic as you had planned.
5. Request that the table groups meet again to review their important words. Invite them to modify their lists, if they choose.
6. Have each group share its list and provide a brief explanation about their word choices. Post the lists around the room.

ALTERNATIVES

1. Provide students with a list of more than 10 words before you teach a lesson and ask students to predict the 10 that they think will be most important (Stephens & Brown, 2000).
2. Use the strategy only at the end of the lesson or unit of study as a way to summarize important learnings.

3. Challenge groups to create a paragraph that uses all 10 of their words. One of the templates found in the Teacher Resources CD includes space for this paragraph.

4. Request fewer or more words. Ten works well because it imposes a limit that forces students to make discriminations among more and less important words. Depending on the density of the content, 5 words may be better, but it may also be too limiting.

5. Build graphic organizers with the words.

TIME ALLOTMENT

Five to 10 minutes to generate and negotiate group lists at the beginning of a lesson or unit of study is generally sufficient. Five to 10 minutes at the end to revisit and revise lists is also ample time. Sharing with the whole group should be quick, and we suggest that you allow each group no more than 1 minute.

EXAMPLE

Figure S9.1 shares some possible topics for the Important Words strategy.

TROUBLESHOOTING

1. Encourage students to generate many words and then select their top 10 words. Otherwise, students may stop after they have thought of their first 10 words. This will limit thinking about the topic and may lead to off-topic conversations.

2. Unless you are using Alternative 1 above, assure the students that you do not have a "right" list of 10 words in mind. Of course, some words choices are better than others, but as long as groups can reasonably defend their selection, they have done well.

3. Use this strategy when students have some background knowledge of the topic.

Second-grade Health: Nutrition

Fourth-grade Language Arts: Poetry

Sixth-grade Social Studies: Newspapers

Eighth-grade Science: Force and motion

High School Biology: Cardiovascular system

Sample Important Words generated by a high school biology student before studying the cardiovascular system:

  pulmonary artery

  left ventricle

  right ventricle

  left atrium

  right atrium

  aorta

  blood

  muscle contractions

  veins

  arteries

Figure S9.1   Sample Topics for Important Words

STRATEGIES FOR ENCOURAGING STUDENT INTERACTION

Learning is a social endeavor. Active teachers provide students with plentiful opportunities to interact with one another. They capitalize on the human resources in their classrooms, organizing instruction so that students share their ideas and understandings with one another. Further, active teachers know that as students share their thoughts and experiences with peers they refine, modify, and extend their own understandings. Strategies that encourage student interaction about the content optimize student learning.

Each of the strategies in Chapter 4 has as its main thrust interaction among students. The strategies provide a structure for student talk. Students turn to neighbors, they cluster together near charts, and they get up and move around the room to engage with peers. Some strategies facilitate the interaction of like-minded students; other strategies provide a structure for students to meet with peers who have different or contrasting perspectives or experiences; still others prompt conversations among students who have been grouped randomly. In some cases, students talk with a peer to frame a response to a question. In other cases, they share relevant experiences with one another or talk about their understandings of the content. Some strategies, such as Graffiti Board (p. 81) and Snowballs (p. 96), allow students to anonymously share ideas.

When students interact, they

✔ Become members of a learning community.

✔ Articulate and refine their understandings.

✔ Bring themselves to the learning.

✔ Learn from one another.

✔ Understand alternative perspectives and interpretations.

✔ Observe the cognitive processing of others.

✔ Learn to value the unique backgrounds and contributions of their peers.

✔ Recognize that they matter in the learning process.

You may wish to review Chapter 2, especially Figures 2.1 through 2.3, for suggestions on using active teaching strategies with students who are not independent readers and writers, students who are learning English, and students who have specific learning needs. You may also wish to review Figure 1.4 for typical cognitive, physical, social, and emotional needs and interests of students of various ages.

STRATEGY 10 Share the Wealth

LANGUAGE DEMANDS	LITERACY DEMANDS
Appropriate for:	Appropriate for:
✔ Early English Learners	✔ Emerging Readers/Writers
✔ Intermediate English Learners	✔ Intermediate Readers/Writers
✔ Advanced English Learners	✔ Proficient Readers/Writers

Talk is associated with power, or, in a sense, classroom "wealth." "Wealthier" people—people with power—have more opportunities to talk, opportunities that usually bring more and richer opportunities to learn. Unfortunately, research on classroom discourse shows that students have limited opportunities to talk in the classroom. In one recent study (National Center for Education Statistics, 2003), for instance, teachers talked *eight times* more than their students did! Further, when they *do* allow students to talk, teachers often use an interaction pattern that puts students in a passive role. Classroom discourse typically follows an I-R-E pattern: The teacher *Initiates* talk with a question, a student *Responds* to the question, and the teacher *Evaluates* the response (Cazden, 1986). When it comes to discourse, then, typical classroom practices tend to leave students "impoverished." Because opportunities to engage in meaningful, higher-level conversations about the subject matter are such powerful promoters of learning (Brophy, 1997), active teachers work to ensure that all students have plenty of rich opportunities to talk. All students need a chance to share and refine their thoughts—and to gain power over their own learning. Share the Wealth is not a single strategy but a group of techniques aimed at increasing the equity of participation and the number of students who respond to a teacher's question or other prompt. The techniques are listed under Alternatives and fall into two categories. Techniques in the first category, Some People Respond, break up the I-R-E (Initiate-Respond-Evaluate) pattern and encourage more equitable participation. The second category, Everyone Responds, includes techniques that hold all students accountable for the information. Rather than encouraging student-to-student interaction, techniques in this category allow all students to share their thoughts, and allow the teacher to check everyone's understanding.

PREPARATION

1. Prepare your questions carefully to ensure that they are asking what you intend to ask and that they will encourage careful thinking from students.
2. Select from among the Alternatives a technique that is appropriate for the class and for your purpose.
3. Prepare the materials required by that Alternative.
4. Decide whether you will allow students to "pass."

IMPLEMENTATION

1. During the lesson, pause frequently (no less often than every 10 minutes) and ask a question, using a Share the Wealth Alternative to facilitate students' responses.

ALTERNATIVES

Some People Respond

1. **Use Wait Time:** Rowe's seminal research (1972; 1986) found that teachers waiting at least 3 seconds before accepting and then evaluating student responses elongated the number, length, and quality of responses. After asking a question, wait at least 3 seconds. (That is Wait Time 1.) After receiving a response, wait 3 seconds before evaluating it. (That is Wait Time 2.) Stahl (1994), noting the important purpose of the teacher's silence, suggests using the term *think time* instead, and he recommends using think time strategically throughout a lesson, not just when asking questions.

2. **Urge Students to Respond:** Do not take the first hand that goes up. Urge more students to raise their hands: "I see three hands up. I'll wait for a few more." If students continue to hesitate, consider changing your questioning technique. See number 4, Tell a Partner First, for a good choice.

3. **Pull Sticks or Cards:** Place each student's name on a craft stick or playing card. Shuffle the sticks or cards and draw one or more after each question you ask. Decide whether you will put cards aside after calling on students or put their cards back into the stack. Students who are learning English or need support in formulating and sharing a response in public can be given extra time when their stick is drawn; call another student and then come back to the student needing support. Additionally, students in need of support can use a "learning buddy" to help them formulate their response.

4. **Tell a Partner First:** Allow students to discuss your question with their partner before you call on one or more respondents. See Think-Pair-Share (p. 76) for an elaborated version of this technique.

5. **Take Five (Morris, 2000):** After any question you ask, select five students, using sticks or cards, if you choose, to answer the question. Try Take Five for both convergent, factual questions and divergent questions. Alternatively, allow students to raise their hands and then name three, four, or five of those students to respond in order.

6. **Toss a Ball:** Use a soft foam ball, a stringy ball (such as a Koosh ball), or a balled up pair of nylons. After asking a question, toss the ball to a student. After responding, the student tosses the ball to a peer for another response. Decide whether you will allow students to request the ball and how many tosses will follow each question.

7. **Have Students Nominate the Speaker:** Tell the student who has just finished speaking to call on the next speaker. Some students need a time limit to make their choice.

8. **Try Audience Plants (Silberman, 1996):** Before the lesson begins, quietly tell just a few students answers to a couple key questions you will ask during the lesson. This technique can foster student discussion and can help students who might otherwise not have or not be willing to share an answer experience success in front of their peers. Alternatively, before class, have a private conversation with one or more selected students and say, "When we review homework, I'm going to ask you to give an answer. Look your homework over and tell me which answer you will be prepared to give."

9. **Invite Responses:** Near the end of a lesson or discussion, state, "Not everyone has said something during this discussion. I invite those who haven't spoken yet to share their ideas." Wait for responses, but do not require them.

Everyone Responds

10. **Use Unison Response:** If your question has one right answer, ask everyone to say the answer when you give a signal. Mark down the items where the response is "muddy" so you can go back to them. This technique is good for checking many

kinds of homework. Unison responses can be nonverbal as well. You might, for instance, ask students to point northeast, draw a symbol or letter in the air, or form a trapezoid with their hands.

11. **Use Visual Responses:** Ask students to give a "thumbs up or down," a number rating using finger signals (remember Finger Ratings, p. 44), or a colored-flash card response at your signal. Individual white boards allow each student to write a response and display it on your cue. Card stock slipped into transparent page protectors are excellent for this purpose.

12. **Conduct a Whip:** If you ask a question where answers vary by individual, and hearing every answer will be useful, "whip" around the class. Each student shares a brief response to the question. Do not evaluate responses. In most cases, it is appropriate to allow students to "pass." After the last response, you may choose to either summarize responses yourself, or ask students to do so.

TIME ALLOTMENT

Using Share the Wealth techniques may increase the time it takes for students to respond to a question, so plan on from 1 to 5 minutes each time you use a technique.

EXAMPLES

See Figure S10.1 for examples.

Technique	Example
1. Use Wait Time.	High School English Lesson: "What novels have we read that seem to be driven by their characters?" [3-second pause] "Brita?"
2. Urge Students to Respond.	High School Western Civilizations Lesson: "In what ways did the geography of Greece influence the development of cities there? I see two hands up. I'll wait for a few more."
3. Pull Sticks or Cards.	Fourth-grade Health Lesson: "What are some reasons we should eat fruits and vegetables? I'll pull some sticks to hear your answers."
4. Tell a Partner First.	Kindergarten Science Lesson: "Think of some animals that live on a farm. When I say 'go,' tell your partner a few of them." [Partners talk.] "Now let's hear the names of those farm animals. I'm looking for raised hands."
5. Take Five.	Sixth-grade Geometry Lesson: "What is pi? I'll take five." [Teacher calls the names of five students from cards and does not comment on their responses until all five have responded.] "Jenn." "Ryan." "Austin." "Marisela." "Jay."
6. Toss a Ball.	High School English Lesson: "What is your idea of *utopia*? Let's toss the Koosh ball to hear some ideas. Remember, look up. Someone can throw the ball to you even if you are looking at your desk!"

Figure S10.1 Sample Uses of Share the Wealth Techniques

Technique	Example
7. Have Students Nominate the Speaker.	Middle School Government Lesson: "What is one of the checks or balances in our system? Wow! Lots of hands are up! You first, Shaun, and when you've finished, pick another raised hand for a second check or balance, please."
8. Try Audience Plants.	Middle School Art Lesson: Before class: "Ramon, in our lesson I'm going to ask how this painting demonstrates a hopeful spirit. When I do, will you please give the answer I have written on this card? Use your acting skills so that no one knows you've read it."
9. Invite Responses.	High School English Lesson: "Many of you have shared your ideas about how Orwell's *1984* seems to have come true—or not—today, but we haven't heard from everyone. I know that people who didn't raise their hands have good ideas, too. If you haven't contributed yet, we'd like to hear what you're thinking. We invite your ideas." [Teacher looks over the class, pausing and smiling, for 20 seconds.]
10. Use Unison Response.	Middle School Mathematics Lesson: "Let's check page 57. When I call the number, together you say the answer. If I hear the wrong answer or a variety of answers for a problem, don't worry. I'll make a mark in my notes to remind us to go back and discuss that problem."
11. Use Visual Responses.	Fifth-grade Mathematics Lesson: "You have a flash card with one pink side and one green side. I'll say a number, and then I'll give think time. When I say 'flash' show me *pink* if the number is *prime* and *green* if the number is *composite*. Get it? *Pink* for *prime*. If you don't know, hold the card sideways like this." [Later.] "Some people are waving their flashcards like flags. Remember: Hold it in front of your chest, like this."
12. Conduct a Whip.	Sixth-grade Health Lesson: "We're starting a unit on exercise. Before we begin, let's use a Whip to find out the favorite types of exercise in this room. Be ready for your turn, and when it's your turn, say your favorite type of exercise. Say two if you like. No 'passes' allowed for this Whip; say 'walking' if you need an answer because I know you love it when we walk laps together."

Figure S10.1 *Continued*

TROUBLESHOOTING

1. Teach students to use the particular technique through direct instruction. Have students practice, under your direction, and provide feedback on their use of the technique. If participation falls apart, stop the activity and reteach the technique.

2. Periodically check participation rates for individual students and for groups of students. Are girls and boys participating evenly? Are students with learning disabilities getting enough time and support to formulate and share their thoughts? You can have a colleague tally participation rates, or you can audio or video record your class and then analyze the transcript yourself.

STRATEGY 11 Think-Pair-Share

LANGUAGE DEMANDS	LITERACY DEMANDS
Appropriate for:	Appropriate for:
Early English Learners	✔ Emerging Readers/Writers
✔ Intermediate English Learners	✔ Intermediate Readers/Writers
✔ Advanced English Learners	✔ Proficient Readers/Writers

Think-Pair-Share engages students individually, in pairs, and as a whole group in the content of the lesson (Lyman, 1981). The teacher poses a question, provides think time for students to consider the question individually (Think), asks the students to discuss the question with a partner (Pair), and then invites them to participate in a whole-group discussion of the question (Share). This activity provides a quick opportunity for students to reflect on and talk about the topic with a classmate and provides a structure that eliminates the problem of only the most verbal students participating in a discussion.

PREPARATION

You can find this template on the accompanying Teacher Resources CD and at the back of the book.

1. Develop lesson-related questions for the participants to consider. Questions should prompt students to think about and discuss ideas presented in the lesson or go beyond the ideas presented by making connections to their own experiences.

2. If you choose, duplicate the template found in the Teacher Resources CD to allow students to record ideas.

IMPLEMENTATION

1. Ask students to individually respond to a question or prompt. Having them do so in writing is optional, but we find that it ensures engagement. Alternatively, they may quietly reflect on the question, jotting notes only if they choose to do so. Provide a minute or two for this step.

2. Have students partner with someone sitting near them to discuss their responses to the question. Allow 2 or 3 minutes.

3. Invite pairs to share key ideas from their discussion, or randomly call on pairs to share their discussions.

4. Repeat steps 1 through 3 at several points in the lesson.

TIME ALLOTMENT

Think-Pair-Share takes a short amount of time, perhaps 5 minutes, and it is a valuable strategy to engage students in talking about the topic throughout the lesson.

EXAMPLES

Figure S11.1 presents prompts for a third-grade class studying fractions and a seventh-grade class studying ancient American cultures.

Third-grade Mathematics Lesson on Adding Fractions with Like Denominators

Think:	Think about where and how you use fractions in your life. Record your ideas on paper, if you like.
Pair:	Turn to a partner and share your thinking.
Share:	Please share with the whole group one idea that you and your partner discussed.
(Later)	
Think:	List the steps involved in adding fractions with like denominators.
Pair:	Tell your partner what you wrote.
Share:	Let's hear from three pairs.
(Later)	
Think:	Now that you know how to add fractions with like denominators, think about how you might subtract fractions with like denominators. How do you think you might subtract fractions?
Pair:	Talk to a partner about your ideas.
Share:	Would anyone like to share with the group some thoughts on subtracting fractions with like denominators?

Junior High Lesson on Ancient American Cultures

Think:	Think about the ways the Mayan culture was similar to modern U.S. culture.
Pair:	Tell a partner.
Share:	Please share the ideas you discussed with the whole group.

Figure S11.1   Sample Think-Pair-Share Prompts

TROUBLESHOOTING

1. The think time and opportunity to test ideas with a peer usually results in increased participation in a whole-group discussion. However, you may encounter a group of students who do not respond when you invite whole-group sharing or who provide only minimal responses when you call on pairs. This may indicate that the students are not secure with the content and may cue you to revisit the material. Alternatively, you may have a group of quiet students. Be sure to provide plenty of wait time both when asking for responses and after hearing a response. Wait time rarely fails to provoke more elaborate responses.

STRATEGY 12 Q Cards

LANGUAGE DEMANDS	LITERACY DEMANDS
Appropriate for:	Appropriate for:
Early English Learners	Emerging Readers/Writers
✔ Intermediate English Learners	✔ Intermediate Readers/Writers
✔ Advanced English Learners	✔ Proficient Readers/Writers

In this strategy, students ask questions in writing, which are then answered by their peers. Q Cards (or Question Cards) allow an opportunity for students to review what they have learned, ask for clarification, and identify implications of their learning. Both the acts of generating questions (Yopp, 1988) and answering questions (National Reading Panel, 2000) and the subsequent conversations support learning. Further, the strategy allows students to learn their peers' perspectives on the content.

PREPARATION

1. Have available index cards onto which students can write questions.
2. Decide when in the lesson or unit of study you would like to invite questions.

IMPLEMENTATION

1. Distribute cards, one per student. Request that, either alone or with a partner, each student generate a question about the content. The question may be a clarifying question, a quiz or review question, an application question, or any other type of question.
2. Collect the cards and scramble them. Distribute the cards to table groups.
3. Ask the students to address the questions orally in table groups.
4. After each table has discussed answers to its questions, ask each table group to read aloud one question and share the table group's answer with the entire group.
5. After sharing, allow students to ask any questions they would like addressed by the entire group. A table group, for example, may want the entire group's thinking on an issue that arose in their discussion, or an individual may want to discuss the question that he posed in writing at the beginning of this strategy. Although there will almost certainly be some question duplication, an individual's question most likely will not be among those discussed at his table. It is important that students be provided with the opportunity to have their question addressed.

ALTERNATIVES

1. You generate the questions and distribute them to tables for discussion. These may be frequently asked questions, questions that address common misconceptions, or questions that you believe are important for the students to discuss. You may wish to provide all table groups with the same set of questions or provide a variety of questions across the room.

2. Ask each student to generate several questions, one per index card, or use self-adhesive notes as they work better for this alternative. Have the students at each table pool their questions and sort them in some way and identify category labels for each group of questions ("These questions are about . . . " "These questions are about . . . "). Depending on the number of students at each table and the number of question categories, have each student or two take responsibility for one category of questions. Some question categories may be omitted if there are more categories than students at a table. Students circulate around the room, looking for peers from other tables who have the same category of questions. Once question-alike groups are formed, students work with these groups to answer the questions.

TIME ALLOTMENT

Depending on the length of the discussion, this strategy takes from 20 to 30 minutes.

EXAMPLES

Figure S12.1 shares questions generated by third graders studying visual arts. Figure S12.2 displays sample questions generated by high school students in a geography class.

TROUBLESHOOTING

1. You may be concerned that students' responses are not the responses you would have provided to questions. We have found this strategy to be an outstanding opportunity for students to "own" the content by sharing their own perspectives and

---

Who are some local artists?

What are some of the tools artists use?

What are some different art media?

Why is van Gogh famous?

How is art used in different countries?

Figure S12.1   Sample Questions Generated by Third Graders Studying Visual Arts

---

How many tectonic plates are there?

What is the Ring of Fire?

What is a subduction zone?

How are earthquakes measured?

What is the largest earthquake on record?

How do communities best prepare for earthquakes?

Where in the world is seismic activity the greatest? Why?

What are some superstitions about earthquakes?

How did early peoples explain earthquakes?

In what ways are earthquakes and volcanoes related?

Figure S12.2   Sample Questions Generated by High School Students Studying Geography

knowledge. Further, it allows us to gain an understanding of—and appreciation for—the beliefs and knowledge of the students, which is often substantial. You should feel comfortable, however, respectfully adding to, or providing alternative thinking about, the responses of the groups.

2. Students may need support in writing questions that demand more than a single-word response. Conversations will be limited if each question has a single, short correct response (e.g., "What is the first odd number?" as opposed to "What are some ways of classifying numbers?"), and a group with five questions with short answers will quickly stray off topic. Share examples of questions that generate more and less thoughtful and in-depth reflection on the content. Do not suggest that narrow, literal level questions are incorrect or inappropriate, however—after all, some students may genuinely wish to know the answers to those questions—but do guide students toward questions that expand their thinking.

STRATEGY 13 Graffiti Board

LANGUAGE DEMANDS	LITERACY DEMANDS
Appropriate for:	Appropriate for:
✔ Early English Learners	✔ Emerging Readers/Writers
✔ Intermediate English Learners	✔ Intermediate Readers/Writers
✔ Advanced English Learners	✔ Proficient Readers/Writers

Humans have been expressing their opinions and ideas through anonymous public writings at least as far back as ancient Rome and Greece. Graffiti Boards are charts in the classroom onto which students can anonymously record, for public perusal, ideas related to a prompt. Students are not provided a specific assigned time to write on the Graffiti Board; instead, they add their ideas to the Graffiti Board during free moments, such as before class begins, during work periods, and at the end of class as they exit the room. This strategy encourages students to continue to think about content or skills they are learning throughout the day and then express ideas for classmates and the teacher to review. It allows the teacher to address the informal curriculum, or the curriculum sparked by students' daily lives (Koch, 2005), in addition to the curriculum required by academic standards. Additionally, a Graffiti Board promotes conversations about the topic as students gather around the board and read the contributions of peers. Short, Burke, and Harste (1995) use Graffiti Boards as a small-group, prereading activity.

PREPARATION

1. Determine the topic of the Graffiti Board. Consider current units of study, skills you are helping the students acquire, the potential for many responses, and space issues. You will want to establish Graffiti Boards that ask for fairly short contributions, such as single words, short phrases, sentences, or sketches.

2. Think about when you would like to receive students' input. Graffiti Boards are often used to elicit topics for discussion or study. They can also be used to track students' continuing interaction with the content.

3. Post a piece of poster paper or butcher paper—your Graffiti Board—in a convenient and obvious location in the room, such as on the classroom door, the side of a bookcase, or a corner of a whiteboard at the side or front of the room. The Graffiti Board will be posted for several days, so do not put it on the whiteboard if you will need the space for other work. Further, using chart paper allows you to save the Graffiti Board for later reference. Ensure easy access to writing instruments by placing several pens or pencils in a box near the Graffiti Board or, better, by tying a couple of pens or pencils to strings and attaching them nearby.

4. Write the topic on the Graffiti Board.

5. Establish ground rules. Consider when students will be permitted to post their ideas on the Graffiti Board. Anytime during the class period or day? Only during independent or group work time? Only when entering or exiting the room? Consider whether mistakes may be corrected by other students. For example, may a student who notices a misspelled word or content error correct it? (It is common practice to allow students to correct the graffiti posted by others, but you and your students may decide not to

allow this practice.) Determine whether you will need to talk to your students about writing only appropriate comments. The Graffiti Board will need to be taken down if profanity or insults are written on the board.

6. Determine how long you will have the Graffiti Board posted. Many teachers keep boards posted for a week or more.

IMPLEMENTATION

1. Point out the Graffiti Board to the students. Tell them that you have posted it for them to record ideas related to a topic under study. Provide an example or two. After a lesson on long-e spelling patterns, for example, tell the students they will see many words with long-e spelling patterns in the books they are reading and in their own writing. As they encounter and notice these words, they should write them on the Graffiti Board.

2. Share your ground rules, or develop them as a class.

3. During the time the Graffiti Board is posted, occasionally read an interesting posting and remind students to make contributions. Although usually little prompting is needed because students are curious about what their friends have posted and often cluster around the board examining and discussing the postings, do encourage them to read the contributions of their peers.

4. At the end of the predetermined time period, discuss the students' contributions to the Graffiti Board.

ALTERNATIVES

1. Let students get credit for their idea or example by having them write their names next to their contributions to the Graffiti Board, or make names optional.

2. Provide each student with a self-adhesive note at the end of a lesson. Tell the students to write one important learning from the lesson onto the note. On their way out the door, have students post their notes on the Graffiti Board. You may then review their notes to gain a sense of their understanding of the lesson and then make adjustments to the next day's lesson based on this input.

3. Ask students to write questions or comments related to the topic on the Graffiti Board instead of something they learned or a response to a specific prompt.

4. Have students develop individual Graffiti Books. Encourage the use of written words and symbols or drawings to express a thought.

5. Have several Graffiti Boards on related topics posted at the same time. At the end of a given period of time, assign each Graffiti Board to a small group to review and summarize for the whole class.

6. Create computer-based Graffiti Boards using bulletin boards or specially designated Graffiti Board spaces.

TIME ALLOTMENT

Graffiti Boards are generally posted for a week or more. However, a board may be displayed for only a day, depending on the purpose and use of the board.

First Grade:	Use the magazines and catalogs in the basket to find pictures of things that start with the sound /b/ and paste them onto the Graffiti Board.
Third Grade:	Write homonym pairs on the Graffiti Board.
Fifth Grade:	Write similes on the Graffiti Board.
Sixth Grade:	Write your idea of one of the biggest issues facing 12-year-olds today.
Middle School:	Record on the Graffiti Board words that you could use instead of "said" in your writing.
Middle School:	Write interesting quotes from *Holes* by Louis Sachar on the Graffiti Board.
High School:	Record interesting vocabulary that you encounter in your reading of *Brave New World*.
High School:	Write anything related to our study of dystopias on the Graffiti Board.

Figure S13.1   Sample Graffiti Board Ideas for Language Arts

EXAMPLES

Figure S13.1 shares sample ideas for language arts Graffiti Boards for several grade levels.

TROUBLESHOOTING

1. Sometimes students are slow to respond to Graffiti Boards. Consider why this might be. Is it a timing issue? If you think so, you might modify your rules about when postings are allowed. If students are only permitted to write on the Graffiti Board when they exit the classroom, they may be already thinking about their next class or activity and not want to take the time to write on the board. Generally, allowing them to write on the board whenever they have a free moment is most effective. Is it because students cannot think of anything to contribute? Consider changing the prompt—making it more specific or, conversely, more open-ended. And, during your lessons, point out information that might be posted and ask a student to go record the information on the board right then during the lesson.

STRATEGY 14 Make the Point

LANGUAGE DEMANDS	LITERACY DEMANDS
Appropriate for:	Appropriate for:
✔ Early English Learners	✔ Emerging Readers/Writers
✔ Intermediate English Learners	✔ Intermediate Readers/Writers
✔ Advanced English Learners	✔ Proficient Readers/Writers

In Make the Point, students use pointers to interact with their peers about the content. Key to English learners' language development is increased interaction (Northwest Regional Educational Laboratory, 2003), and using pointers to refer to visual information helps embed content conversations within a rich context. This facilitates comprehensible output for all students, including English learners. Further, most students enjoy the novelty of using pointers, and many feel a heightened sense of comfort in speaking when they hold a pointer.

PREPARATION

1. Determine the number of pointers required by deciding on the size of groups you will use. Gather or make pointers suitable for your students' age and interests. Some examples include:
   a. Novelty fly swatters
   b. Yard or meter sticks
   c. Dowels with simple rubber erasers or toys glued to their tips
   d. Pictures or objects that students use to point at materials at their desks
   e. Laser or light pointers (check with local policy for rules)
   f. Translucent plastic pointers for the overhead projector (cut from report covers or duplicated from the template found on the Teacher Resources CD)
   g. Dry erase markers (to point and leave a record)
   h. Mouse cursors on computer screens

> ◉ **You can find this template on the accompanying Teacher Resources CD and at the back of the book.**

2. Decide on the timing of when students will use pointers. You might, for instance, set up a permanent center for Make the Point (see the second-grade example in Figure S14.1) so that students can visit it during spare moments, using pointers to review and share content with their peers. You might, instead, decide to use Make the Point as part of your day's opening exercises so that a small number of students use pointers while the rest observe. Or you might have students use pointers during the warm-up or practice section of particular lessons (see the high school examples in Figure S14.1).

3. Teach students to Make the Point: Discuss appropriate use of pointers for safety considerations, and remind them that Make the Point is to encourage conversations among students as they address the content together.

IMPLEMENTATION

1. Present the students' task. Tell them when and how to use the pointers.
2. Monitor carefully as students Make the Point.

ALTERNATIVES

1. Use Make the Point to *practice information* rather than to *encourage student interaction*.
2. Distribute a few pointers among students during a lesson to encourage students' overt participation within a whole-class discussion.
3. Combine Make the Point with Graffiti Board (p. 81) by having students point to information on the Graffiti Board.

TIME ALLOTMENT

Use Make the Point in short, focused periods, such as 5 to 10 minutes.

EXAMPLES

Figure S14.1 gives sample Make the Point uses in two grade levels: second grade and high school.

Second Grade

- During Opening Exercises: Students discuss in small groups how to form an equation that equals the target number, the date. One group's equation for 14 is "one hop of ten and two hops of two," or $14 = 10 + 2 + 2$. Several groups come up to the class's number line to demonstrate; they use a dowel with a plastic grasshopper glued to the end for this purpose. Others demonstrate their equations using plastic grasshoppers on the small number lines at their desks.
- During Center Time: In pairs, students use meter sticks to read the words on the class Word Wall. (A Word Wall is a dynamic bulletin board filled with individual word cards.) They discuss their favorites and quiz each other on reading the tougher words.
- During Center Time: In pairs, students use flashlights to read the wall book they created in science, "I Didn't Know That . . . A Force is a Push or a Pull" (see "I Didn't Know That . . ." Response Frames, p. 218).
- During Independent Work Time: At the neighborhood map posted in the social studies center, partners use as pointers paper dolls colored to look like themselves. They describe possible journeys, practicing the letter-number grid system to name locations, and they use directional words such as *north* and *south*.

High School

- In Chemistry Class: The class warms up by pointing to periodic tables in response to questions from the teacher. Sometimes students point toward the class chart with lightpointers or with their fingers, tracing responses in the air while seated. Sometimes they point at individual charts on their desks.
  ✔ "Point at *cobalt*. Move your pointer: Where are the other members in cobalt's *period*? Its *group*?"
  ✔ "Point at *iridium*. Which direction would you travel to find the closest *noble gas*? Which direction would you travel to increase the element's *nuclear radius*?"
  ✔ "With your partner, point to every element name that refers to a *place*. What other interesting patterns do you find in element names? Be ready to share with the class." Partners discuss before pointing.
- In World Cultures Class: The teacher accesses students' prior experiences at the beginning of a lesson to introduce New Imperialism. The teacher states, "Almost all of us in this room—and in this nation!—have family members who came from some other place—somewhere back in time, either yesterday or hundreds of years ago. Last night you talked about your own history with your families. In your groups, please tell your partners about the places from which your family members or ancestors came. Use your dry erase markers to trace these stories on your globes." Later, the teacher refers to the marked globes to draw on students' own connections with countries or continents affected by New Imperialism: Africa, Southeast

---

Figure S14.1 Sample Make the Point Uses

Asia, China, India, Latin America, and the Philippines. (Note: Students are allowed to "pass" and complete an alternate activity if they do not feel comfortable sharing their ancestors' travels.)

- In Art Class: Students end a lesson on *contrast* by moving throughout the room in small groups, each with a meter stick, discussing works on permanent display in the room. The teacher prompts, "When you hear the chime, move to the next work of art and point to and discuss the *visual contrasts* you find there. Remember to look for contrasts in subject matter, color, line, light, and texture. I'll be watching and listening." The teacher allows 2 minutes at each work and requests that a different person hold the pointer when each group rotates to a new work.

Figure S14.1   *Continued*

TROUBLESHOOTING

1. Think carefully about management so that you maximize academic learning time, or the time students spend successfully mastering the lesson objective. Ensure that everyone has an instructionally relevant task during Make the Point.

2. If pointers are new or of great interest to the students, give them a few minutes to explore the pointers' capabilities before using them as tools. Students will be better able to use the pointers as tools as a result.

3. Store pointers near point of use. Keep pointers at a permanent center hung on a hook near the center, for instance, and keep overhead pointers stored with other overhead transparency materials. Place high-interest pointers such as flashlights or laser pointers in more secure areas.

STRATEGY 15 Carousel

LANGUAGE DEMANDS	LITERACY DEMANDS
Appropriate for:	Appropriate for:
Early English Learners	Emerging Readers/Writers
✔ Intermediate English Learners	✔ Intermediate Readers/Writers
✔ Advanced English Learners	✔ Proficient Readers/Writers

This strategy requires students to respond to topics or prompts on charts posted around the room. Small groups of students circulate from chart to chart, writing notes on the chart paper as they brainstorm (Osborn, 1953) about the topic. The purposes of this strategy are to elicit topic-related conversations among students, activate students' background knowledge on a topic or review information learned in the lesson, and assess students' understandings of key ideas.

PREPARATION

1. Develop topics or prompts and write one each at the top of a piece of chart paper. Prompts should be related to the topic of the lesson and be broad enough to allow for many responses. Prompts may be written in the form of questions, short phrases, or single words.
2. Post the charts around the room, with sufficient space between the charts to allow for small groups to comfortably cluster at each chart.

IMPLEMENTATION

1. Assign students to a chart, or allow them to stand by a chart of their own choosing. If students select their own charts, ensure that the students are distributed fairly evenly among the charts. You may need to request that several students move to another chart. Assure them that they will have the chance to work on the chart they first selected.
2. Give each group a different colored marker and allow them 2 or 3 minutes to respond to the prompt by recording their ideas on the chart.
3. Call time, and ask the students to move in a clockwise direction to the next chart, where they read the new prompt and the previous responses. The group's task is to add to the work of the previous group or to clarify or record questions about the previous group's contributions.
4. The groups continue moving from chart to chart as time is called until all have had the opportunity to respond to each prompt and have arrived back at their original chart.
5. Students read other groups' responses to their first chart, and one student is selected to share one or two ideas listed on the chart.
6. As each group shares, students are given the opportunity to briefly respond or clarify if they wish.
7. Finally, the students are given the opportunity to ask questions about any of the responses on any of the charts. Colored markers are useful in that they allow groups to identify their own responses and thus respond to queries from other groups.

If there is any concern that this is a high-risk strategy for some students and complete anonymity is preferred, then all groups should receive the same color marker.

8. Finally, respond to any ideas on the charts that merit special attention.

ALTERNATIVE

1. Provide a prompt that asks for drawings rather than writings. For instance, students can draw examples of things such as shelters or modes of transportation during a social studies lesson.

TIME ALLOTMENT

The time you allot for this strategy depends on the number of prompts, the number of students in each group, and the time allowed at each chart. Typically, about 20 minutes is adequate.

EXAMPLES

Figure S15.1 presents prompts used after a fourth-grade unit on forms of fiction. Figure S15.2 provides prompts on key topics in a unit on India in a middle school social studies class. Notice that the prompts are broad topics that will elicit many and diverse responses.

TROUBLESHOOTING

1. If prompts are too narrow, the final groups to rotate to the charts will have little to contribute because duplication of ideas is not allowed.

What do we know about . . .

Myths

Fables

Legends

Folk Tales

Short Stories

Figure S15.1 Carousel Topics Used After a Sixth-grade Language Arts Unit on Forms of Fiction

---

British Rule

Gandhi

Hinduism

Pakistan

Bangladesh

Islam

Figure S15.2 Carousel Topics Used After a Seventh-grade Social Studies Unit on India

2. The number of charts should be determined by the number of students as well as by the topic. Too few charts will increase the size of the groups at each chart, resulting possibly in some disengaged students. Additionally, too few charts may limit conversations, as some students will take a few minutes to get warmed up. Too many charts may result in a lack of participation by the time the students finally get around the room. Five to seven charts have worked effectively for us. Students have ample opportunities to contribute and still have things to say by the time they reach the last chart.

3. If most students have exhausted their ideas and are unproductive at the charts, you may choose to stop the rotation before they arrive back at their starting point and share one or two ideas from the chart where they are standing.

4. A happy medium in terms of time at each chart must be found. Too much time may result in off-task behavior or an exhaustion of ideas so there is little left for later groups to contribute. Too little time can be frustrating to students who want to talk and share their ideas. We have found that it is preferable to err on the side of too little time, however. Although some students groan when time is called because they have had to rush, this fast pace keeps the strategy alive, reduces off-task behavior, and leaves enough unsaid that other groups can contribute. Our recommendation is no less than 1 and no more than 3 minutes. The younger the group, the more time should be provided.

5. Some individuals require think time before participating in a strategy like this. If you know you have students who may have difficulty rapidly articulating ideas, you might allow students a moment to quietly read and think about each prompt prior to engaging in the Carousel. Be careful not to provide too much time, however, or you will find that the charts become filled early in the process and later groups will be left with little to contribute.

STRATEGY 16 Magnetic Quotes

LANGUAGE DEMANDS	LITERACY DEMANDS
Appropriate for:	Appropriate for:
Early English Learners	Emerging Readers/Writers
✔ Intermediate English Learners	✔ Intermediate Readers/Writers
✔ Advanced English Learners	✔ Proficient Readers/Writers

Students read quotes posted around the room and stand by one that interests them. The purpose of this strategy is to have students respond to a statement or idea and discuss it with peers. This strategy is useful prior to learning about a topic as it prompts students to think about the topic or is likely to cause them to generate questions about the topic. It is also useful during or at the conclusion of a unit of study in that it allows students to identify what is important to them and summarize their understandings, beliefs, or attitudes about the content. Whether used before, during, or at the conclusion of a unit, Magnetic Quotes promote student discussion about content they will or have learned during their study of the topic.

PREPARATION

1. Select quotes related to the topic. Quotes may come from a single source or from a variety of sources. Feel free to paraphrase the thinking of experts and even invent a few quotes of your own.
2. Record each quote on a separate piece of chart paper and post the charts around the room.

IMPLEMENTATION

1. Ask students to quickly read (or you may read to them) the quotes posted around the room and then to select one that draws them to it (i.e., has a "magnetic pull" for them). You might ask them to read the quotes from their desks and then, at a signal, move directly to the quote of their choice. Or, you might allow students to circulate around the room to examine the quotes and then stand next to the one they find most appealing or interesting.
2. Once students have each selected a quote, ask them to discuss their understandings of, response to, or thinking related to the quote with peers standing by the same quote.
3. Invite each group to share one or two responses to the quote with the entire group.
4. Make information related to the quotes available for students to examine or study later if they wish.

ALTERNATIVES

1. Use a prompt other than quotes. Examples include reproductions of artwork, movie posters, or book titles.

2. Have students provide you with quotes from interesting texts that they are reading or on topics that they have studied or with which they have experience and expertise. Without identifying the contributor, post the quotes and engage in the strategy as described. Afterwards, contributors may be identified and share their knowledge. Quotes in languages other than English may provide an opportunity for English learners to share their expertise.

3. For English learners, consider providing students with instruction in the quotes sometime before the whole-class lesson, perhaps including translations of the quotes, or allowing students to take quotes home for examination.

TIME ALLOTMENT

This strategy takes about 15 minutes, depending on how much discussion you wish to encourage.

EXAMPLES

Figure S16.1 displays quotes from works of children's literature. Fifth-grade students discuss the quote of their choice—why they find it appealing and what it may reveal about the book—prior to selection of books for literature circles. Figure S16.2 shows quotes related to a unit of study on bacteria and viruses in a high school biology class to spark students' interest in concepts they will soon encounter in a unit of study.

"A specialist named Dr. Bang-Jensen diagnosed her as a *selective mute*: a person who chooses not to speak." (*Flying Solo* by Ralph Fletcher, p. 5)

"A ping of guilt hit Lerner, but she ponged it away by remembering that she hadn't intended to get everybody in trouble." (*The Word Eater* by Mary Amato, p. 55)

"For Mae Tuck, and her husband, and Miles and Jesse, too, had all looked exactly the same for eighty-seven years." (*Tuck Everlasting* by Natalie Babbitt, p. 12)

"*Mayday! Mayday!* This is Cessna 6-7-Z-RAY at Virginia Falls on the South Nahanni River. Have landed on a river, engine out, floating toward the falls. *Mayday! Mayday!*" (*Far North* by Will Hobbs, pp. 41–42)

"He reminded himself, 'I will never be allowed outside again. Maybe never again as long as I live.'" (*Among the Hidden* by Margaret Peterson Haddix, p. 1)

"Going to die, Brian thought. Going to die, gonna die, gonna die—his whole brain screamed it in the sudden silence." (*Hatchet* by Gary Paulsen, p. 25)

Figure S16.1 Magnetic Quotes from Children's Literature Used in a Fifth-grade Language Arts Lesson

---

". . . the virus that causes smallpox in humans is thought to have evolved from a virus that causes a disease in cattle called cowpox." (p. 643)

"You may not realize it, but at this very moment, a battle might be raging inside your body." (p. 638)

"Bacteria are adapted to be transmitted from one host to another in a variety of ways." (p. 640)

"Since viruses were first isolated in 1935, a large number have been discovered and studied." (p. 642)

"Your body possesses several lines of defense against diseases." (p. 644)

Figure S16.2 Magnetic Quotes Used in a High School Biology Class
Source: Orem (1998).

TROUBLESHOOTING

1. Students may not distribute themselves evenly among the quotes. That is okay! Respect students' choices and allow them to be drawn to any quote. If all students stand by the same quote, you might have them break themselves into small groups for discussion. If no one stands by one or more of the quotes and you think the quotes merit attention, ask the entire group to comment on them at the end of the strategy.

2. If quotes are controversial, ensure that you have established a safe tone in your classroom so that diverse viewpoints are respected.

3. If students repeatedly appear to simply cluster with their close friends rather than to select a quote for personal reasons, try the following: Number each quote. Have students read the quotes (or listen as you read them aloud) and record on a piece of paper the number of the quote they find interesting. Then ask them to move to the quote with their papers in hand. Once there, they quickly show group members their numbers. Be sure that this does not become a policing practice, however! Tell students you are encouraging them to respond personally. You want their individual reactions.

STRATEGY 17 Stand and Share

LANGUAGE DEMANDS	LITERACY DEMANDS
Appropriate for:	Appropriate for:
✔ Early English Learners	✔ Emerging Readers/Writers
✔ Intermediate English Learners	✔ Intermediate Readers/Writers
✔ Advanced English Learners	✔ Proficient Readers/Writers

Stand and Share calls for each student to generate a response to a prompt or question and allows for each student to feel that his response is heard. In this strategy, described by Kagan (1994), students first engage in a discussion about the topic under study. This discussion supports the students in constructing understandings of the content, clarifying their thinking about the content, and acquiring ideas they might not have independently considered. The teacher then asks a topic-related question, and students independently generate a response, perhaps recording it on paper. When students have decided on their response, they stand. The teacher calls on a student to share her response. After sharing, the student sits down, and all other students who had the same response also sit down. The teacher calls on another standing student who gives a different answer to the question and then sits down, as do peers who have the same response, until all students are seated. This strategy engages all students in the lesson because it supports their ability to respond through the discussion that precedes the question, it requires all students to have an answer, and it encourages them to listen carefully to the responses of their classmates so they know whether their answer has been shared. It even includes some movement (standing and sitting), and physical activity is counter to passivity and disengagement.

PREPARATION

1. Determine size of discussion groups. Pairs increase each student's responsibility to participate but may limit exposure to ideas. Small groups of four to six allow a relatively safe environment for students to share their ideas, and they also allow increased opportunities for more students to participate in the discussion than do whole-class discussions. Small-group environments are also more supportive of English learners who may be less inclined to take risks with their new language in a whole-class discussion. However, whole-class discussions can have the benefit of increasing the students' opportunities to hear more diverse responses.

2. Determine whether you want the students to record their response in writing or whether it is acceptable for them to simply formulate a response and remember it.

3. Design a prompt for which there are many possible responses that are fairly brief. The prompt need not be entirely open-ended, but it should allow for more than just a few responses, depending on the size of the group. With larger groups, you will want to have more possible responses.

IMPLEMENTATION

1. After or as part of a learning experience, engage the students in a discussion about the content, allowing them to share information and ideas and to listen to the thinking of others.

2. Pose a question or provide a prompt related to the topic.

3. Provide the students with think time to independently generate a response to the question or prompt. Tell them that you want every student to be ready with a response and that they must select one response only from the several they may be ready to share. Ask the students to confirm they have selected one response by use of a signal, such as looking up at you or nodding their heads.

4. When all students have a response, ask the class to stand.

5. Call on one student—either randomly, in a specified order (such as the student at the head of table number one in your classroom), or by asking for a volunteer—to share his answer. When the student answers the question, thank him, briefly comment on the answer, and ask him to be seated. Tell the students that everyone who had the same answer is to also be seated.

6. Call on the next student to share her answer. She then sits, along with all other students who had the same response.

7. Continue in this manner until all students are seated.

ALTERNATIVES

1. Some students will not want to be limited by choosing one response. Allow the students to record in writing as many responses to the prompt or question as they like. After students have generated their lists of ideas, have them select one to Stand and Share. Students may not be seated until all ideas on their list have been shared by someone in the class.

2. Allow students to select one idea with a partner. Students Stand and Share with their partner.

TIME ALLOTMENT

Depending on the length of the discussion, this strategy generally takes from 5 to 15 minutes.

EXAMPLES

Figure S17.1 provides a list of Stand and Share prompts across several grade levels and content areas.

TROUBLESHOOTING

1. One purpose of Stand and Share is to allow every student to feel his voice is heard. His idea is acknowledged even if he does not share it. Therefore, you must allow every response to be heard. That means that the question must invite a brief enough response that you have time to call on all students until none is left standing. If you find that the first one or two students are taking too much time to share their responses, you have probably phrased the question poorly. Thank the students for their contributions and then rephrase the question so that remaining contributions are briefer.

2. You may find that all students sit after the first one or two students share their response. You might ask the students to select another response to the prompt and stand again. Consider the possibility that your prompt is too narrow and broaden

your questions in the future. Or, if you are concerned that students are sitting because they do not really have a response, you might increase accountability by asking them to write their response and then randomly spot check the written responses as the students sit down. Or, as students sit, they display the paper they are holding to reveal that they have the same response.

First-grade Fine Arts (Dance): After participating in a dance lesson in which students are taught the labels for various movements, such as skip, slide, stretch, and roll, students experiment with the movements and the vocabulary in small groups. Each student is asked to pick one movement, then Stand and Share.

Third-grade Mathematics: After appropriate instruction, students meet in small groups to talk about various ways to represent the number 10 (e.g., $9 + 1$, $20 \div 2$, $21 - 11$). The students then independently identify one way to represent the number, and they Stand and Share.

Middle School Language Arts: After the students have read a chapter of *Johnny Tremain* (Forbes, 1943), they meet in triads to discuss the main character. What do they know about him? What kind of person is he? What words might describe him? The students each then pick one word that describes Johnny, and they Stand and Share.

High School French: After a lesson on French words related to foods, students discuss foods that might be eaten for breakfast, lunch, and dinner. Then the teacher asks students to Stand and Share the French word for their favorite food.

Figure S17.1   Sample Stand and Share Prompts

STRATEGY 18 Snowballs

LANGUAGE DEMANDS	LITERACY DEMANDS
Appropriate for:	Appropriate for:
Early English Learners	Emerging Readers/Writers
✔ Intermediate English Learners	✔ Intermediate Readers/Writers
✔ Advanced English Learners	✔ Proficient Readers/Writers

Students write a response to a prompt on a piece of paper, crumple the paper into a ball, and on cue toss it across the room for a peer to read. This strategy allows students to express an idea or feeling anonymously and read what someone across the room thinks or feels. Additionally, it adds a bit of fun to the content, possibly relieves some stress, and provides the teacher with insights into the learnings or feelings of the group.

PREPARATION

1. Be prepared with a stack of blank paper.
2. Prepare a prompt or spontaneously generate one as the circumstances dictate.
3. If necessary, discuss the rules for safely tossing snowballs and define the parameters for appropriate written responses.

IMPLEMENTATION

1. Ask the students to respond to a prompt on paper. Tell them not to identify themselves, and alert them that their statement may be shared with the group, including you.
2. When everyone is finished, ask students to wad their paper into a ball, and, on the count of three, toss it gently across the room so the papers fall like snowballs around the room. Enjoy this moment of chaos!
3. Once the paper Snowballs have landed on the floor and tables around the room, ask students to each pick up, smooth out, and silently read one Snowball.
4. Invite students to share interesting Snowballs with the group.
5. Foster discussion in response to comments shared.

TIME ALLOTMENT

This strategy takes about 5 minutes, unless comments warrant more elaborate discussion.

EXAMPLE

Our favorite Snowball prompt asks students to write one sentence about how they are feeling at the moment. This prompt allows students to express their concerns, frustrations, or enthusiasm. Reading and listening to the comments of anonymous peers can validate an individual's feelings and provide students with insights into different ways people respond to the same experience.

ALTERNATIVES

1. Other prompts we have used include the following:
   • "Write one question you have about [the topic]."
   • "Write one thing you know about [the topic] that you did not know before."
   • "Write what you find most interesting about [the topic]."

2. Allow students to draw a picture that captures their learnings or feelings. When students receive the tossed Snowballs, they share the drawings with neighbors and discuss what they may mean. They then share their interpretations with the entire class.

3. Consider asking students to use numbers to rate their level of interest in or understanding of the topic. Students raise their hands, after retrieving a tossed Snowball, if they hold a "1," for instance. At a glance, the teacher and students will learn how others are feeling.

4. Snowballs can be used as an icebreaker. Ask students to write three things about themselves that they would not mind sharing with others. They should not write their names on their papers. After Snowballs are thrown, each student talks with the others to match the Snowball they caught with the person who threw it.

TROUBLESHOOTING

1. If you open yourself up to feedback about students' feelings (and we hope you do), you must be prepared to hear negative comments. "I'm very frustrated." "I don't know how I'm going to learn all this." "I can't imagine getting all this work done." "I didn't learn anything." How you respond to negative feedback will speak volumes to the students about you, and we have never seen defensive posturing work. We recommend that you be a good listener, ask for more sharing, and encourage students to support each other in working out issues that may arise. More often than not, the responses will be overwhelmingly positive, and the one or two individuals who write negative comments will learn that their feelings are not the group norm. Their concerns are legitimate, however, and should invite reflection on the part of the teacher who should seek ways to address them, either now or later. If many Snowballs are negative, you need to work with the entire group to problem solve. If you are concerned about the negativity of a group and you do not want to allow them to air their complaints, consider carefully how you phrase a prompt. Ask for something specific or for something that encourages ownership, such as "Write one thing about the topic that you think you could share with younger students" and "Write one thing you could do that would help you understand the content better."

2. Although we have never experienced a problem, throwing wadded paper around the room may incite too much enthusiasm and energy with some groups. Know your group, and make a decision to use this strategy accordingly.

STRATEGY 19 Four Corners

LANGUAGE DEMANDS	LITERACY DEMANDS
Appropriate for:	Appropriate for:
Early English Learners	Emerging Readers/Writers
✔ Intermediate English Learners	✔ Intermediate Readers/Writers
✔ Advanced English Learners	✔ Proficient Readers/Writers

Cooperative learning has positive effects on student achievement and other outcomes (Good & Brophy, 2000). Four Corners is a cooperative learning strategy that provides students with the opportunity to think about their own opinions and then discuss those opinions with others. Students make decisions about whether they strongly agree, agree, disagree, or strongly disagree with a series of statements and then stand in corners of the room so labeled to discuss their ratings with others. Four Corners enhances student interaction and encourages high-level cognitive talk, important because task-related social interactions support students' cognitive development (Bruner, 1986; Vygotsky, 1978). It is a good warm-up or team-building strategy that can also provide information about the students' knowledge and attitudes at the beginning of a lesson or unit.

PREPARATION

1. Develop a series of statements and record them in the left column of a paper. How many statements you develop is up to you. We have used as many as 20 and as few as 5. Using 20 will spark students' interest in your topic and alert them to the learning ahead, but you will not address all of the statements. In the right column, write the abbreviations SA, A, D, and SD beside each statement, leaving space between them. Provide a key at the top or bottom of the page explaining that the initials stand for Strongly Agree, Agree, Disagree, and Strongly Disagree. You may choose to use the template provided on the Teacher Resources CD. Reproduce the paper for each student.

2. Use chart paper to label corners of the room Strongly Agree, Agree, Disagree, and Strongly Disagree.

You can find this template on the accompanying Teacher Resources CD and at the back of the book.

IMPLEMENTATION

1. Ask students to take a few moments to complete the form, indicating their level of agreement with each of the statements.

2. When most or all of the students have completed this task, point out that the corners of the room are labeled. Read the first statement (or the first statement you wish to have the students discuss, which may not be number one on your list) and ask the students to move to the corner that represents their level of agreement with the statement.

3. After students have moved to corners of the room, ask them to discuss their rating with their corner-mates.

4. Provide only a couple of minutes and then ask a representative from each corner (SA, A, D, SD) to summarize the group's comments. Thank them for their comments but do not provide your thinking on the statement. However, do allow responses or questions from students in other corners.

5. Read aloud the next statement that you would like the students to discuss and ask them to move from their current corner to the corner that coincides with their rating for this statement.

6. Again, ask the groups to share their thinking with corner-mates and then request a quick summary from each group.

7. Repeat this process for each statement that you wish to have the students discuss. We generally discuss only four or five statements—just enough to engage the students in the process and stimulate the use of academic language.

8. Have the students return to their seats. You may choose to collect the papers and develop a chart sharing group data, or you may allow students to keep their papers and comment that the statements will all be addressed as part of the lesson and so they may want to keep the paper and reconsider their ratings as the lesson progresses.

ALTERNATIVES

1. Rather than asking students to rate their level of agreement, ask them to respond to some other dimension. Examples include degrees of likelihood, times of day, directions on the compass, and kinds of animals.

2. Modify the discussion so that students from different corners have the opportunity to talk with each other about their ratings. Students begin by gathering in their respective corners and then seek out one or two classmates who are not in the same corner.

TIME ALLOTMENT

Four Corners takes approximately 20 minutes, depending on the number of items you choose.

EXAMPLES

Figure S19.1 provides examples from a third-grade mathematics lesson. Figure S19.2 provides examples from a middle school physical education class.

1. I use mathematics everyday, even on the weekends.	SA	A	D	SD
2. You need a paper and pencil to do mathematics.	SA	A	D	SD
3. Math is only about numbers.	SA	A	D	SD
4. Many people I know love mathematics.	SA	A	D	SD
5. The best thing about math is getting the right answer.	SA	A	D	SD
6. Everyone can learn mathematics.	SA	A	D	SD
7. People who are really good readers are usually not really good at mathematics.	SA	A	D	SD
8. Being good at mathematics means memorizing your multiplication facts.	SA	A	D	SD

Key:
SA = Strongly Agree
A = Agree
D = Disagree
SD = Strongly Disagree

Figure S19.1   Four Corners Statements Used in a Third-grade Mathematics Lesson
Source: Statements 1, 2, and 3 are from Guillaume (2005).

1. The best sports are team sports.	SA	A	D	SD
2. Competition is what makes sports great.	SA	A	D	SD
3. What I like best about playing a sport is pushing myself to achieve.	SA	A	D	SD
4. Winning is very important in sports.	SA	A	D	SD
5. Watching sports is more fun than participating in sports.	SA	A	D	SD
6. Girls and boys should be allowed to play on the same team in all sports.	SA	A	D	SD
7. I can picture myself playing a sport when I am an adult.	SA	A	D	SD
8. The best thing about playing a sport is getting (and staying) in shape.	SA	A	D	SD
9. I like sports more than most people I know like sports.	SA	A	D	SD
10. Soccer is the world's best sport.	SA	A	D	SD

Key:
SA = Strongly Agree
A = Agree
D = Disagree
SD = Strongly Disagree

Figure S19.2 Four Corners Statements from a Middle School Physical Education Class

TROUBLESHOOTING

1. If you develop your statements carefully, students are likely to be well distributed for most of the statements. One interesting occurrence in this strategy, however, is that sometimes a corner will have no students standing in it, or occasionally a corner will have all the students standing in it. Students are generally fascinated to observe how they are distributed among the corners and amused by the consensus or lack of consensus for various statements. When a large number of students moves to one corner, ask them to break into smaller groups to discuss their rating. When a single person is in a corner (and it does happen!), applaud her for her courage and ask her to prepare—without benefit of discussion with peers—a brief explanation of her rating. Once in a while, we work with a student who is a bit too intimidated to do this, and we allow him to move to the group most closely aligned with his rating.

2. Occasionally, students express frustration with rating an item and want to write "neutral" or "don't know" rather than select one of the choices (SA, A, D, SD). We tell students that they need to limit themselves to the choices available; they may interpret the statement in whatever way makes sense to them. Remind them that you are not judging their responses, nor do you expect them to remain committed to their response once they have thought about the item more or heard others' responses to the item. New interpretations of the statements often arise as students engage in conversation.

3. Some students want to know the "right answer." Sometimes this depends on the way the statement was interpreted. Let students know that the upcoming unit of study will address the statements, but that you appreciate learning their current interpretations and reactions.

4. Our experience is that students enjoy the opportunity to discuss their ratings with peers and hear the thinking of other groups. They also appreciate the opportunity to move around. They may plead with you to discuss more statements. You will have to make the decision whether to conclude the activity based both on time and benefit you perceive the students are receiving from the strategy.

STRATEGY 20 Up and Out

LANGUAGE DEMANDS	LITERACY DEMANDS
Appropriate for:	Appropriate for:
✔ Early English Learners	✔ Emerging Readers/Writers
✔ Intermediate English Learners	✔ Intermediate Readers/Writers
✔ Advanced English Learners	✔ Proficient Readers/Writers

Most teachers are in constant motion throughout the school day. They choose different locations in the classroom to stand, sometimes circle the entire room, move around as they make points and demonstrate concepts to students, pace back and forth, and navigate from one group of students to another. A key to effective classroom management is, indeed, thoughtful movement on the teacher's part (Jones, 2000). Students, on the other hand, spend most of their school hours sitting in desks. In fact, many classroom management techniques address how to minimize student movement.

Physical activity can provide a welcome change in the classroom for students, and it can reduce the likelihood of passivity and disengagement (Apel, 1995; Middendorf & Kalish, 1996). Movement in the classroom is stimulating and serves to recapture students' attention, which is key to learning. Further, movement can be a vehicle for social interactions, which can facilitate understanding of content (Vygotsky, 1978). Thus, opportunities for movement are desirable for all students, and they may be especially important for some students. For instance, among the suggestions that Vaughn, Bos, and Schumm (2003) offer for students with attention deficit hyperactivity disorder are the use of novelty and movement and postures other than sitting. Likewise, Linksman (2005) notes that kinesthetic learners experience frustration and diminished learning when asked to sit for extended periods. Finally, active teaching techniques that encourage student movement and interaction promote—for all students—the establishment of a community by ensuring that students talk with different members of the class, not just those with whom they have close friendships or those sitting nearby.

Strategies for getting students up and out of their seats to talk with one another are presented here. See Kagan (1994) for some of these and additional examples of participation strategies that encourage student movement.

PREPARATION

1. Select one of the Up and Out strategies described below. Your selection will be determined partly by whether you wish students to talk in pairs or larger groups.

2. Determine the points during the lesson at which students will get Up and Out.

3. In some cases, you may need to be prepared with supplies, such as a deck of cards.

4. If needed, determine a signal and what it will communicate to the students. The signal might indicate that the students are to switch partners, stop talking and listen for further directions, or return to their seats. Auditory signals include a bell, rain stick, gong, or rhythmic handclap. You might quickly turn off and then on a bank of classroom lights for a visual signal. Practice with students beforehand so that they understand exactly what response you expect. Do not begin the Up and Out strategies until students have demonstrated that they understand what to do when the signal is given.

5. Establish ground rules. How loud may student conversations be? How quickly do students need to terminate their conversations once you give the signal? Some

teachers give a 30-second warning; some teachers expect students to stop talking with one another immediately. Will students be permitted to remain in their seats or must everyone get up and move around the room?

IMPLEMENTATION

During your lesson, pause occasionally and have students get Up and Out of their seats to interact with one another to respond to a prompt or question or to review the information. Use one of the following Alternatives (and review Figure 1.8, Quick Ideas for Grouping Students Within a Lesson) to get students Up and Out.

ALTERNATIVES

1. **Reshuffled Partners:** Distribute playing cards so that every student has one. Because you are unlikely to have 52 students in your classroom, you may wish to stack the deck by using approximately the same number of cards—and the same cards—from each suit. For example, if you have 28 students, use only the ace through the seven of each suit. At an appropriate point in the lesson, when you are ready for students to meet with one another, ask students to get Up and Out of their seats, carrying their cards with them, to find one or more peers who have a card of the same suit. Later, when you want students to interact again, ask them to move around the room and this time to find someone with a card of the same number or color (or color *and* number; thus the 10 of hearts would meet with the 10 of diamonds). The advantage of using playing cards is that you can vary the feature students use to identify a partner, and so cards may be used several times while maintaining student interest and suspense.

2. **Line Up:** Have students form a single line across the front, and perhaps down the side, of the room according to some criterion, either unrelated or related to the content. For instance, you might ask students to line themselves up according to birth date, with January birthdays at the front of the line. If two or more students have the same birthday, allow them to decide their order in the line. Other criteria, unrelated to the content, by which students might order themselves include the following:
   - The number of letters (or syllables) in their full names
   - Alphabetically, by first name (or last name or city of birth)
   - Alphabetically, by the name of their favorite fruit (or food, sport, or movie)

   Using line-up criteria unrelated to the content, once students have lined up, they turn to their neighbors to respond to a prompt you provide or question you ask. Content-related criteria for lining up include the following:
   - A rating, on a scale of 1 to 5 (or 10—anything more gets difficult to discriminate) that represents the amount of background the students believe they have on the upcoming topic (e.g., "We are going to be talking about symphonies this week. Rate the amount of knowledge you believe you have on this topic, with 1 being that you are not even sure what the word means and 5 being that you are well versed in the topic and that you have a wealth of information you could share with us"). All those with a 1 will go to the head of the single file line, followed by 2s, and so forth.
   - A rating that represents the amount of experience a student has in a particular area (e.g., "Rate yourself from 1 to 10 on the amount of time you have served as a referee for a sport, with 1 being no experience and 10 being that you are a trained referee of an organized sport and have served nearly every weekend for years!").
   - A rating of the strength of their feelings on the issue you have been discussing (e.g., "We have been learning about nuclear energy. Think about your reaction to

our use of this energy source and rate your feelings regarding its continued use in the years to come. A rating of 1 means that you think it should be discontinued immediately, and a rating of 5 means that it is important that we continue, even increase, our use of this energy source").

Once students have formed the line, they talk with their neighbors about their background knowledge, experiences, or opinions on the topic. Then, or alternatively, break the line in half in the middle and have one half of the line move next to the other half so that students stand across from someone who (likely) gave himself a different rating. Rich conversations can occur when students talk with others who have different backgrounds, experiences, or opinions on a topic.

3. **Inside-Outside Circles:** Ask students to form two circles, one inside the other. There should be the same number of students in each circle. If you have an odd number of students, then you should take a position in one of the circles so that the numbers in the circles match. Students in the two circles turn to face one another: Students in the inside circle face outward, and students in the outside circle face inward. Students should position themselves so that they are directly across from their partner in the other circle. You will need to practice having students get into circles quickly. Have students interact with their partner on the topic. For instance, in language arts, ask students to tell their partner something interesting from a book they are currently reading. Or, have the students quiz their partner on vocabulary the class has been studying. Then have students move to a new partner. You may ask students in the inside circle to move two people to their right or students in the outside circle to move five people to their right. Vary the means by which new partners are established. Keep the pace fairly rapid. Students need time to talk but not so much time that they get off topic.

4. **Overhead Spinner:** Overhead spinners allow students to watch in anticipation as the spinner turns. The number on which the arrow lands determines the size of the groups that will meet. "Ah, the spinner has landed on 3. You'll need to get up and meet in groups of 3." Because you are unlikely to have the number of students in your classroom that can be evenly divided by the number on the spinner, you should have a plan. For example, you have 26 students in your class and the spinner lands on 4. This means that you will have six groups of four students with two students remaining. Do the additional students each join a group so a few groups (in this case, two) become larger? Or, if there are at least two students, do they form their own group? An alternative to the spinner determining the size of the group is to have the spinner identify partners. For example, if the spinner lands on a 2, you might ask all students who have a 2 in their address (or phone number or student identification number) to stand up and quickly select a partner from among those who are standing. If you want students to meet in pairs and there is an odd number of students, then one student sits down. Spin again, and the pattern is repeated until all students have been matched with a partner.

5. **Wander and Freeze:** Have students circulate silently around the room for a few seconds, passing peers as they move. When you say "freeze," students stop where they are and talk to peers who are in close proximity. You may shorten or lengthen the amount of time they wander depending on how much of an activity break you think students need. Repeat the moving and freezing as many times as you wish, determined by the number of opportunities you wish students to have to share with a partner.

6. **Change Seats:** Ask students to clear their desks of materials. Depending on the discussion topic, have them take their notes, materials, or textbook with them when they move. Tell students that on your signal, they must get up and move to a different seat. Once seated, they work with nearby peers. You may repeat this several times if you wish students to have conversations with multiple peers. Or, you may simply tell students that you wish them to have a "new perspective" on their learning;

Fourth-grade Literature Lesson: Spend a few minutes thinking about your favorite novel from this year. In a minute, we will form Inside-Outside Circles to discuss our reasons for selecting favorites.

Middle School Environmental Studies Lesson: Rate your level of agreement (0–5) with this statement: Recycling is the most important thing that consumers can do to combat environmental degradation. In a minute, we will line up, in numerical order, to discuss our ideas with others.

High School Chemistry Lesson: Write down three ways that understanding chemistry is important to the average consumer. In a minute, we will Wander and Freeze to share these ideas with each other.

Figure S20.1   Examples of Up and Out Prompts

they will "see it from a different angle" by situating themselves in a new location in the classroom. They remain in their new location for the next part of the lesson or the remainder of the period. This helps get students out of the routine of always sitting by the same group of peers.

Engage your students in a debriefing after the Up and Out strategy. What did they learn? What new perspective did they gain? What new ideas do they have as a result of talking to peers about the topic?

TIME ALLOTMENT

Keep sessions fairly brief or students may lose focus. Many Up and Out sessions are brief, rarely exceeding 10 minutes.

EXAMPLES

Figure S20.1 gives examples at several grade levels for Up and Out.

TROUBLESHOOTING

1. If students do not respond to your words or the predetermined signal, stop the sharing and have them return to their seats. Talk about the signal and ensure that it was heard or seen. Obtain consensus on the need for a signal and the importance of responding to it. Provide an opportunity for student input by asking students if a different signal would be more effective and encouraging their suggestions. Practice again a few times, without being punitive.

2. Occasionally teachers find that so much of students' energy is spent on locating a partner that conversation and the content take a back seat. Remember to keep these sessions lively. Quicken the pace so that you do not lose significant time for the lesson's objectives. The movement is primarily to reenergize your students, provide them with some variety and novelty, and give them the opportunity to interact with peers and express their thinking.

STRATEGIES FOR GENERATING AND TESTING HYPOTHESES

Active teachers strive to improve student learning and students' control over that learning. According to poet and teacher Mark Van Doren, "The art of teaching is the art of assisting discovery." Chapter 5 contains 10 strategies that active teachers can employ to assist students in building knowledge through the processes of discovery. Each of the strategies in this chapter asks students to pose hypotheses, or tentative explanations, and then to test and refine those hypotheses as they confront additional information.

These 10 strategies capitalize on humans' struggle to make sense of the nearly constant stream of information that washes over us and to solve the myriad of problems we face. Chapter 5's strategies help students build invaluable content knowledge by finding patterns, drawing accurate conclusions, and using information to solve problems and make sound decisions. Students learn important facts, concepts, and generalizations. However, the strategies also foster students' growth as theory builders instead of as mere receptacles of information. By focusing on students' abilities to ask and pursue productive questions, the strategies in Chapter 5 encourage students to become adept at improving their explanations of the world, managing their learning, monitoring their progress, and setting new and challenging learning goals. These strategies help students as knowledge builders to hone their skills at using and analyzing information resources via the processes of investigation. When students generate and test hypotheses they

- ✔ Work within rich physical and social environments.
- ✔ Confront their limited understandings of the world and build more sophisticated ways of thinking.
- ✔ Fuel their interests and motivation to learn by facing interesting challenges and puzzles.
- ✔ Use language in authentic contexts, which is important both for students growing in their ability to read and write and for students acquiring English.
- ✔ Often pursue learning that is appropriate for a range of student needs. Self-directed Learning and Problem-based Learning are, for example, advocated for use with gifted students.
- ✔ Process information deeply through careful observation and explicit attention to the generation of appropriate inferences.
- ✔ Get feedback on their performance along the way.

You may wish to review Chapter 2, especially Figures 2.1 through 2.3, for suggestions on using active teaching strategies with students who are not independent readers and writers, students who are learning English, and students who have specific learning needs. You may also wish to review Figure 1.4 for typical cognitive, physical, social, and emotional needs and interests of students of various ages.

STRATEGY 21 Concept Attainment

LANGUAGE DEMANDS	LITERACY DEMANDS
Appropriate for:	Appropriate for:
✔ Early English Learners	✔ Emerging Readers/Writers
✔ Intermediate English Learners	✔ Intermediate Readers/Writers
✔ Advanced English Learners	✔ Proficient Readers/Writers

In the Concept Attainment strategy (Bruner, Goodnow, & Austin, 1956), the teacher shares items and identifies them as examples or nonexamples of a set. These items might be words, statements, pictures, or concrete objects. As the teacher identifies whether the items do or do not belong in the set, students attempt to determine the rule for grouping. The purpose of this strategy is to inductively build understanding of a concept or skill by requiring students to test their own ideas about it.

PREPARATION

1. Develop or collect items that are examples and nonexamples of a concept or skill.

2. Prepare the items for the students either by collecting or making copies for individuals (or small groups) to manipulate at their desks or by providing single large examples for the entire group to manipulate. Ten to 15 items is usually an appropriate number.

IMPLEMENTATION

1. Tell the students that you are going to put items into groups and their task is to figure out the rule you are using for grouping the items.

2. Identify the items, one at a time, as examples or nonexamples of the concept and put them in two different places at the front of the room. Or, ask several students to each hold an item as you direct them to the "yes" and "no" sides of the room.

3. Invite students to share their initial thinking about the sorting rule. Present more items and ask students where they should be placed. If they guess wrong, tell them so and put the item where it belongs. Encourage students to continue generating hypotheses and ask them whether the placement of new items supports their developing hypotheses.

4. If the students have their own set of materials, guide the entire group through sorting several of the items, as in step 3, then allow them to explore the remainder of the items on their own.

5. As students induce the sorting rule, confirm it, and ask them to generate one or two more examples that you could add to your collection.

TIME ALLOTMENT

This strategy generally takes 10 to 20 minutes.

Figure S21.1   Picture Cards Used by a First-grade Teacher to Help Students Distinguish Between Living and Nonliving Things

EXAMPLES

Chapter 2's sample kindergarten language arts lesson (Figure 2.5) uses concept attainment. Figure S21.1 identifies pictures used by a first-grade teacher to initiate a discussion of the characteristics of living things. Figure S21.2 presents names of states used by fifth graders studying the 50 United States and discovering those with international borders.

TROUBLESHOOTING

1. If students identify a rule that fits the data, but it is not the rule you wanted them to discover, applaud their work and then ask them if they can identify another rule. Or, if you are a quick thinker, generate a couple of items that do not fit their rule but do fit your rule.

Examples	Nonexamples
Montana	Arkansas
Texas	Oregon
Arizona	Colorado
Minnesota	Florida
New Mexico	Massachusetts

Where should each of the following states be placed? Alaska, California, Maine, Hawaii, Kentucky

Figure S21.2   State Cards Used by Fifth Graders Studying the 50 States, Discovering States with International Borders

2. You may avoid the potential problem noted in item 1 through careful planning. Ensure that you have a broad selection of examples and nonexamples. For the examples, the only commonality should be the rule you have in mind. For instance, if the rule is "triangles," you should have triangles and other shapes that vary by a number of nonessential characteristics such as size, texture, color, and material.

STRATEGY 22 Mystery Bags

LANGUAGE DEMANDS	LITERACY DEMANDS
Appropriate for:	Appropriate for:
✔ Early English Learners	✔ Emerging Readers/Writers
✔ Intermediate English Learners	✔ Intermediate Readers/Writers
✔ Advanced English Learners	✔ Proficient Readers/Writers

Many educators have discovered the power of mysterious objects placed in a paper bag to tantalize students (e.g., Horak & Horak, 1983; Spurlin, 1995). Mystery Bags (adapted from Yopp & Yopp, 2006) may be used to arouse curiosity and generate thinking about lesson or unit content and to stimulate language. Each small group receives a bag containing objects that are related to the topic. Students work together to generate hypotheses about the relationship between the object and the topic and discuss how the objects may relate to one another.

PREPARATION

1. Gather four or five objects related to the topic. Objects may be a literal representation of content or metaphorical in nature.
2. Put the objects into a bag so they cannot be seen.
3. Prepare a bag of the same set of objects for each student group.

IMPLEMENTATION

1. Provide each group with a bag of objects.
2. Explain to the students that the objects in the bag tell something about the content of the lesson or unit of study. Each group's job is to examine the objects, one at a time, and then in relation to each other, and make inferences about what the objects reveal about the topic.
3. Allow 5 to 10 minutes for groups to study the objects and develop several hypotheses.
4. Ask each group to share its thinking. Respond with interest, but do not indicate whether hypotheses are right or wrong.
5. Allow students to keep the objects at their tables while you teach.
6. At the conclusion of the lesson or unit of study, ask students to reconsider the meanings of the objects. Although you may ask students to discuss in their small groups, it is also effective to have a whole-class discussion.

ALTERNATIVES

1. You might give each group a different set of objects. If you do, ask groups to pool their understandings after step 4 above and generate some whole-class hypotheses.

2. Rather than giving each group a bag, you might lead a whole-class session by drawing objects from a single bag and eliciting discussion from the class as a whole.

3. Sometimes, such as during a science lesson, part of the mystery may be the number and type of items found in the bags. Allow students to predict and hypothesize before opening the bag.

4. Mystery bags are so popular with students that the bags can be used for a number of purposes in addition to arousing curiosity about an upcoming lesson or topic. Bags stuffed with familiar items can be used to help students form connections among ideas near the end of a unit or course, for instance. Given bags filled with common objects such as a magnet, a small candy bar, a mirror, and a leaf, students may be asked to choose the item that best represents
   - What they learned about the content.
   - What they learned about working together.
   - What they learned about themselves.

TIME ALLOTMENT

The initial examination and small-group discussion about the objects should take no more than 10 minutes. Sharing thoughts with the entire class may take another 10 minutes or more if you have an enthusiastic class. The final discussion may be briefer—perhaps 5 minutes.

EXAMPLES

Figure 2.7, a high school history lesson, uses Mystery Bags. Figure S22.1 lists objects that might be contained in bags for a variety of topics.

TROUBLESHOOTING

1. Each group of students will certainly pull their items out of the bag in a different order, thus perhaps spoiling the surprise element for observant peers in different groups. We have never found this to be a problem. Students usually are very engaged with the task and seeing what is happening at another table sometimes only serves to spark more curiosity.

2. Students tend to become very engaged during Mystery Bags. Have your attention signal ready so that you can regain their focus easily when you need to.

3. If you intend to reuse your bags with another set of students, you can cut down on your preparation time for the next use by being very specific in your directions for cleaning up. Do all items need to go back into the bags? Should they have another group verify that all items are in place before returning the bags?

First-grade Lesson on Weather: thermometer, rain gauge, sock, miniature fan, sealed plastic bag containing ice

Fifth-grade Lesson on the Media as Sources of Information and Culture: magazine advertisement, newspaper article, printout of a Web page, clothing label displayed on the outside of a garment, advertisement page from a telephone directory, movie advertisement

Sixth-grade Lesson on Geology: trowel, rock, rock candy, thermometer, chalk

Middle School Lesson on Motion: ball, incline, doorstop, mini skateboard (or any small toy on wheels), wooden block

Figure S22.1 Sample Objects for Mystery Bags

STRATEGY 23 Question Only

LANGUAGE DEMANDS	LITERACY DEMANDS
Appropriate for:	Appropriate for:
Early English Learners	✔ Emerging Readers/Writers
✔ Intermediate English Learners	✔ Intermediate Readers/Writers
✔ Advanced English Learners	✔ Proficient Readers/Writers

Students spend years in classrooms *answering* questions posed by teachers and text-books, yet it is the *asking* of questions that lies at the heart of learning and motivation (Chin, Brown, & Bruce, 2002). The act of generating questions has been demonstrated to enhance students' comprehension of text material (National Reading Panel, 2000; Rosenshine, Meister, & Chapman, 1996; Singer, 1978; Wong, 1985; Yopp, 1988) and their learning in content areas (Chin et al.). Unfortunately, classroom observations reveal a scarcity of student-generated questions (Dillon, 1988b). The good news is that students can be taught to ask questions, and posing questions gives students a sense of control over their learning, stimulates active engagement with the content, and contributes to problem solving and comprehension monitoring. Question Only is a strategy that prompts students to ask questions about an upcoming topic of study (Manzo & Manzo, 1997).

PREPARATION

1. Become very familiar with the content of your lesson or unit of study so that you are able to respond to questions. You may have notes available, but if you have to refer to them often, the pace of the strategy will be slow and students likely will become disengaged.

2. Identify key learnings and prepare a test that covers what you have identified as the most pertinent information.

3. Prior to using the strategy, work with students on generating questions. Talk about the five W and H questions: Who? What? When? Where? Why? How? Most students, including young ones, will be able to generate these types of questions. A template found in the Teacher Resources CD can be used to help students generate and organize their questions during the lesson. A second Question Only template found in the Teacher Resources CD can help students record their revised questions, as described below.

4. Consider sharing Bloom's (1956) taxonomy as a model of different kinds of questions for older students (see Figure S23.1).

You can find these templates on the accompanying Teacher Resources CD and at the back of the book.

IMPLEMENTATION

1. Announce the topic that you will soon be studying and state that there will be a test at the end of the period. If you work with younger students who would appreciate it, tell them that they are detectives and their mission is to uncover as much information on the topic as possible solely by asking you questions. For all grade levels, the test will be given whether or not the students have asked the questions that reveal the

Levels	Description	Examples
Knowledge	Recalling information	• How many elements are on the periodic table? • List the events that led up to the French Revolution. • Define "adjective."
Comprehension	Understanding the information; translating it into one's own words or providing examples	• Describe in your own words the process by which archeologists determine the age of an artifact. • Given what you know about amphibians and reptiles, how would you classify a tortoise?
Application	Using information to solve problems; applying information to new circumstances	• Using what you know about place value, write a five-digit number with the digit in the thousands place less than 7, the tens place equal to 0, and the ones place greater than 2. • Build a lunch menu utilizing what we just learned about nutrition.
Analysis	Breaking down the material into its parts and examining its structure	• Identify the poetic devices used in this poem and consider their roles in the poem. • Examine each aspect of the argument for electric-powered automobiles. Which have a basis in fact and which are opinion?
Synthesis	Putting parts together and creating new patterns or structures	• Use what you know about kinetic and potential energy to design an experiment that illustrates both. • Create a set of guidelines to address water pollution in our community.
Evaluate	Judging the value of material; critiquing information based on criteria for a specific purpose	• Explore at least two ways of solving this mathematics problem and decide which is most elegant. Tell why. • Listen to three musical compositions and rate them in terms of their appeal to your emotions. On what will you base your ratings?

Figure S23.1   Levels of Bloom's Taxonomy of Thinking Skills

information. You may only provide information in response to questions that have been asked.

2. Encourage students to begin asking questions immediately. Alternatively, allow students to work in small groups or pairs to generate some initial questions together. After a few moments, open the session to questions.

3. Answer each question fully, without providing information that goes beyond the question. Keep the pace lively. Students may take notes if they wish, perhaps on one of the Question Only templates found in the Teacher Resources CD.

4. Pause after you have responded to several questions and have students put their heads together to identify additional questions, given what they have learned up to

this point. One of the Question Only templates found in the Teacher Resources CD has space for students' subsequent questions.

5. After students have depleted their questions, provide students with the test, which they may respond to individually, in pairs, or in small groups. If you find that the questioning session is becoming so long that students are losing interest, announce that you will permit three final questions before the test. Encourage students to talk with one another to make wise selections of final questions.

6. Grade the test with the students. Talk about what questions they might have asked that would have enhanced their performance on the test. The test will provide you with information about the students' understanding of the content at this point and can be used to guide your planning.

7. Debrief the entire process. How did your students feel about generating questions? What questions provided the most information? What might they do differently the next time you engage in Question Only? Did the asking of their own questions contribute to their learning and interest?

8. Continue with the topic. Be sure to provide students with the opportunity to explore any questions they found interesting.

ALTERNATIVES

1. Have small groups of students become experts in one area of the content and let them lead a Question Only session with their peers. Be sure that they have developed a test prior to taking questions from their peers and that they only provide information in response to questions.

2. Tell students the topic and have them brainstorm questions about the topic. You can record their questions on a chart or overhead transparency, or students may record them on paper or in journals. Then, rather than asking you their questions, have them search the World Wide Web for the answers to their questions prior to taking your test. Be sure that your topic is specific enough that students' questions and subsequent searches are on target with the content. For instance, the specificity of "Causes of the American Revolution" will lead to more relevant and focused questions than the more general topic of "The Revolutionary War."

You can find this template on the accompanying Teacher Resources CD and at the back of the book.

3. You may wish to follow a Question Only session with the development of a Know-Want-Learn (K-W-L) chart (Ogle, 1986). A blank chart is available in the Teacher Resources CD. Students record what they *know* as a result of responses to their questions, what they *want* to know, and, later—after additional interactions with the content—what they *learned*.

4. Encourage question generation by keeping an in-the-classroom or an online question bulletin board. Students may post questions related to any topic under study. Occasionally examine the questions and respond to them or use these questions as options for group research projects.

5. Make the test a whole-class activity, especially if you work with younger children or any group of students that would find the test stressful. (See Troubleshooting item 1 for more advice if you work with such students.) Tell students you have a list of questions you will ask after they have asked their questions, and you will all find out how many of your questions they can answer as a group. You may find that the first time you use Question Only, students do not do well on the test. Keep a record of the score. Compare this score to subsequent times you engage in Question Only. Students will develop their ability to ask meaningful questions.

6. Consider having a student record all the questions that have been asked so that you may review them together later.

Depending on the age of the students and the content, the questioning session will take approximately 15 minutes. The test will also take some time—the amount depends on its length and your students.

EXAMPLES

Figures S23.2, S23.3, and S23.4 share examples of questions generated by first graders, sixth graders, and high schoolers, respectively.

TROUBLESHOOTING

1. Some of your students (perhaps those with specific learning disabilities, for instance) may not respond well to the pressure of hearing that there will be a test within the hour. Plan accordingly. For instance, you may pair students, choose a culminating activity other than a test, elect to have students complete the test as homework, or tell them that the test is worth only a very limited number of points (if any).

2. You may need to model question asking. As noted earlier, students typically have substantially more experience answering questions than asking them, so they may need support generating worthwhile questions. Games such as 20 Questions may be used as a warm-up. Students strategically ask up to 20 yes-no questions to identify something you are thinking about. Younger students may especially have difficulty generating questions. Frame your responses to their questions in a way that blatantly or subtly prompts more questions until they build more skill (e.g., "Magnets attract some materials, but not all. Ask me another question about the materials magnets attract" or "Yes, ice is the solid form of water. How a solid becomes a liquid is another question!").

3. If you find the same few students are dominating the question asking, encourage students to collaborate with peers for a few moments and tell everyone to be ready with a question: one of their own or one they heard during their small-group discussion. Then call on individuals. Or, use one of the techniques for encouraging participation found in Share the Wealth (p. 72).

What animals don't have teeth?

Are teeth used for anything besides chewing?

Do all animals have the same number of teeth?

How are some animals' teeth different from other animals' teeth?

Do all animals have baby teeth?

Are any animals born with teeth?

Some animals' teeth have poison in them, right?

Test Questions

1. Tell three ways animals are the same or different in terms of their teeth.
2. How do animals use their teeth?
3. How do animals change over time in terms of their teeth?
4. Here is a drawing of an animal's tooth. What does the animal eat?

Figure S23.2 Questions Generated by First Graders on the Topic of Animal Teeth

What do you mean by "underground water"?

How much water is underground?

Is there water under our school?

How does water get underground?

How deep under the ground is water?

If I dig down 10 feet, will I find water? Is underground water the same depth all over the world?

Are geysers the way underground water gets out?

When it rains a lot, is there more underground water? Is that good or bad or neither?

Sometimes when it rains a lot, water just sits on top of the ground instead of soaking in. Does that mean there's already a lot of underground water in that area?

Are there any benefits of underground water? What?

Is it dangerous to live above underground water? Why or why not?

Will the earth eventually soak up all our planet's fresh water so we won't have any more available for use?

How did we learn about underground water?

Who studies underground water? Who works with it?

Is underground water polluted? How does it get polluted?

Can water be pumped out of the ground?

Is the water in wells from underground water?

My friend's family has a water pump on his property. I think they are not on a city water system. Are they tapping underground water? What can a family do if the well runs dry?

Test Questions

1. Define "underground water." Give three specific details to support your definition.
2. Explain why underground water is important.
3. Give two ways we can protect our underground water supply.
4. What is an aquifer?

Figure S23.3   Questions Generated by Sixth Graders on the Topic of Underground Water

What are five key terms related to the topic and what do they mean?

Why are we studying Theatre of the Absurd? What is its relevance to our understanding of theatre?

Is there any relationship between this movement and any of the other theatrical movements we have studied?

Who is most associated with this theatrical movement?

What makes a work of this type unique? How can one identify a work of this type?

Is there any controversy related to Theatre of the Absurd, and if so, what is the nature of the controversy?

What is an example of a work from this movement? What is a nonexample?

How do we know a good example of this type of drama when we see it?

When was Theatre of the Absurd most popular?

Why was it popular during this period?

Is Theatre of the Absurd unique to certain cultures? If so, which ones?

What political or societal circumstances contributed to this theatrical movement?

What are the roots of Theatre of the Absurd?

What is the dominant characteristic of Theatre of the Absurd?

How can we use our understanding of this theatrical movement?

Figure S23.4   Questions Generated by High School Students on the Topic of Theatre of the Absurd

Test Questions

1. Describe Theatre of the Absurd and explain its origins.
2. Contrast Theatre of the Absurd with another type of theater we have studied.
3. Take the position of a director hoping to stage a work of Theatre of the Absurd. Argue in a paragraph for the importance of this work.

Figure S23.4 *Continued*

4. If you have talked about question types, some students may think they need to stick to the types you mentioned. This will restrict their thinking and limit their sense of ownership over the content and the direction of the discussion. You may choose to remind them of question types, and even encourage their consideration if students are stumped. Prompting students with "Does anyone have a *why* question regarding this topic?" or "Think about the application level of Bloom's taxonomy. Are there any questions you have on this topic that might tap that level of thinking?" can stimulate good questions. However, do not limit their questions.

5. If you observe that students' questions stray far from the content you were hoping to address, you may choose to gently refocus them with a comment like "Hm. Really interesting questions you have been asking—someone write them down!—but we are moving into topics that I was not planning to address yet. How about trying some different questions? Think more about the *effects* of the war."

6. Question Only works best if you have a solid grasp of the content. Be prepared!

STRATEGY 24 Inquiry Training

LANGUAGE DEMANDS	LITERACY DEMANDS
Appropriate for:	Appropriate for:
Early English Learners	✔ Emerging Readers/Writers
✔ Intermediate English Learners	✔ Intermediate Readers/Writers
✔ Advanced English Learners	✔ Proficient Readers/Writers

The heart of discovery lies in asking questions sparked by one's curiosity. In Suchman's Inquiry Training model (1962, 1964), students are presented with a discrepant event or a puzzling phenomenon. They ask the teacher questions that can be answered "yes" or "no" to first verify what they observe and to then determine causal relationships. Finally, they explain what they observed and analyze their questioning strategies to improve them for next time. Inquiry Training helps students learn habits of mind and processes of scientific thought that can help them devise and test hypotheses across many fields of study—and throughout life.

PREPARATION

1. Determine the major concept or generalization to be addressed during the Inquiry Training session.

2. Select, related to that major idea, a discrepant event or puzzling phenomenon that will capture students' curiosity. To be effective, the event or phenomenon must spark a genuine desire to acquire additional information or explain what students see. A discrepant event is something that behaves counter to one's expectations. For example, in science you might drop two unopened cans of soda into an aquarium filled with water and watch as one can floats and the other sinks. Or, you might display a can that rolls up hill or a pin that floats in midair. If you are working in an area such as social studies, you might select an object or artifact that is puzzling to students because they cannot explain a central idea such as its origin, function, or age. Preparing the discrepant event or puzzling phenomenon may entail gathering additional materials that allow students to test their hypotheses by examining other data.

3. Be very clear on the explanation you have in mind. This may entail conducting additional research so that you will not be caught off guard by students' questions.

IMPLEMENTATION

1. Present the discrepant event. Allow students to witness it as many times as they wish.

2. Tell the students that their job is to ask you yes-no questions in order to determine an explanation for what they see. Students should first ask confirming questions that verify their observations and then move to causal connections that seek out the explanations for the discrepant event.

3. If students need to test an idea that cannot be physically manipulated, give—or better yet, show—them additional information to allow them to reject or confirm their conjectures.

4. Support students in asking questions.
   a. If students struggle to ask yes-no questions, allow peers to assist them.
   b. Use partner sharing ("Tell your neighbor what you're thinking") to encourage students to formulate and revise hypotheses.
   c. Use wait time.

5. Ignore students' outbursts that do not fit your instructions for acceptable questions.

6. If students ask causal questions early in the sequence, remind them to ask those questions later: "That is a causal question. Save it until we verify what we see here."

7. To conclude the session, have students reflect on their questioning practices and how they might learn from the current session to improve their questioning in the future.

ALTERNATIVES

1. Use technology to present a discrepant event that may not be available otherwise. For instance, show a video clip that utilizes stop-action or time-lapse photography sequences.

2. Allow students to develop their own Inquiry Training sessions. Require them to practice in front of you or another knowledgeable adult before presenting to the class.

TIME ALLOTMENT

The time spent depends on students' curiosity and persistence with their questions. Young students may focus for 10 minutes or so, and older or more persistent students may focus for 20 minutes.

EXAMPLES

Figure S24.1 lists brief ideas for Inquiry Training sessions across the lower and upper elementary grade. Figure S24.2 describes in detail a discrepant event for a middle school class studying density. Figure S24.3 describes a discrepant event for an Inquiry Training session for a high school class studying the Middle East.

TROUBLESHOOTING

1. Students may not have had much practice testing causal connections by asking questions. Practice by playing games such as 20 Questions. Remember, though, that mere guessing is not the same as scientific inquiry, and games like this should be used to foster inquiry skills.

2. Occasionally one or two students will begin the lesson completely aware of the explanation being sought. These students may present causal questions that explain the phenomenon early on. Rather than appearing upset that they would "give away the answer," treat these students' questions and explanations merely as additional data. Do not respond emotionally to their input.

3. Sometimes students do not arrive at the explanation of an event before your time for the lesson runs out. Rather than sharing the explanation at that time, commend students for the productive questions they have asked thus far. Tell students that you will leave the object out for their exploration, and assure them that you will

Lower Elementary Grades

Problem: Where is the quarter?

The teacher displays a quarter and then "accidentally" drops it. She bends to pick it up, straightens, and says, "Poof!" When she opens her hand, the quarter is gone. The teacher leads an Inquiry Training session to discover what happened to the quarter. Students eventually arrive at the explanation: The teacher slid it under her shoe instead of picking it up. This Inquiry Training session leads into a discussion about careful observation and logical explanations for events that appear to be magical. Enthralled, students begin to bring in their own magic tricks to lead Inquiry Training sessions.

Problem: What is this tool?

The teacher presents the most unusual object found in his house, similar to the one found in Photo A. He leads an Inquiry Training session wherein students attempt to discover the function of the tool. Through their questioning, they discern the explanation: The tool is a cheese plane, used for shaving thin slices of cheese off the larger block. A cheese plane is a type of blade, or a double wedge, and this Inquiry Training Session leads into the study of simple machines.

Photo A
Source: Andrea M. Guillaume

Problem: What do you see?

The teacher presents a photo of an animal or object, the scale of which prevents the viewer from immediately recognizing the identity of the animal or object (see Photo B). Ranger Rick magazine often prints photos like this, or sections of existing noncopyrighted photos can be enlarged. An Internet image search with the term "photos taken with an electron microscope" yielded Photo B. Students ask yes-no questions to determine the subjects of the photograph. Their teacher guides them to the explanation: Photo B shows conodonts, or fossilized teeth of ancient, microscopic animals, photographed on the head of a pin.

Photo B
Source: Mark A. Purnell, University of Leicester

Figure S24.1 Sample Inquiry Training Sessions for the Elementary Grades

Upper Elementary Grades

Problem: What is my number?

The teacher presents a 100s-chart (a 10 × 10 grid with the numbers 1 through 100 written in order) on the overhead projector. He instructs students to guess his secret number using a variety of yes-no questions. They are required to use strategic questions rather than simple ones such as, "Is it 63?" The first three questions students ask are: "Is your number greater than 50?" "Is your number a multiple of 3?" and "Is the sum of the digits in your number even?" The teacher crosses out numbers on the overhead transparency as students eliminate them.

Problem: Who done it?

The teacher presents a "morbid inquiry" for students' solution: "A man was found dead in his bed. Next to him were two sticks in a small pool of liquid. How did he die?" Through an Inquiry Training session, students discover the explanation: He choked to death on a Popsicle. Beside him lay the Popsicle sticks and the melted remains of the Popsicle. This session launches lively investigations into an avocation popular with the students: forensic science.

Problem: What's their story?

The teacher presents pairs of tweezers to each table and announces that ancient versions of these implements—2,000 years old—were pulled from the Roman Baths in cities like Bath, England. Students' Inquiry Training session goal is to determine: What is the story of these implements? Why were they found among the remains in Roman Baths? By asking careful questions, students determine the explanation: Many Ancient Romans apparently detested body hair. Slaves, called depilators, plucked the body and underarm hair of other Romans as they lounged at the baths. This session heightens students' skills not only in interpreting evidence but also in connecting ancient societies' values and practices to those of their own society.

Figure S24.1   *Continued*

Generalizations

1. Some liquids do not readily mix. These are immiscible liquids.
2. Some liquids are denser than others. These liquids have a greater mass per unit of volume.

Discrepant Event or Puzzling Phenomenon

1. The teacher first presents a Density Bottle (Sarquis, Sarquis, & Williams, 1995). A Density Bottle is a container such as a one-liter water bottle filled half with tap water (plus a few drops of food color) and half with baby or mineral oil. Because water and oil are immiscible, the denser liquid (colored water) sinks to the bottom. As an alternative, the teacher can add oil and water to the bottle before the lesson, out of students' view, and then add coloring as students watch (Guillaume, 1997). The food coloring (which is water soluble) will drop through the oil and spread into the water. (See the drawing, below, of a Density Bottle.)

2. After students have asked questions to discern the nature of the Density Bottle, the teacher presents a Frustration Bottle (Sarquis, Sarquis, & Williams, 1995). The Frustration Bottle contains water and oil, but this time the oil is colored (such as lamp oil, purchased at a grocery or discount store). As a result, the clear layer (the water, which is denser) is on the bottom, and the colored layer (oil, which is less dense) is on top. The teacher leads an Inquiry Training session to help students determine why the clear layer is on bottom in one bottle and on top in the other. (See the drawing, below, of a Frustration Bottle.)

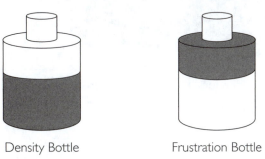

Density Bottle   Frustration Bottle

Figure S24.2   Inquiry Training Session for Middle School Lesson on Density

Generalizations

1. Ancient civilizations have made contributions that are often attributed to more recent Europeans.
2. Existing evidence limits the possible conclusions of those who study ancient history.

Discrepant Event or Puzzling Phenomenon

1. The teacher presents a photo of the "Baghdad Battery" found online (similar to that found in the first frame below). She presents the task: "What can we conclude about this object?"
2. As students require additional information, the teacher presents a cutaway illustration of the object, found online, similar to that found in the second frame below.
3. The teacher leads students to the conclusion that, based on best guesses, the artifact is an ancient battery.

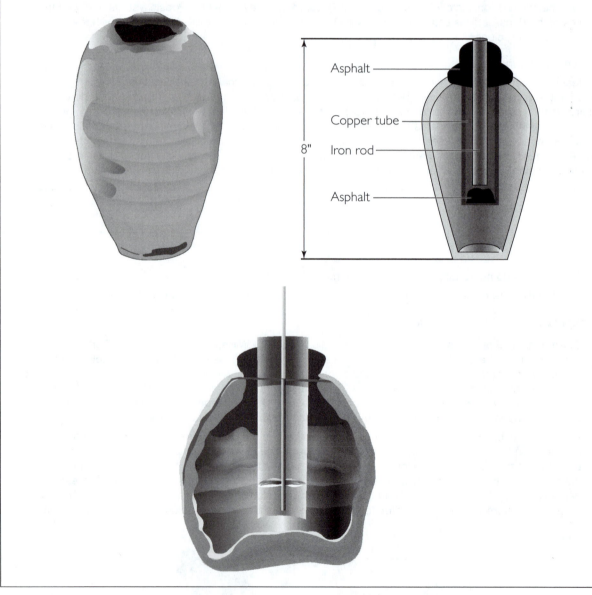

Figure S24.3 Inquiry Training Session for a High School Lesson on the Middle East

continue your investigations later. This gives you the opportunity to consider whether you need to provide additional information to help students ask effective questions.

4. Yes-no question formation can be difficult for students acquiring English. Pair English learners with friends who are fluent in English and allow them to talk before posing the question to you. You may wish to record some of the students' yes-no questions in writing and look for patterns in questions as a later language development lesson.

STRATEGY 25 Object-based Inquiry

LANGUAGE DEMANDS	LITERACY DEMANDS
Appropriate for:	Appropriate for:
✔ Early English Learners	✔ Emerging Readers/Writers
✔ Intermediate English Learners	✔ Intermediate Readers/Writers
✔ Advanced English Learners	✔ Proficient Readers/Writers

All students should engage in inquiry in order to develop the abilities to ask questions, conduct investigations using appropriate tools, and think critically about evidence (National Research Council, 1996). By interacting with everyday yet interesting objects, students can pursue central questions under the guidance of their teachers (Alvarado & Herr, 2003). Object-based Inquiry uses items to spark students' curiosity and the study of important concepts and questions, and it allows students to refine the processes of investigation as they generate and test hypotheses. As a result, student motivation increases and students deeply process information; thus, they construct richer understandings. Using objects from daily life builds background knowledge, which is essential to future learning. Further, hands-on instruction increases access to core concepts for all students.

PREPARATION

1. Build collections of interesting objects. Examples include feathers, shells, rocks, small toys, and postage stamps. If you teach more than one subject, you may notice that your collections can address academic standards or outcomes for a number of areas. For example, shells can be useful for teaching science concepts, measurement skills, and descriptive writing techniques.

2. Study the outcomes (standards) your students are to master and plan initial questions that can incorporate several concepts, perhaps from more than one subject area.

3. Write specific objectives and initial questions. Questions should be open-ended and flexible and should encourage higher-level thinking.

4. Gather materials that can assist students in their explorations. Examples include hand lenses, scales, rulers, and graph paper.

5. Store items so they will be safe and consume minimal space between uses.

6. Arrange students in small groups and provide easy access to materials. If materials are limited, plan to circulate small collections of different sorts among the groups. Or, place the collection in a center for small-group interaction during set work periods.

You can find this template on the accompanying Teacher Resources CD and at the back of the book.

7. Consider duplicating the template found in the Teacher Resources CD to help students structure their notes during the inquiry.

IMPLEMENTATION

1. Present the objects and your initial questions. Heighten student interest by conveying your own sense of enthusiasm and wonder about the objects. You might use Quick Draws (p. 50) before distributing the objects as a way to entice students into the investigation. Invite careful observation once you distribute items.

2. Elicit students' questions: What are they wondering about these objects? Help them focus on questions that can be answered through empirical study (such as observation and experimentation). Record students' questions.

3. Guide students in addressing their questions through careful observation and research. Provide texts and Internet access so that students can address questions that cannot be answered through observation alone.

4. Draw conclusions and present results. Consider using strategies such as Invented Dialogs (p. 210) and "I Didn't Know That . . ." Response Frames (p. 218) to share students' knowledge.

ALTERNATIVES

1. Online museums can also be used for study of virtual objects through Object-based Inquiry.

2. Invite students to contribute items for a class museum. Create an investigation center where students can continue their studies during independent work time.

TIME ALLOTMENT

Allow plenty of time for Object-based Inquiry, as students' curiosity tends to intensify as the lesson proceeds. A basic session takes approximately 45 minutes.

EXAMPLES

Figure S25.1 presents objects and questions used in a kindergarten class. Chapter 2's sample fifth-grade science lesson (Figure 2.6) uses Object-based Inquiry.

Content Areas

Mathematics (Counting objects)

Social studies (Recognizing national symbols)

Language arts (Distinguishing letters, words, and sentences)

Science (Observing and sorting common objects)

Lesson Description

1. Before the lesson, the teacher has placed a variety of U.S. coins and coins from Canada and Mexico in a box with a lid.

2. To begin the lesson, the teacher gathers students near her and says, "I have a surprise. Last night I cleaned out my car and my dresser, and I filled this box. Listen as I shake it." She engages the students in a discussion of what type of object might be in the box, how many objects might be in the box, and other related questions. She dramatically removes the lid to show students: "Coins!" "Money!" they exclaim.

3. The teacher prepares students for inquiry: "Everyone will have two coins to examine. At your tables I have placed hand lenses and paper. You may wish to trace and draw the coins. Be careful with the coins so that we can put them into our learning center later. Study your coins for 5 minutes, and then I will call us back to the rug to focus our investigations."

Figure S25.1   *Object-based Inquiry in a Kindergarten Class*

4. After 5 minutes, the students report their findings and develop the following list of questions for further investigation:

How many animals are on the coins?

Why do the coins have people?

Are Spanish and English the only languages on the coins?

Why are the coins different colors?

How much do the coins weigh?

Why do some coins have crinkly edges?

How much could we buy with the coins?

How much do we have altogether?

5. The teacher records students' questions on a chart, and their investigations continue for a number of days.
6. The students create a Graphic Organizer (p. 204) to display their findings.

Figure S25.1 *Continued*

TROUBLESHOOTING

1. Be certain to create a sense of intrigue in sharing the objects. The set-up you provide plays an important role in students' engagement in the lesson.

2. Not every question students ask can be answered via scientific observation. Be ready to help students distinguish scientific questions from other types of questions.

3. Be prepared for the fact that not every student (or class) will find every set of objects interesting. Have a Plan B in mind: Consider providing an alternate source of materials or prepare to truncate your lesson in favor of objects that arise as interesting to the students.

4. Teach students to handle collections carefully.

STRATEGY 26 Problem-based Learning

LANGUAGE DEMANDS	LITERACY DEMANDS
Appropriate for:	Appropriate for:
✔ Early English Learners	✔ Emerging Readers/Writers
✔ Intermediate English Learners	✔ Intermediate Readers/Writers
✔ Advanced English Learners	✔ Proficient Readers/Writers

In Problem-based Learning, students work in cooperative groups to solve realistic problems. Advocates report that Problem-based Learning fosters students' comprehension of the content, their thinking skills, their ability to find and analyze resources, and their social skills (Rhem, 1998). Because they tackle contextualized problems, students perceive learning as more authentic and report higher interest in the subject matter (Torp & Sage, 2002). Problem-based Learning follows a general set of steps: Students meet the problem, make a plan for solving the problem, gather information, generate possible solutions, select a solution, and debrief.

PREPARATION

1. Prepare the problem. It needs to be ill-structured, meaning that its solution—and the strategies to solve it—are not obvious at first inspection. The problem should stem from a real or realistic context. It should feel genuine. One way to capture a problem is to start with an actual problem experienced by real people in the local setting. Another way to structure a problem is to examine the content standards or outcomes of interest and imagine what type of real-life problem a person who has mastered that content could solve.

2. Prepare Know-Need-Do (KND) charts. A blank chart is found in the Teacher Resources CD. These charts will be used as students analyze the problem. They can be constructed on chart paper, on writing paper, or on the computer.

3. Brainstorm the types of resources students may need to access to understand and solve the problem. A variety of resources should be used. Examples include Internet research, library research, interviews of peers and experts, and other kinds of data such as surveys and observation. Ensure that such resources are available.

4. Decide on student groups. Consider students' strengths and needs so that members can contribute their strengths and help each other. If you use a variety of problems, you may also consider students' interests as you establish groups.

You can find this template on the accompanying Teacher Resources CD and at the back of the book.

IMPLEMENTATION

1. Help students get to know the problem. Be certain to create a sense of importance and intrigue as you introduce the problem. It may help to dress in a uniform befitting a relevant role or to read real requests for help from others, such as letters from city council members or the school principal.

2. Help students analyze the problem. Use the KND chart from the Teacher Resources CD to record what is known, what is needed, and what students will do. Students define the problem statement after completing the analysis.

3. Guide students in gathering information. Help students access resources. Students may need to make phone calls, survey their peers, and read newspaper articles, for example. Help students to analyze and share their information.

4. Direct students to list all possible solutions, and then help them determine which solution has the best fit for the problem.

5. Allow students to present and defend their solutions, perhaps using presentation software, posters, or other visual displays of information. If the problem is real, share the research and proposed solution(s) with people of interest.

6. Discuss the problem and the learning that came from Problem-based Learning.

ALTERNATIVES

1. If time is short, or as a warm-up, do informal group problem solving in place of Problem-based Learning. In these informal sessions, the problem may be more obvious, or students may be required to collect fewer (or no) resources to solve it. Figure S26.1 gives a sample problem for an informal group problem-solving session in the language arts. This example presents an informal session, falling short of a fully developed Problem-based Learning experience, because the problem is set by the teacher (not the students), and it does not have a wide range of potentially useful or accurate solutions. Still, it gives students the opportunity to work together to solve an interesting puzzle. Notice that no one student is given all the information needed, so collaboration continues to be critical.

2. Ask students, families, and the community for input on generating problems.

TIME ALLOTMENT

A full Problem-based Learning session can take a week or two to complete. Briefer versions can take just 20 minutes.

EXAMPLES

Figure S26.1 gives a sample problem for an informal group session in the language arts. Figure S26.2 gives a variety of problems for Problem-based Learning across the grade levels and curriculum.

Build-A-Word: All students have a set of letter tiles; each tile contains one letter of the alphabet. Each small group of students receives an envelope full of clues for building a word. Each group member receives only one clue. First the students individually build words that meet their own criteria, then they together build a word that meets all criteria. The clues read:

1. Build a word with seven letters.
2. Build a word that rhymes with "ease."
3. Build a word with a total of four vowels.

Figure S26.1   Sample Problem for Informal Group Problem-solving Session in a Third-grade Language Arts Lesson

4. Build a word with three e's.

5. Build a word that means "to grasp" or "to crush."

Students discover that the word is *squeeze*. A short debriefing discussion focuses on questions such as, "Are there other words that fit all criteria?" and "Which of these clues is absolutely necessary to arrive at the word? Which could be deleted?"

Figure S26.1   *Continued*

First-grade Social Studies: Several students reported not feeling safe on the playground because some children frequently played rough and said mean things. The students wondered, "What can we do to make the playground a happier, safer place?"

Third-grade Art: Third graders, in studying their local community, had the mayor in as a guest speaker. She expressed her concerns that the downtown area was not a uniformly colorful or welcoming place. What could the students do to improve their community and address the mayor's concern? The mayor invited the students to present a plan to the City Council.

Sixth-grade Environmental Studies: When the sixth-grade classes went to environmental education camp, they learned that the average American wastes approximately 3 pounds of food each day. The entire camp worked hard to get the camp's food waste down to zero pounds per day. The sixth graders came back to school highly motivated to discover how much food waste was occurring at school and what they could do to reduce potential food waste.

Middle School U.S. Government Class: As a tradition at the local middle school, students took a trip to Washington, DC, to visit museums and watch government in action. The school district's administration decided that the trip is not worth the time and effort because so few students could afford the trip and so few cultural and governmental sites could be visited in one trip. This year's seventh graders were anxious to go on the trip during their eighth-grade year. How could they make the trip accessible for more students? How could they fit more sites into the trip? They needed to present a compelling case to the school district.

High School Physics Class: A class watched video footage of the Tacoma Narrows Bridge disaster, a spectacular collapse caused by improper use of building materials given the forces on the bridge. The teacher challenged his students to form small teams and build "the best" bridge with limited materials.

Figure S26.2   Sample Problems for Problem-based Learning at Various Grade Levels

TROUBLESHOOTING

1. There is a degree of uncertainty in Problem-based Learning, given the fact that answers are not predetermined. Remember to think about your role as a guide rather than as a dispenser of knowledge, and be sure you use sticky points or stumbling blocks as teachable moments for problem-solving skills. Ensure that your schedule has enough flexibility that you can complete the experience without worry.

STRATEGY 27 Revealing Information

LANGUAGE DEMANDS	LITERACY DEMANDS
Appropriate for:	Appropriate for:
✔ Early English Learners	✔ Emerging Readers/Writers
✔ Intermediate English Learners	✔ Intermediate Readers/Writers
✔ Advanced English Learners	✔ Proficient Readers/Writers

Too often, students perceive that school is about knowing the right answer on the first try. Instead, the constructivist approach emphasizes that teachers should foster students' growth as *theory builders* who learn by conjecturing and then revising their ideas as they reconcile conflicting information and gather more data (Chaillé & Britain, 2003). In Revealing Information, the teacher divulges information, bit by bit, until students accurately identify the concept or rule. The revealed information can be in the form of words—printed or spoken—or in other forms such as numerals (Coates & Stenmark, 1997), music, or visual images. Revealing Information not only teaches students the concept or rule of interest; it is also useful for teaching processes (such as prediction and estimation) and for increasing students' factual stores.

PREPARATION

1. Begin by selecting the target based on your learning goals. Whether it is a concept, fact, person, song title, letter, shape, country, or something else, the target is a single right answer.

2. Develop clues that will allow students to identify the target. Preparation may be as simple as creating an overhead transparency to be covered with a paper that is slowly pulled down (Coates & Stenmark, 1997), or it may entail finding subconcepts or facts that lead to the target.

3. Sequence the clues as appropriate. If clues entail factual hints, order them from least to most directive so that the last clue provides the most specific information about the target.

4. Decide how students will provide their responses. They may, for instance, use Unison Response (p. 73), or they may use number or letter tiles that they display. Unison Response takes the least time but has low accountability for individual students.

IMPLEMENTATION

1. Present the task. For instance, you might state, "Discover which shape I have hidden here on the overhead projector."

2. Tell students how they are expected to respond. As an example, you might say, "Think first. When I lower my arm, everyone will say a guess at the same time."

3. Provide clues and ask for revised predictions. "Okay! Many people think *triangle*. Watch as I pull this cover sheet down a bit. Just watch; don't guess yet. When I give the signal, say your new guess."

4. Continue to reveal information until all students have discovered the target. Celebrate students' success and ask about the strategies or processes that were helpful to them. Because students' ability to solve future problems resides largely in their ability to develop and employ strategies appropriately, be sure to discuss thought processes. Looking back, according to Wilson (1993), may be the most important step in problem solving.

ALTERNATIVE

1. Allow students to develop the targets and clues. Before using their clues with the class, check accuracy to ensure the class's success.

TIME ALLOTMENT

As a quick lesson opener, Revealing Information takes fewer than 5 minutes. As the major portion (or body) of the lesson, it may take as long as 15 minutes, especially if time is spent discussing students' ideas.

EXAMPLES

Figure S27.1 gives sample Revealing Information prompts for a variety of grades and topics.

TROUBLESHOOTING

1. Be certain that you have enough clues that students can arrive at the target.
2. Double-check clues for factual accuracy, as students' success depends on their ability to draw accurate conclusions.

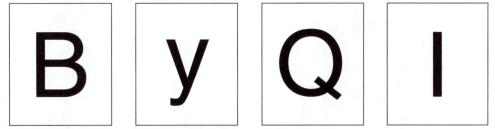

Kindergarten Lesson on Identifying Letters: For each letter, below, the teacher displays a single enlarged letter on the overhead and conceals it with a coversheet. The teacher reveals the letter bit by bit, and students predict the identity of the letter. She varies her clues by pulling some coversheets from the top down, some from the bottom up, and some from side to side. The teacher pauses frequently to say, "What else could it be? How do you know?"

B y Q I

Third-grade Math Lesson on Identifying Linear Patterns: The teacher shows the following patterns on a projected computer screen or on an overhead transparency with all terms individually covered by small

Figure S27.1 Sample Revealing Information Clues for a Variety of Grades and Topics

self-adhesive notes. The teacher reveals the terms from left to right or, for some patterns, at random. At the teacher's prompting, students hold up number tiles to show their predictions for the next number in the pattern.

0, 2, 4, 6, 8	98, 97, 96, 95, 94	15, 16, 15, 16

High School Lesson on the Geography of Iraq: The teacher tells students that their job is to identify a country that meets all of the given criteria in a game called, "I'm thinking of a country . . ." They will discuss each clue as partners, and they will list their guesses in order. They will submit their list of guesses, though accuracy in their responses along the way will not factor into their grades for the assignment. The class views globes as they discuss each clue.

Clues

1. I'm thinking of a country consisting of mountains in the north and plains, often marshy, in the south.
2. I'm thinking of a country that has one very short border that touches a gulf.
3. I'm thinking of a country that was once a part of the Ottoman Empire.
4. I'm thinking of a country fed by two major rivers.
5. Those rivers are the Tigris and Euphrates.
6. I'm thinking of a country known as the Cradle of Civilization.
7. I'm thinking of a country found at 33°N, 44°E.
8. I'm thinking of this country (displays map): Iraq.

Figure S27.1 *Continued*

3. Some students, eager to share their hypotheses, may shout out ideas that are less than carefully formulated. Remind students that, although enjoyable, Revealing Information is not a guessing game but an opportunity for students to refine their ability to use information (data) to make reasonable and increasingly accurate hypotheses. If students make wild guesses, ask, "What in the data presented so far supports that guess?"

STRATEGY 28   Photo Analysis

LANGUAGE DEMANDS	LITERACY DEMANDS
Appropriate for:	Appropriate for:
✔ Early English Learners	✔ Emerging Readers/Writers
✔ Intermediate English Learners	✔ Intermediate Readers/Writers
✔ Advanced English Learners	✔ Proficient Readers/Writers

As we are bombarded with visual images, the ability to analyze visual information becomes increasingly important in our image-driven society (Kellner, 2002). Visual literacy, or the ability to find and make meaning through imagery, develops slowly and with careful support (Yenawine, 1997). Photo Analysis helps students scrutinize photographs to determine their meanings and messages. Analysis of images can help students to generate or test hypotheses about people, places, and times and can reveal much about history and actual events, which is useful for social studies lessons or other lessons that focus on historically accurate and objective understandings of events. Photo Analysis can also focus on the artistic qualities of a work—its inferred and personal meanings and messages—which may be useful in visual arts lessons or lessons in such areas as language arts where universal themes such as joy, despair, or isolation are explored.

PREPARATION

1. Obtain one or more photographs related to the upcoming lesson. Select photos that are intriguing, such as those containing people engaged in particular activities, perhaps surrounded by objects that deepen intrigue or provide clues. If you are analyzing photographs for artistic purposes, see Figure S28.1 for guidelines on selecting artworks for school-age viewers. Consider using illustrations from students' textbooks that are rich and capture ideas that are central to the content. You may also use photographs from your own collection, students' collections, the library, or the Internet. If you use the Internet, try first conducting an image search using a search engine such as Google (www.google.com), Alta Vista (www.altavista.com/image/) or PicSearch (www.picsearch.com). Figure S28.2 provides some additional suggestions for Web sites with plentiful images.

2. Study background information on the image and, if relevant, the artist in enough detail that you can guide students' inquiries and provide accurate information.

3. Determine how you will display the images and prepare them for display. Overhead transparencies are effective and can easily be stored and transported. Electronic images stored on a computer or the Internet and projected on a screen offer many advantages. Public domain photographs, such as many of those posted on the Web by the U.S. government, can be photocopied and distributed to students. Be sure to have a class-size image available even if students have their own copies.

4. Develop questions and prompts to lead students in analyzing the images. As a general rule, focus students first on prominent visual features, then on their background knowledge related to the period or subject, then on inferences or conclusions they draw. End with unanswered questions. Figure S28.3 offers prompts for factual or historical Photo Analysis, and Figure S28.4 gives prompts for artistic Photo Analysis.

5. If you choose, duplicate either the Historical Analysis or Artistic Analysis template found in the Teacher Resources CD.

You can find these templates on the accompanying Teacher Resources CD and at the back of the book.

IMPLEMENTATION

1. Present the image. Photos can be used at any point during a lesson, but they are often effective for focusing attention during a lesson's opening. For example, Photo Analysis can serve as a powerful prereading activity because it allows students to test their newly discovered knowledge and to seek additional supporting details (Bower & Lobdell, 2003).

2. In presenting the image, emphasize students' role as detectives, or inquirers, who are being asked to "read" a scene from a particular time and place (Bower & Lobdell, 2003). Magnify a portion of the projected image by holding a blank paper in front of the desired portion.

3. Guide students in analyzing the image using prompts developed earlier (step 4, in preparation), emphasizing the process of discovery and of testing inferences to tell a story or share meanings.

ALTERNATIVES

1. Use reproductions of famous paintings or other visual works instead of photographs. Try using high-quality art in children's literature (see Frohardt, 1999).

2. Once students learn to analyze images, a number of images can be analyzed within one lesson, either at stations or within student groups. Then students can draw conclusions across images.

3. Provide students with cameras and ask them to take photos that capture a certain concept or event. They can close a lesson this way, or you can open a future lesson with their images. Digital photos can be easily collected, stored, and manipulated.

4. Combine Photo Analysis with other strategies such as Quick Writes (p. 48), Q Cards (p. 78), or—to enact new understandings—Dramatizations and Tableaux (p. 212).

TIME ALLOTMENT

Depending on the age of the students and the number of prompts you plan to use, Photo Analysis can take from 5 to 30 minutes.

EXAMPLES

Figures S28.5 and S28.6 provide sample photographs and accompanying protocols for two contrasting lessons.

TROUBLESHOOTING

1. Pay attention to copyright restrictions. Check fair use policies, and look for information to order reproductions if necessary.

2. Be certain that photos are displayed in a manner that allows all students to see them. If images are projected, ensure that the room is dark enough to provide strong contrast.

3. Help students separate inferences from observations so that they do not rush to conclusions. Ask students to supply evidence to support their knowledge claims.

Accessibility:	Can viewers connect to what they see? Does their background experience allow them to recognize and understand what they see?
Expressive Content:	Is the image open to several interpretations? While accessible, are there also puzzling elements? Is the subject matter inherently interesting to young people?
Narrative:	Is there an intended story that viewers can make sense of?
Diversity:	Do images present a range of experiences in time and culture? In media, material, and styles? Can students of different races and ethnicity find themselves among the various images?
Realism:	Do the images represent a range within the general category of "realistic"?
Series/Themes:	If there are multiple images, are they presented in a series connected by a common theme?
Media:	Do the media subject themselves well to reproduction? (Photos, paintings, and drawings all reproduce well; sculpture and architecture less well.)
Artistic Genre:	Do works, over time, represent a range of genre scenes, portraits, self-portraits, landscapes, and so on?
Key Artists and Works:	Are well-known artists and well-known works among those presented?
Sequences:	When multiple images are used, are they presented in a sequence from simple to complex?

Figure S28.1 Guiding Questions for Selecting Images for Young Viewers

Note: This process should be done as thoughtfully as one selects reading material for beginning readers. (*Content summarized and reworded from VUE, 1998, with permission.*)

http://www.thinker.org	Fine Arts Museums of San Francisco
http://lcweb2.loc.gov/ammem/	The Library of Congress: American Memory
http://www.metmuseum.org/home.asp	The Metropolitan Museum of Art
http://www.nationalgeographic.com/	National Geographic
http://www.cr.nps.gov/	The National Park Service
http://www.nmpft.org.uk/	National Museum of Photography, Film and Television
http://www.loc.gov/rr/print/catalog.html	Prints and Photographs Reading Room of the Library of Congress
http://americanart.si.edu/	Smithsonian American Art Museum
http://smithsonianimages.si.edu/siphoto/ siphoto.portal?_nfpb=true&_pageLabel=home	Smithsonian Images
http://www.archives.gov/	U.S. National Archives and Records Administration
http://www.ibiblio.org/louvre/	The Web Museum

Figure S28.2 Web Sites with Plentiful Photographic Images

Note: Many sites describe the images, their creators, and their histories. Check for descriptions as you review sites.

Select some prompts from each category.

First Impressions

1. Study the photo for 15 seconds.
2. What is your overall impression? Describe the photo in one or two sentences.

Observations

1. What do you see?
2. What is the subject of the photo? (Examples include buildings, people in daily life, people posed, and landscapes.)
3. Who is depicted? Describe the people. (Focus on number, age, clothing, expressions, apparent relationships, and economic status.)
4. Describe the objects you see. Make a list.
5. What is the action? What is happening in the photo?
6. When was this photo taken? What time of day, season, or year?
7. Where was this photo taken? What is the setting?
8. What are the unique physical qualities of the photo? (Examples include notations, photographer's imprint, and color—black and white, sepia, half tone, full color.)
9. To focus observations, divide the photo into quadrants and study individual quadrants. Or, magnify parts of the image. If the image is projected onto a screen, use a white piece of paper in front of the screen, brought forward to bring sections into sharper focus.

Background Knowledge

1. What do you know about this time period?
2. What do you know about the event, people, and objects that appear?

Inferences and Conclusions

1. What is memorable or intriguing about this photo?
2. What, if anything, can we conclude about the event, life, or the time period in the photo?
3. Why did the photographer take this photo?
4. How might this photo have been used originally?
5. What is the message, idea, or thought suggested by the photo?
6. What memory does the photo call to mind, either of actual events, sights, and smells or something less tangible such as a feeling or attitude?
7. Is this photo is a valid historical document?

Next Steps

1. What questions has the photo raised?
2. What more do you want to know?
3. What are some sources you can use to find out?

Figure S28.3   Prompts for Historical or Factual Photo Analysis

Use just a sampling of prompts from each category, selecting prompts that are relevant to the work.

First Impressions

1. Study the photo for 15 seconds.
2. What is your overall impression? Describe the photo in one or two sentences.
3. What do you see and how do you know?

The Photograph's Design

Stand in the photographer's footprints: What decisions did the photographer make regarding the arrangement of things?

1. **Angle:** What was the vantage point? High or low?
2. **Framing:** What did the photographer choose to include? What does the framing draw your attention to in the photograph?
3. **Dominance:** Which object or part of the photo draws your eye? How does your eye move through the photo?
4. **Contrast:** Are there strong visual contrasts?
5. **Repetition:** What elements are repeated? Do they contribute to a sense of unity?
6. **Variety:** Can you see a variety of visual elements such as values, shapes, and textures?
7. **Balance:** Is the visual weight balanced top to bottom? Side to side? Diagonally?

The Photograph's Creation

1. What do you know about the method or techniques the photographer used?
2. What do you know about the equipment used to create the image?

The Photograph's Visual Elements

1. **Light and shadow:** Where is the light source? Describe the shadows.
2. **Value:** Is there a range of tones from light to dark? Squint your eyes. Where is the darkest value? The lightest?
3. **Focus:** What parts of the image are clearly in focus? Are some parts out of focus?
4. **Space:** Do overlapping objects create a sense of space? Is the space shallow, deep, or both?
5. **Shape:** Do you see geometric or organic shapes? Are there positive shapes, such as objects, or negative shapes that represent voids?
6. **Line:** Are there thick, thin, curvy, jagged, or straight lines?
7. **Scale:** Does the scale or size of objects appear to be natural?
8. **Color:** What colors do you see, if any?
9. **Texture:** Do you see visual textures within the photograph? Is there an actual texture on the surface of the photograph?

Impact

1. What is the message or meaning of the photograph, based on your observations?
2. What does the photographer attempt to communicate?

Figure S28.4   Prompts for Artistic Photo Analysis

(These prompts are based on text from online educators' guides created by Cass Fey, Curator of Education at the Center for Creative Photography, the University of Arizona. Used with permission.)

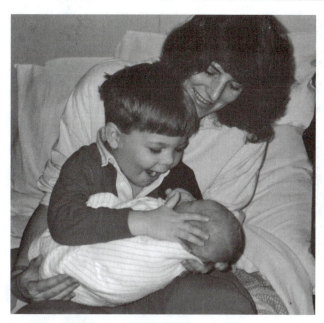

Teacher's Note:

This photograph depicts a 4-year-old boy (Alex) meeting his younger brother (Zach) for the first time. They are sitting with their mother in her hospital room. Alex and Zach's grandmother took the photograph.

Source: LuAnn Burghardt Munns Berthel

You can find a color version of this photo on the accompanying Teacher Resources CD.

First Impressions

1. I'm going to show you a photograph. Ready? First just look quietly.
2. Tell your partner what you think. Now tell me.

The Photograph's Design

1. **Angle:** Was the photographer right in front of, above, or below the people in the picture?
2. **Dominance**: Put your index finger in the air, and when I say "go," trace in the air the path your eye takes when you look at this photo. Where did you start? Where did you end?

The Photograph's Creation

1. What do you know about how the photographer created this picture?

The Photograph's Visual Elements

1. **Value**: Where is the darkest part in this picture? The lightest?
2. **Space**: How close together are the people in the picture? How do you know? (overlap)
3. **Line**: Tell about the lines you see. Who can find a straight line? Who can find a curve?

Impact

1. Tell a story that goes with this photo.

Figure S28.5   Photo and Protocol Used During a First-grade Language Arts Lesson on Telling Stories

Source: Thomas L. D. Edwards

You can find a color version of this photo on the accompanying Teacher Resources CD.

> **Teacher's Note:**
> This photo depicts members of a work crew who are resting after clearing brush to create firebreaks. Firebreaks stop the spread of fire.

First Impressions

1. Take a look at this photo. For the next 15 seconds, just study it.
2. Describe it in a sentence. What do you see?

Observations

1. Describe the people in the photograph.
2. What objects do you see? Let's make a list. I can magnify portions that you need to see more closely.
3. What is happening in the photo? Which quadrant(s) provide the most information about the action?
4. When do you suppose this photo was taken? What clues do the objects in the photo provide? (Check our list [step 2].)

Background Knowledge

1. What do you know about the event that appears here?

Inferences and Conclusions

1. What can we conclude about the event in the photo?
2. What message, idea, or thought is suggested by the photo?
3. Why did the photographer take this photo?
4. What memory does the photo call to mind for you?

Next Steps

1. What more do you want to know? Let's see whether those questions are answered by our lesson. We'll pursue the remaining questions in our research later.

Figure S28.6 Photo and Protocol Used to Open a Sixth-grade Environmental Studies Lesson on Forest Fire Management

STRATEGY 29 Structured Decision Making

LANGUAGE DEMANDS	LITERACY DEMANDS
Appropriate for:	Appropriate for:
Early English Learners	✔ Emerging Readers/Writers
✔ Intermediate English Learners	✔ Intermediate Readers/Writers
✔ Advanced English Learners	✔ Proficient Readers/Writers

The ability to make sound decisions is a critical skill; it guides students' actions throughout their lives both in and out of school (Elias, 2003). According to Elias, making sound decisions requires students to manage their emotions so that they become useful tools in reaching decisions, to understand the circumstances involved in decision making, to set goals and plan accordingly, and to solve problems creatively. Additionally, decision-making activities afford students with opportunities to generate and test hypotheses as students examine and refine their decisions or predictions with a growing store of insights provided by content knowledge and the structured decision-making process (Marzano, Pickering, & Pollock, 2001). One format for Structured Decision Making includes the following steps:

- Describe the problem, situation, or decision to be made.
- List the possible alternatives or options.
- Decide on the criteria for evaluating the alternatives.
- Evaluate the alternatives.
- Make a decision.
- Evaluate the quality of the decision.

PREPARATION

1. Select or devise a decision-making situation related to the content. Figure S29.1 lists six examples, most based on student content standards. Real-life or realistic decisions, or those with which students have some meaningful connection, will likely result in the richest decision-making sessions.

2. Determine student groupings. Will you lead a whole-class session, or will students work in small groups or independently?

3. Structure your lesson or unit to allow students to engage in the steps of the decision-making process as they gain more information throughout the lesson or unit.

4. Prepare any charts that will support the decision-making process, as described below. Blank charts for Structured Decision Making are found in the Teacher Resources CD. They include a Weighted Sum chart; a Plus, Minus, Interesting (PMI) chart; and a Six Thinking Hats mat.

You can find these templates on the accompanying Teacher Resources CD and at the back of the book.

IMPLEMENTATION

Phases of implementation are presented according to the steps in the structured decision-making process.

1. **Describe the problem, situation, or decision to be made:** Provide a context for the decision. Heighten students' interest by using vivid language and building a sense of importance about the decision. In some cases, exploring the issue to ensure student understanding is necessary. Close this phase by asking students to state the problem or decision to be made in their own words. If students have sufficient background knowledge of the issue, you may also ask them for a tentative decision, which will be revisited and perhaps revised throughout the lesson.

2. **List the possible alternatives or options:** In a closed-ended situation, present the options (for instance, yes or no, for or against, or a brief list of choices). In an open-ended situation, have students list potential alternatives. In open-ended situations, push students to think beyond the most common or predictable alternatives into the more unusual; creative thinking often enhances decision making even if only by providing an enriching twist to more traditional solutions.

3. **Decide on the criteria for evaluating the alternatives:** Ask students to state the criteria by which they will judge the alternatives they have listed. They may consider, for example, the impact of an alternative on themselves, on others, and on society in general. Figure S29.2 shows an example of a computer spreadsheet created by a small group of students in a high school class studying current social issues; their criteria are found in the top row. It may be appropriate to assign a weight to the criteria in order to prioritize them. The most important criterion can be weighted more heavily than the least important criterion. Figure S29.2—social issues—shows student-assigned weights. As students begin to consider evaluation criteria, any early decision they considered may begin to shift. Thus, you may wish to ask students to report on their evolving decisions.

4. **Evaluate the alternatives:** Determine the worth of each option. Numerical ratings can be used in many cases. (In Figure S29.2, A gives unweighted totals, and B gives weighted totals.) As Figure S29.2B shows, if students weight their criteria, they multiply their numerical ratings by the weighting factor for a total rating for each option.

5. **Make a decision:** Have students select the best option, given their evaluation of the alternatives. In numerical analyses, students select the option with the highest score.

6. **Evaluate the quality of the decision:** Spend a few minutes reflecting on the decision-making process. Potential prompts include: What new insights into the content did students gain? Into the decision-making process? Which techniques might transfer to their own lives right now? What would they do differently next time?

ALTERNATIVES

1. PMI (Plus, Minus, Interesting) charts can help students explore issues in greater detail before making any decision (De Bono, 1994). In PMI charts, students brainstorm and record benefits, drawbacks, and neutral yet interesting points or questions related to the issue. Note that what some students consider a Plus, others might consider a Minus. Figure S29.3 contains a partially completed PMI.

2. Another technique for evaluating options in a decision-making session is considering possible consequences. Students can list the likely immediate, short-term, and long-term consequences for each of the options.

3. Sometimes decision making is a question not of *what to do* but what to do *first*. Help students set priorities by first brainstorming lists of necessary actions and then ordering them in terms of when each action should be accomplished.

4. Older students can construct tree diagrams (similar to those constructed in probability problems in mathematics) to help them determine promising courses of action.

TIME ALLOTMENT

Depending on the age of the students and the complexity of the decision to be rendered, Structured Decision Making can take from 15 to 60 minutes.

EXAMPLES

Figure S29.1 provides sample issues for decision making. Figure S29.2 gives an example of a numerical analysis for decision making, using a spreadsheet. Figure S29.3 presents the beginnings of a PMI (Plus, Minus, Interesting) chart.

First-grade Language Arts: Students in Room 16 must decide which book, from among the many they read this year, to put forward as their selection of "Room 16's Best Book" in celebration of Read Across America Day.

Third-grade Mathematics Lesson: Students are asked to select the most promising strategy for solving a challenging mathematics problem.

Sixth-grade Science Lesson: In studying renewable and nonrenewable energy sources, students must recommend one promising alternative to fossil fuels.

Middle School Homeroom Discussion: After reading an unsettling report of bullying in the local paper, the teacher leads her students in deciding on personal courses of action if they witness bullying or other antisocial behavior at their own school.

Middle School Social Studies Unit on Ancient Rome: From among ancient Rome's many contributions to today's society, students select and justify one as the most significant.

High School Health Class: Students select a health product from a number of alternatives. As part of the decision-making process, they analyze the products' advertising approaches.

Figure S29.1 Some Opportunities for Structured Decision Making

---

A. What Is Our Most Pressing Social Issue? (Unweighted)

	Number of People Affected	Degree to Which "Victims" Are Affected	Degree to Which We as a Society Suffer	Total
Homelessness	1	3	1	5
Drugs	2	1	2	5
Racism	3	2	3	8

B. What Is Our Most Pressing Social Issue? (Weighted)

Weight	Number of People Affected (x 2)	Degree to Which "Victims" Are Affected (x 1)	Degree to Which We as a Society Suffer (x 3)	Weighted Total
Homelessness	2	3	3	8
Drugs	4	1	6	11
Racism	6	2	9	17

(Note: The higher the rating, the greater the concern.)

Figure S29.2 Computer Spreadsheet Composed by High School Students Selecting the Most Pressing Social Issues

Plus	Minus	Interesting
+ Parents can have another child whose cells might help one of their existing children who is ill. + It could be seen as a way to achieve immortality. + Many people could be saved by cloned tissues.	− No one has the right to play God in creating human life. − Our court system is not prepared to handle the legal fallout from human cloning. − It would be far too easy to clone humans for the wrong reasons.	? Don't we already have human clones? (identical twins) ? What have been the downsides of animal cloning that might apply to human cloning? ? Would a clone of me think just like I think?

Figure S29.3   A Partially Completed PMI Chart for High School Science Students Studying Human Cloning

TROUBLESHOOTING

1. Students who talk less, who have little social power with their peers, or who have particular learning needs may need explicit support to ensure that their perspectives are not overlooked during the decision-making process. Consider using a Share the Wealth technique (p. 72) to ensure that every student's perspective gets fair consideration.

2. Some students are likely to make their decisions based predominantly on what their peers think or on what they believe the most popular decision will be. To develop decision-making skills, avoid techniques such as voting as a method for decision making and instead emphasize the *processes* of arriving at sound decisions.

3. We have seen instances of students of all ages making a swift decision and shutting down further thinking. You may need to emphasize step 2 in implementing this strategy by requiring students to identify multiple alternatives (pick a number if you must!) for consideration and evaluation. Some students believe there is an obvious decision and resist pursuing the problem or issue further. Build the consideration of alternatives as a habit of mind over the course of your time with your students. When students provide an explanation or response to an issue, routinely ask questions such as the following:
   - What else might explain this phenomenon? Anything else?
   - Give three other interpretations.
   - How might someone with different experiences than you respond?
   - What are two other choices people might make in this circumstance?
   - Give another point of view on that issue.

4. Most of us need support in viewing situations from a number of perspectives, a skill that enriches the decisions we make. You can suggest stakeholders who may have varying views on an issue. Also, De Bono's (1985) Six Thinking Hats can help students examine the effects of potential decisions from multiple perspectives. Each hat (presented either literally or figuratively) requires students to use a different type of thinking:

White:	Pure facts; objective data
Red:	Emotions and feelings
Yellow:	Why these are good ideas
Green:	Creative thinking; no judgments
Blue:	Ideas for organizing
Black:	Cautions

STRATEGY 30 Self-directed Learning

LANGUAGE DEMANDS	LITERACY DEMANDS
Appropriate for:	Appropriate for:
Early English Learners	Emerging Readers/Writers
✔ Intermediate English Learners	✔ Intermediate Readers/Writers
✔ Advanced English Learners	✔ Proficient Readers/Writers

A recent survey ranked "helping students become self-directed learners who take responsibility for their own academic performance" as a very high priority by a large majority of educators (Northwest Regional Educational Laboratory, 2004). Self-directed learners own and manage their learning, pursuing personally relevant questions and monitoring their own progress. Self-directed Learning, a strategy advocated for adults, gifted students, and students using computer-based technology, can help teachers in many K–12 classrooms to differentiate instruction and assist students in taking control of their own learning. In Self-directed Learning, students pursue questions and goals of interest to them, gather and study resources related to those goals, scrutinize their work along the way, and present their learning in a format they (in consultation with their teachers) deem appropriate. Teachers take an active role in each step of Self-directed Learning. In addition to fostering positive attitudes toward the learning process, they model strategies, facilitate peer interactions, and provide structure appropriate for each student. In doing so, teachers help students shape their goals, consider their resources, get information, and monitor and assess their own learning.

PREPARATION

1. Examine the content to determine a good fit for Self-directed Learning experiences. Self-directed Learning can be useful to address content standards that provide flexibility in the knowledge students convey as evidence of meeting the standard. Figure S30.1 provides a variety of examples of such standards.

2. Determine the scope of the Self-directed Learning experience. How much time will be dedicated to Self-directed Learning? Will all students be involved? Are all topics acceptable, or do you intend to offer a range of possible projects?

Third-grade Language Arts Standard: "The learner will be able to differentiate among a variety of texts, including lists, newsletters, and signs, and the purposes they serve." (Texas; www.statestandards.com)

Fifth-grade Mathematics Standard: "The learner will be able to organize and present data; make an interpretation; apply the data to obtain solutions to problems; and find the most suitable data display." (Florida; www.statestandards.com)

Middle School Health Standard: "Students should be encouraged to develop a personal nutrition plan based on food choices and calorie levels that promotes health and reduces the risk of disease." (California Department of Education, 2003, p. 99)

High School Science Standard: "The learner will be able to explore the knowledge, preparation and experience needed in science, math and technology for career interests." (Washington, grade 10; www.statestandards.com)

Figure S30.1   Sample Student Content Standards that Can Serve as Springboards for Self-directed Learning

3. Anticipate resources that may be used and ensure that they are accessible. Although students will be guided to select their own appropriate resources, ensure that access to specialists, library materials, and the Internet are available.

4. Consider setting up peer discussion groups (Leal, 1993) as avenues for students to share their inquiries and seek advice from peers on how to proceed productively.

5. Think about how Self-directed Learning products will be assessed. You may wish to develop a scoring rubric in advance, or you may choose to draw students into a discussion of how their work should be assessed.

IMPLEMENTATION

1. Discuss the content and range of Self-directed Learning options with students. Ensure that you build interest and emphasize students' choice of avenues for inquiry.

2. Help students select questions and goals for investigation. Check that students' questions can be answered through scholarly inquiry.

3. Collaborate with the students to decide deadlines, acceptable products, and requirements. Revisit these expectations along the way.

4. Begin the Self-directed Learning experience. Provide time in class, or ensure that students take time outside of class, to begin their studies.

5. Heighten students' awareness of their own learning at multiple points throughout the experience. How aware are students of their own strengths (and progress) in capitalizing on their curiosities, persistently pursuing their interests, finding appropriate resources, and developing other relevant skills? Discuss these skills—and self-awareness of the skills—as factors that enhance learning.

6. Model and support students in using a variety of resources and strategies to approach their questions (Many, Fyfe, Lewis, & Mitchell, 1996). For example, you might need to teach students to use the atlas, an online search engine, or the newspaper to gather information.

7. If you plan to use peer discussions throughout the learning experience, hold one or more discussions, directed by guidelines as appropriate for your students. Sample prompts for speakers include:
   • State your question.
   • Describe what you have done thus far.
   • Tell what you have learned thus far.
   • Give a stumbling block you have experienced.

   Peers may be instructed to respond:
   • Summarize what you have heard.
   • Share one thing you find interesting.
   • Give either a suggestion or something that you wonder too.

8. At the close of the Self-directed Learning experience, guide students in assessing both their learning and their increased capacity to pursue future inquiries.

ALTERNATIVE

1. Independent studies and learning contracts are variations of Self-directed Learning.

TIME ALLOTMENT

Self-directed Learning experiences can range from a brief experience of perhaps one class session to term-long projects for more advanced learners.

EXAMPLES

Figure S30.2 provides sample projects for Self-directed Learning.

TROUBLESHOOTING

1. A number of students may possess limited skills for pursuing independent inquiry. Assist these students by introducing Self-directed Learning gradually and on a small scale. Two ideas to help students become accustomed to more independent learning include offering students a small set of choices from which to select and keeping the time frame brief during early Self-directed Learning experiences. Another is explicit instruction and modeling on the skills needed to ask and answer personally meaningful questions.

2. In a related vein, some students, particularly those who are more accustomed to teacher-directed learning projects, may need assistance in focusing their studies and using their time wisely. You may assist students by helping them break the project into small tasks and by using manageable deadlines to accomplish their learning.

3. Journals can be used to help students track their learning and allow the teacher and students to converse about the students' inquiries (Corno, 1992).

Second-grade Social Studies Project: Select one way in which life is different for you today than it was for your family members (or other people in our city) earlier in time. The difference you choose should be interesting to you. Explore that interesting difference and present your findings.

Middle School Visual Arts Inquiry: Many artists use their works to make a social comment. You have two choices for this project:

1. Select a number of works from a favorite artist and investigate the social comments made by those works.

2. Select a social issue that is important to you and investigate the comments made by a number of artists' works regarding that issue.

High School Web Quest on the Bill of Rights: Choose one of the first 10 amendments that is of most interest to you and conduct a Web quest to explore how it affects students' lives in schools today—and throughout U.S. history.

Figure S30.2 Sample Self-directed Learning Experiences

STRATEGIES FOR ORGANIZING INFORMATION AND MAKING CONNECTIONS

Active teachers help students organize information and make connections among concepts they are learning. When students organize information and think about how ideas are related, they process information deeply and engage in elaboration. Understanding and retention of the content are facilitated. Organizing information increases the likelihood that students will make sense of it and that it will transfer from working memory to permanent memory where it can be used by students now and in the future.

Chapter 6 presents nine strategies that prompt organization of information and identification of relationships among ideas. Students arrange information hierarchically, categorically, sequentially, or in other ways. They discover and depict the overall structure of the material as well as how discrete pieces of information fit together. They organize and reorganize generalizations, principles, concepts, and facts. They explain their thinking to partners or groups and listen to alternative perspectives. Many of the strategies presented in this chapter can also be used as pre- and postassessments to determine what students already know and what they have learned. However, in our view, their primary purposes are to help students understand and remember the content, and so we describe them with those purposes in mind.

When students participate in the strategies in Chapter 6, they

✔ Distinguish between major ideas and important details.

✔ Identify superordinate, subordinate, and parallel ideas.

✔ Consider similarities and differences.

✔ Analyze critical features.

✔ Categorize information.

✔ Discuss their thinking about how information is organized with peers.

You may wish to review Chapter 2, especially Figures 2.1 through 2.3, for suggestions on using active teaching strategies with students who are not independent readers and writers, students who are learning English, and students who have specific learning needs. You may also wish to review Figure 1.4 for typical cognitive, physical, social, and emotional needs and interests of students of various ages.

STRATEGY 31 Sequencing Cards

LANGUAGE DEMANDS	LITERACY DEMANDS
Appropriate for:	Appropriate for:
Early English Learners	✔ Emerging Readers/Writers
✔ Intermediate English Learners	✔ Intermediate Readers/Writers
✔ Advanced English Learners	✔ Proficient Readers/Writers

The ability to organize information has long been recognized as critical to learning (Gage & Berliner, 1975; Wingfield, 1979), and one way of organizing information is sequencing. The ability to sequence contributes to understanding in every area of the curriculum. In mathematics, we work through steps to solve a problem. Thinking about the chronology of events is critical to the study of history. The sciences demand an understanding of sequence: In biology we explore topics such as life cycles, cellular respiration, and the process of digestion; in chemistry we examine chemical reactions—what happens first? second? next? Musicians create melodies by arranging notes in a sequence. Steps are followed in engaging in any sport. In literature, we attend to the development of characters and their relationships and to the events that build to a climax. We think about the order of sounds in spelling, decoding, and phonemic awareness.

In Sequencing Cards, students play an active role in ordering information that they have been studying. Students may work in teams to manipulate a set of cards that contain information, or each student may have a single card and contribute to a class sequence.

PREPARATION

1. Decide on the content for sequencing.
2. Determine whether you will have students work independently, in pairs or small groups, or as a single large group.
3. Prepare the cards, using text, illustrations, or both. You may need multiple sets.

IMPLEMENTATION

1. After instruction, provide students with the cards you have developed. Tell them that their task is to put the cards in sequential order. For instance, middle school students may be asked to order cards that display the steps of the scientific method. High school geometry students may be asked to order cards that have the individual steps of the proof of a theorem.
2. Students manipulate the cards to place them in order. If students are working independently, encourage them to think on their own and then allow them the opportunity to check their work with a neighbor. The conversations that occur as students consider the order will contribute to students' understanding of the content.
3. Alternatively, if the class is working as a whole, distribute cards so that each individual receives one card. Then ask students to line up in order across the front of the classroom. Students will need to talk with one another as they find their places

in the line. Ideally, you have enough cards for every student to participate. If not, prepare two sets of cards and divide the class in half. Have each half work to line up in order. The two lines then can compare their results. Or, you may provide cards to a smaller group of students who stand in front of the class. Their seated peers talk about the content of the cards and instruct the students holding cards where to move in the line.

4. Encourage students to look at their notes, text, or the Internet to confirm the sequences they created.

5. Debrief with students about the content and the process. Which events did they find easiest to sequence? Why? Why is sequencing information important? How did this strategy help them build a better understanding of the content? Was it helpful to talk with peers? Were their notes useful?

ALTERNATIVES

1. Have students examine and sequence cards *before* you begin instruction, encouraging them to use what they already know about the content and to make hypotheses about the time-order relationships among the cards. If cards are small strips of text that can remain on students' desks, have students keep the strips in front of them and reorder them as the lesson proceeds. If the cards are large, display them along the whiteboard ledge or bulletin board. Pause occasionally or wait until after the lesson or unit of study and ask students to reorder the cards to reflect what they learned.

2. Have the students work in small groups to develop sets of cards themselves that capture the content under study. Students may challenge another group to sequentially order the cards, providing feedback when their peers have completed the task. Or, each student or small group may read a segment of text that contains only one part of a larger sequence, make a card for it, and later work with the class to create the larger sequence.

3. Use this strategy with content that has any kind of order, not just time sequence. For instance, students may order cards of the planets in terms of proximity to the sun. Students may order units of measurement from smallest to largest.

4. Integrate the content of two or more curricular areas. After students have ordered one set of cards, ask them to consider what they have been learning in a different curricular area and develop cards that match the approximate times of the events in the original set. For instance, what artistic movements were occurring about the time of the American Revolution? What global explorations were occurring? Links among subject matter help students see the bigger picture of the human experience.

TIME ALLOTMENT

Depending on the number of cards you give students, the Sequencing Cards strategy may take from 5 to 20 minutes.

EXAMPLES

Figures S31.1, S31.2, and S31.3 share examples from first grade, middle school, and high school.

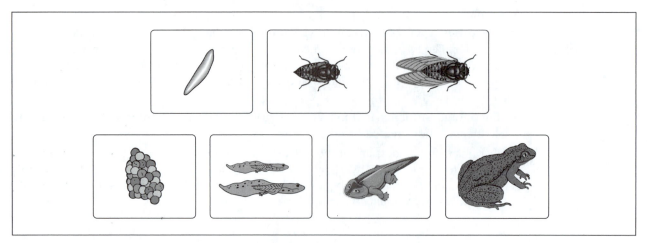

Figure S31.1   Two Sets of Picture Cards for Sequencing by First Graders Studying Life Cycles

Abraham Lincoln is elected President.
Southern states secede from the Union.
Jefferson Davis is named President of the Confederacy.
Shots are fired at Fort Sumter.
The Union army suffers defeat at the First Battle of Bull Run.
The battles of the Merrimac and Monitor occur.
Lee and his army are stopped at Antietam.
Lincoln issues the Emancipation Proclamation.
Lee's forces at Chancellorsville defeat the Union army.
Stonewall Jackson dies.
The Confederate army is defeated at the Battle of Gettysburg.
Frederick Douglas urges Lincoln to offer full equality for Union Negro troops.
General Grant is appointed to command all Union armies.
Lincoln is reelected President.
Sherman launches the March to the Sea.
Congress approves the Thirteenth Amendment to the Constitution.
Lee surrenders to Grant at Appomattox, Virginia.

Figure S31.2   Strips for Sequencing by Middle Schoolers Studying the U.S. Civil War

TROUBLESHOOTING

1. If students are having difficulty sequencing cards, consider reducing the number of items they sequence, giving them the most obvious events first. Then, provide additional cards and support them in inserting them in the correct order.

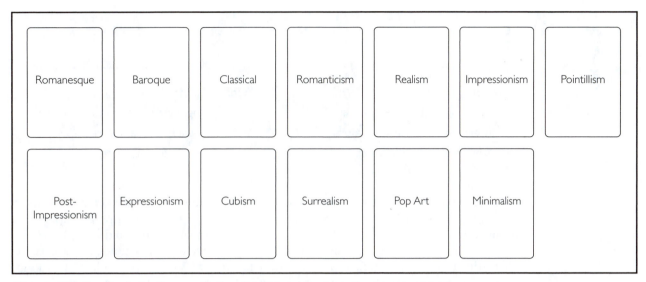

Figure S31.3   Cards for Sequencing by High School Students Studying Art History

STRATEGY 32 Content Structures

LANGUAGE DEMANDS	LITERACY DEMANDS
Appropriate for:	Appropriate for:
Early English Learners	Emerging Readers/Writers
✔ Intermediate English Learners	✔ Intermediate Readers/Writers
✔ Advanced English Learners	✔ Proficient Readers/Writers

In Content Structures, small groups of students work together to organize content strips in meaningful ways. Each group is provided an envelope containing strips of paper with information relevant to a unit of study written on them and asked to build a display of the strips that shows how the ideas are related. Students consider which concepts or facts are superordinate to others, which are subordinate, and which are parallel. The strategy prompts the students to discuss major ideas and important details and requires them to think deeply about how ideas are interconnected. Thinking about the content of each strip and determining its relationship with the content of other strips demands a depth of processing that facilitates understanding and retention of content (Anderson & Armbruster, 1984). This strategy differs from Graphic Organizers (p. 204) in that all the information is provided for the students by the teacher. The students' task is to organize the information. Content Structures differ from Concept Maps (p. 158) in that Content Structures address more types of information than do Concept Maps. Additionally, Concept Maps explicitly emphasize propositional knowledge by linking concepts with verbs whereas Content Structures do not.

PREPARATION

1. Identify important concepts, generalizations, and other information on the topic under study.
2. Record terms or short phrases representing the concepts, generalizations, and other information on paper and make multiple copies, enough for each group of three or four students to have a copy.
3. Cut the paper into strips so that each concept, generalization, or other piece of information is by itself. Scramble the strips and put them into an envelope, one for each group.

IMPLEMENTATION

1. Organize students into small groups of three or four and provide each group with an envelope.
2. Explain that each group is to build a graphic organizer of the strips so that the relationships among the strips are evident. Assure the students that there is no single right answer and that no two groups' graphic organizers are likely to be identical as there are several ways to think about the content represented on the strips. Tell the students that they should be prepared to explain the reasons for the organization of their strips.
3. Provide glue and markers so strips can be attached to a piece of poster paper and lines can be drawn to connect strips.

4. Depending on the complexity and number of strips, provide 10 to 20 minutes for the groups to work.

5. When all groups are ready, invite them to post and explain their Content Structure.

ALTERNATIVES

1. You may wish to impose a bit of structure on the graphic organizers or provide support to students by color coding the strips. For example, let students know the hierarchy of the ideas by printing all the terms and phrases of the same level on the same color of paper. Inform students that terms and phrases on pink paper, for instance, are superordinate ideas and that terms and phrases on green are the next level, and so forth.

2. Have students brainstorm key ideas about the content under study. Students then organize their thinking into a hierarchy demonstrating their understanding of the relationships among the ideas.

3. Have students compose electronic Content Structures with software that creates graphic organizers. Inspiration and Kidspiration are examples. Students can add a variety of media, such as sound, movie clips, and images, to their structures by creating them through multimedia presentation software such as HyperStudio.

TIME ALLOTMENT

Often this strategy takes 30 minutes from beginning to end. It may take longer if the topic is complex. Less complex material will take less time.

EXAMPLES

Figure S32.1 shares words and phrases from a fourth-grade unit on music and part of one group's Content Structure. Figure S32.2 shares words and phrases from a sixth-grade social studies unit on Ancient China and presents how one group began organizing its strips. Note that these strips include a variety of kinds of information, including facts, concepts, and generalizations.

TROUBLESHOOTING

1. A common occurrence with this strategy is that one group finishes well before the others. The teacher can attempt to pace the groups by nudging the slower groups to move more rapidly but runs the risk of hindering important conversations that may be occurring in those groups. We find it preferable to acknowledge the faster group for their work and then encourage them to stretch themselves by thinking of another way to organize their strips. Have an extra set of strips (or two) on hand for this purpose. You may also be prepared to hand them an envelope that has different strips. For example, you may provide strips that are related to the content but are more sophisticated or difficult in some way and ask them to add these strips to their Content Structure.

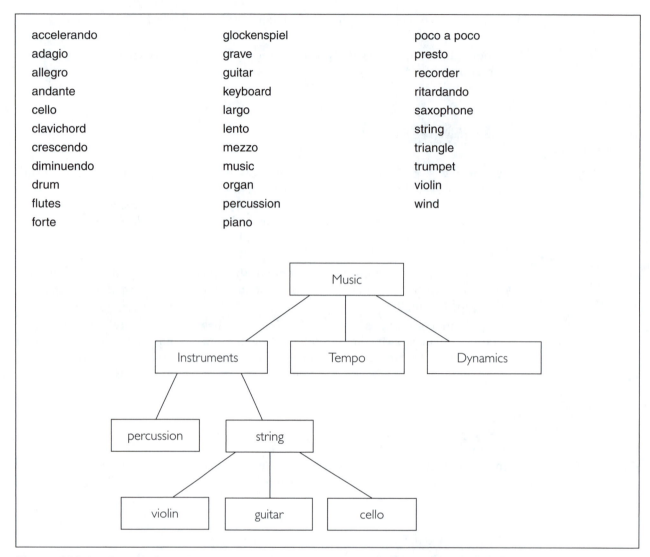

accelerando
adagio
allegro
andante
cello
clavichord
crescendo
diminuendo
drum
flutes
forte

glockenspiel
grave
guitar
keyboard
largo
lento
mezzo
music
organ
percussion
piano

poco a poco
presto
recorder
ritardando
saxophone
string
triangle
trumpet
violin
wind

Figure S32.1   Content Strips Provided during a Fourth-grade Music Unit and One Group's Initial Content Structure

ancient China

Anyang

canals

China is low in the east and high in the west.

China's topography affected the development and spread of Chinese civilization.

Chinese writing

classical age

Confucianism played a significant role in the shaping of Chinese society and government.

Daoist teachings focused on the individual and nature.

dynasty

erosion

Figure S32.2   Content Strips Given to a Sixth-grade Social Studies Class and the Beginnings of a Content Structure

geography

Huang He

levees

loess

nobles

The cracks in oracle bones were read to foretell the future.

schools of thought

Shang

steppe

Tibet, a region in China, was once an independent country.

Two-thirds of China is composed of high plateaus and mountains.

Xia

Zhou

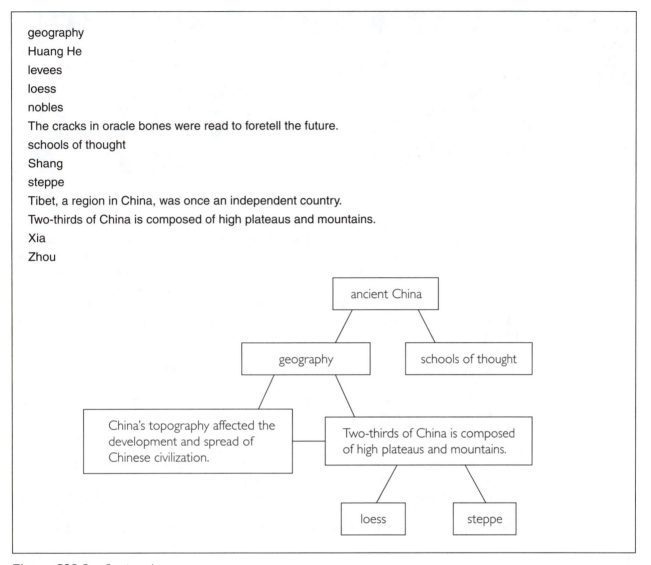

Figure S32.2   *Continued*

STRATEGY 33 Concept Maps

LANGUAGE DEMANDS	LITERACY DEMANDS
Appropriate for:	Appropriate for:
Early English Learners	✔ Emerging Readers/Writers
✔ Intermediate English Learners	✔ Intermediate Readers/Writers
✔ Advanced English Learners	✔ Proficient Readers/Writers

Concept Maps are a type of graphic organizer, or visual display of information, with particular power for helping students organize and represent their knowledge (Edwards & Fraser, 1983; Novak, 1990; Novak & Gowin, 1984). Concept Maps take the building blocks of knowledge—that is, concepts or ideas—and place them into meaningful structures by linking concepts into propositions that reveal the creator's understanding of relationships among concepts. Using Concept Maps as an instructional tool has been shown effective for enhancing both student achievement and attitude (Horton et al., 1993).

Although Concept Maps exist in a number of forms, Concept Maps are typically webs with nouns (representing concepts at various levels of detail) linked to each other by verbs written on lines or arrows. As the example in Figure S33.1 shows, concepts are found in "nodes," usually ovals or rectangles, that are organized hierarchically so that the overarching idea is near the top of the map or is visually prominent. Verbs are found on line segments or arrows that can be unidirectional or bidirectional, depending on the relationship that exists between concepts. Also, concepts can be cross-linked so that multiple arrows connect them. At the lowest level on a Concept Map are supporting details, or terms that represent examples of more central concepts.

Concept Maps differ from Content Structures (p. 154) in that, although Content Structures emphasize the structure of knowledge, they do not focus on propositions or the explicit links among concepts. This is evident in the labeled links of Concept Maps.

PREPARATION

1. Determine size of student groups. In the early stages, you may be creating all or most of a map with the students in a whole-class setting. Later, they can work in small groups or independently to create their maps.

2. Select materials to be used in creating the maps. Self-adhesive notes are effective because they can be repositioned readily, and using them on a white board allows for easy revision of links. Index cards held to a white board with magnets are also useful for whole-class mapping activities. Some classes have access to computers and concept mapping software (see Alternative 1 below). For individually created maps, students might use small slips of paper or self-adhesive notes. However, paper and pencil may be all that are required.

3. At least initially, generate the list of concepts to be mapped before the lesson. Review the chapter or materials for key concepts. After students have become skilled at concept mapping, they can help you generate the list of concepts, or they can generate it independently. For early experiences, the list of concepts should be brief (approximately five terms).

4. Think about the terms that might be used to link those concepts. Sample linking words can be found in Figure S33.2.

IMPLEMENTATION

1. Present the concepts to be mapped, or generate them with the students.

2. Provide direction appropriate for students' current skill level as you create the map. Begin by identifying the major concept. Place others below that one, near concepts that relate to each other. Then add links by asking the question, "How are these two ideas related?" Also ask, "Can we add other links? What other terms are related?" Allow for revision as ideas begin to take shape.

3. Read the map's statements to ensure accuracy. Begin with one concept, read its link, and conclude with the concept(s) to which it is linked.

4. Require students to use the information in their maps in some way. For instance, they may write a paper, compose an Interactive Journal entry (p. 201), do a Partner Share (p. 56), or create a Dramatization (p. 212).

ALTERNATIVES

1. Computer-based concept mapping offers many advantages. For instance, maps can include enriching hypertext (or nested) features and sophisticated, yet easily created, symbol systems. Some software translates visual maps to outlines with the click of a mouse. Several software programs can assist students in creating computer-based Concept Maps. Examples include Kidspiration and Inspiration, produced by Inspiration Software Inc.

2. Use different shapes and colors to identify different types or levels of information or to indicate information that is added or revised over time.

3. Use Concept Maps as assessment tools (Mintzes, Wandersee, & Novak, 2000). Ask students to construct a Concept Map to reveal their understanding of concepts and propositions before and after a lesson or unit.

4. Many teachers build their own Concept Maps of an entire course or of unit content as a first stage in curriculum planning. Using Concept Maps as a planning device allows you to distinguish major ideas from minor ones, determine important relationships, and select appropriate instructional examples (Novak, 1991).

TIME ALLOTMENT

Students who are already familiar with concept mapping will require approximately 15 minutes to construct a map with 5 to 10 terms. However, the length of time required to complete a map varies with the age of the students, their familiarity with the concepts, your choice of class structure (will students create individual maps, or will you create one as a class?), and the number of concepts to be mapped.

EXAMPLES

Figure S33.1 presents a Concept Map on Concept Maps, created by high school students who were learning to use them as a study tool. Figure S33.3 gives a Concept Map created by a third-grade class studying the solar system.

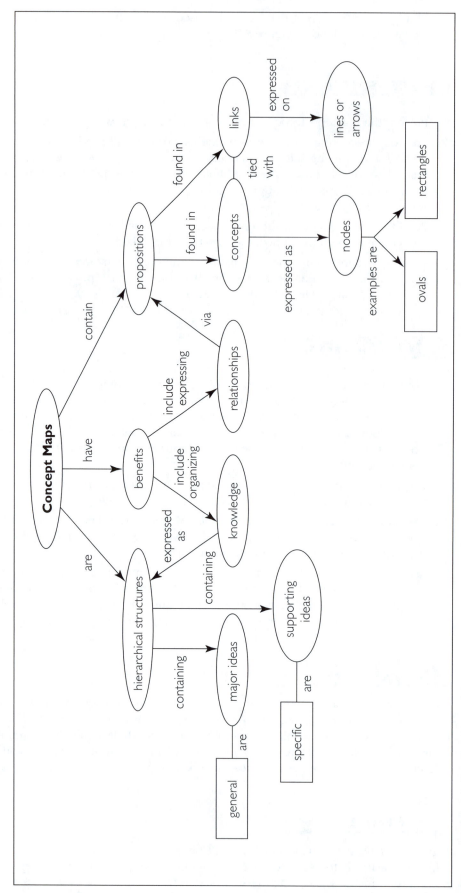

Figure S33.1 A Concept Map of Concept Maps

Figure S33.2 Sample Linking Words

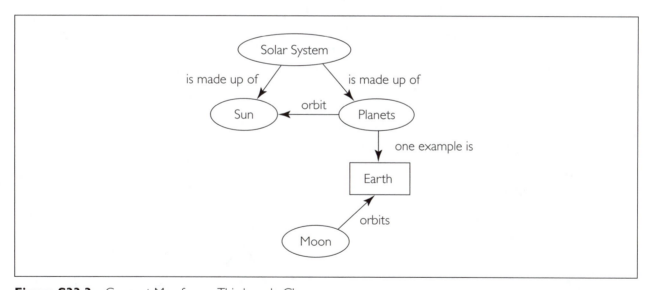

Figure S33.3 Concept Map from a Third-grade Class

TROUBLESHOOTING

1. Teach concept mapping as a skill before using it with your targeted content. To do so, lead a directed lesson on concept mapping using four or five related terms from a subject that is highly familiar to students. If all students are familiar with a particular food, such as a peanut butter sandwich, you might use these terms for your lesson: *peanut butter sandwich, bread, peanut butter, knife,* and *jelly.* For a class with great familiarity with a place, such as the seashore, a sample map can be built using related terms: *beach, sand, ocean, birds,* and *sun.*

2. Practice creating your own map before asking students to create maps. Try creating more than one map for the same terms to help you think flexibly about students' maps.

3. Sometimes students create "string maps" where concepts are linked in one long chain dangling down the paper. String maps often indicate poorly structured knowledge. Work individually with students to restructure string maps using cross-links and fewer levels in their hierarchies. Teaching them additional linking words can help. You may wish to present a class bank of choices of linking words that can get them started.

4. No Concept Map is ever finished because every concept has more concepts related to it than can appear on a single map, and there are different yet accurate ways to depict one set of concepts. Help students focus on the accuracy of their propositions, and be sure to discuss maps that represent the same content in different ways.

5. Encourage students to utilize Concept Maps as a study tool that helps them organize information for future topics, or the power of Concept Maps may not go beyond your lessons and into students' repertoire of learning strategies for organizing information.

STRATEGY 34 Picture Sorts

LANGUAGE DEMANDS	LITERACY DEMANDS
Appropriate for:	Appropriate for:
✔ Early English Learners	✔ Emerging Readers/Writers
✔ Intermediate English Learners	✔ Intermediate Readers/Writers
✔ Advanced English Learners	✔ Proficient Readers/Writers

Pictures Sorts allow students to use visual information to discuss their understandings of or experiences related to the lesson or unit content. In this strategy, small groups of students each receive a set of pictures that they discuss and sort into meaningful stacks. The visual input contributes to students' learning and retention as it provides a nonverbal representation of content that complements or extends verbal representations (Paivio, 1971, 1986) and may evoke affective reactions that contribute to understanding and motivation (Hibbing & Rankin-Erickson, 2003). Sorting serves to deepen students' conceptual understandings of the content as they consider similarities and differences, analyze critical features, look for connections among a number of seemingly discrete events or objects, and ponder superordinate concepts. Learning is aided as students categorize information and build networks of associations (Bruner, Goodnow, & Austin, 1956).

PREPARATION

1. Collect pictures related to your topic from magazines, newspapers, clip art, the Internet, and whatever other sources you have available.

2. Put 10 to 20 pictures into each of several large envelopes or folders, ensuring that you have a sufficient number of envelopes to provide one for each small group of students. Depending on your purposes and resources, each group does not need to have the same collection of pictures. In fact, the strategy might be more interesting if pictures are not identical. You may wish to randomly distribute the pictures into envelopes, or you may wish to ensure that each group has pictures representing subtopics that you want addressed in group discussions.

IMPLEMENTATION

1. Organize students into small groups of three to five. Provide each group with an envelope of pictures and ask them to view and discuss the pictures among themselves. What do they see in each picture? How is the picture related to the topic? How are the pictures related to each other?

2. After several minutes of small-group discussion about the pictures, ask the students to sort the pictures into related stacks. Although some groups will intuitively begin sorting pictures during the discussion without prompting from you, we prefer to provide initial discussion time prior to directing the students to sort the pictures because open-ended discussion opportunities seem to result in more diverse thinking about the topic. However, do not tell students who spontaneously sort to stop. Allow them to approach the pictures in a way that feels right to them.

3. After all groups have sorted their pictures, conduct a Whip around the room so groups can share their categories for sorting and provide examples from the pictures (see p. 56 and p. 74 for descriptions of a Whip).

ALTERNATIVES

1. Rather than pictures, use objects. Provide each group with a bag or small box containing objects that are relevant to the unit of study. Students follow the same procedure, sorting and discussing their thinking.

2. Use content-specific images such as political cartoons or reproductions of oil painted artworks.

3. Present images to students electronically. For example, you might have pasted drawing objects into a word processing document. Students can move the images around into groups and annotate the groups. Programs such as Kid Pix can be useful for this purpose.

4. Conduct the Picture Sort as a *closed sort*. In other words, ask students to find examples of the categories you name after they have had a chance to sort them into their own categories (an *open sort*).

5. After students sort the images one way, ask them to re-sort in another way. This increases students' flexibility in thinking.

6. Ask students to create the pictures that will be sorted. Collect students' pictures throughout instruction. Students may create pictures electronically using a drawing program, for example.

7. Consider using Content Links (p. 173) with the images, wherein students travel the room and find someone whose image forms a link with their own.

8. Ask students to use what they learned through the Picture Sort in a new way. They might, for instance, create a Graphic Organizer (p. 204) to demonstrate their understanding.

TIME ALLOTMENT

This strategy takes from 15 to 30 minutes.

EXAMPLES

Figures S34.1 and S34.2 present suggestions for pictures that might be used by third graders in a geography lesson as they study human modifications of the environment and by sixth graders studying erosion and deposition. Figure S34.3 shares pictures of objects that middle schoolers studying simple machines may sort.

TROUBLESHOOTING

1. It will take time to develop a library of pictures related to the content. If you have center time, or time built into your schedule for independent work, provide magazines (check appropriateness) or Internet access for students to find pictures that relate to the content at hand. Build students' finds into your collections. Families might, similarly, be entreated to help you build your collections. Asking students' families to supply images has the added bonus of representing the diversity of your students' experiences.

2. While you are building your collection, you can use one or two pictures for small-group discussions (Photo Analysis, p. 134, might work here) and postpone the sorting portion of this strategy for use with future groups when you have more pictures.

Figure S34.1   Pictures for Sorting by Third Graders Studying Human Modifications of the Environment

3. You may wish to laminate the pictures or put them in plastic sheet protectors to reduce the wear that comes with handling.

4. Some pictures may be too abstract for students to make direct connections with the content. You may need to guide groups who are unable to see the content reflected in the picture by sharing what you see in the picture as it relates to the content.

5. If students' sorts seem limited to an obvious type of categorization, be prepared to help them sort in new ways by thinking of the different ways that images may be sorted. Examples include chronology, structure (how things are built), function (how things are used), size, importance, and prevalence in daily life.

Figure S34.2   Pictures for Sorting by Sixth Graders Studying Erosion and Deposition

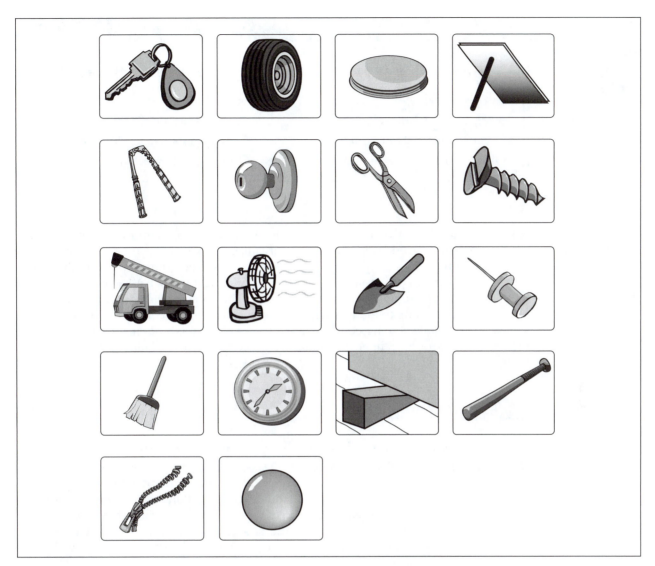

Figure S34.3   Objects for Sorting by Middle School Students Studying Simple Machines

STRATEGY 35 List-Group-Label

LANGUAGE DEMANDS	LITERACY DEMANDS
Appropriate for:	Appropriate for:
Early English Learners	Emerging Readers/Writers
✔ Intermediate English Learners	✔ Intermediate Readers/Writers
✔ Advanced English Learners	✔ Proficient Readers/Writers

Students draw on their experiences and prior knowledge to brainstorm as many words as they can on a given subject and then organize the words into meaningful groups. Higher-order thinking is required as students then label the groups. What do the words in this group have in common? Why do they belong together? What is the superordinate idea? This strategy prompts personal responses to the content as students reflect on their own knowledge and experiences, and it facilitates links between the students and the subject matter. Links among concepts are also developed as students group words and then label the groups. Students formulate new concepts by examining their groupings (Taba, 1967).

PREPARATION

1. Identify the prompt you will provide based on the unit of study.

2. Decide whether students will work as a class, in small groups, or independently. We have the greatest success when students work in small groups. When students work together, one student's ideas spark another student's thinking and more words are generated. Although the entire class may work together, we find that more students are likely to actively participate in the strategy when they are in small groups. (See Troubleshooting item 1 if you have not yet used List-Group-Label with your students.)

3. Decide on the listing format you will use and gather materials. For example, some teachers place terms on index cards and manipulate them either in a pocket chart or on a magnetic board. Provide index cards or paper scraps, or ensure that each group has paper and pencil.

IMPLEMENTATION

1. Ask the students to think of as many words as they can that are related to a topic that you provide. If students are working in small groups, one student should be designated the record keeper.

2. After students have developed extensive lists of words, ask them to group the words in any way, as long as the words in a group are meaningfully related to one another. Refrain from naming the groups at this point. Students will likely need a second piece of paper as they record their groups of words.

3. Once all the words are grouped, ask students to provide a label, or name, for each group.

4. Have students share with the entire class their groupings. For example, in listing words in response to "inside our bodies," one group of students may have put words

related to the circulatory system together, words related to the respiratory system together, and words related to the nervous system together, and labeled them as such. Another set of students may have placed terms into "soft tissue" and "hard tissue" groups. Another may have grouped by "symmetrical body parts" and "asymmetrical body parts." Students share their labels with the class and provide some examples of words that are included in each group.

ALTERNATIVES

1. Require students to group terms in more than one way. This helps them see new relationships and encourages them to see more than one viable "answer." Each new grouping that is required stretches students more.

2. You provide words that are relevant to the upcoming unit of study. Give each small group of students the list of words and have them create their own groupings of your words. Allow student groups to share their way of grouping the words.

3. You may wish to ask students to write a paragraph that uses the major topic and each of the group labels. Or, ask students to select one of the groups of words and write a brief paragraph about the category.

4. Have students List-Group-Label words after a unit of study as a means of reviewing and consolidating their knowledge.

5. Although the power of List-Group-Label comes from the inductive formation of new ideas, it can be modified for use as a deductive strategy as well. Encourage students to think of group labels first. You may even choose to provide those labels. For instance, in preparation for studying Olympic Games, you may ask students to think of different categories, prompting them with suggestions such as "water sports," "snow sports," and so on. Students then use these groupings to generate exemplars.

TIME ALLOTMENT

Provide ample time for the generation of words. If you end this step of the strategy too quickly, you will not stretch your students. Too much time means that students stray off task and begin talking about unrelated topics. Five to 10 minutes is often adequate for listing words. You will need to monitor your students and make the judgment call. The grouping of words can take longer as students work to create meaningful categories. The final step of labeling the groups is usually rather swift if students have thoughtfully grouped words. The entire strategy takes about 15 to 30 minutes, longer if you ask students to form multiple groupings or write paragraphs at the conclusion of the strategy.

EXAMPLES

Figure S35.1 shows a list of words that young children contributed to a whole-class discussion when the teacher asked them what words they think of when they hear the term *science*. Students grouped the words. Then, with the teacher facilitating the process, students developed terms to label the groups. Figure S35.2 shares an example of words generated by sixth graders who were beginning the study of measurement. One group of students categorized words they generated according to what was being measured: length, weight, and so on. Another group, not shown in the example, categorized words by whether the words were metric or English units. Figure S35.3 shares an example of this strategy in a high school English class that was beginning the study of poetry.

Topic: Science

List: Teacher says, "What words do you think of when you hear the term *science*?" Teacher records students' ideas on an overhead transparency, on the board, or on index cards placed in a pocket chart.

microscope	curious
bacteria	measuring cups
examine	diseases
test tube	explore
watch	laboratory
water life	animals
dissect	test
question	

Group: Teacher says, "Which of these words go together in some way?"

Tools	*Content*	*Attitudes*	*Processes*
microscope	bacteria	curious	examine
test tube	water life	question	watch
measuring cups	diseases		dissect
laboratory	animals		test
			explore

Label: Teacher says, "Let's think of a label for each of the groups you made." With teacher support, they add the labels (above) to their groups.

Figure S35.1   List-Group-Label for a First-grade Science Lesson

Topic: Units of Measure

List:

mile	liter
quart	bushel
pint	tablespoon
foot	teaspoon
inches	kilometers
ton	pounds
decibels	ounce
acre	square meter
bushel	yard
cup	kilogram
pint	
cubic inch	
centimeters	
carat	
grams	
square yard	
square foot	
gallon	

Figure S35.2   List-Group-Label for a Sixth-grade Mathematics Unit on Measurement

Groupings (with labels):

Length	Mass or Weight	Sound	Area	Volume
centimeters	ton	decibels	acre	bushel
mile	grams		square foot	cubic inch
foot	pounds		square yard	cup
inches	ounce		square meter	pint
kilometers	kilogram			gallon
yards	carat			liter
				quart
				tablespoon
				teaspoon

Figure S35.2   *Continued*

Topic: Poetry
List:

love	sonnet	assonance
Shakespeare	laughter	Maya Angelou
Carl Sandburg	Shel Silverstein	Emily Dickinson
metaphor	Robert Frost	onomatopoeia
personification	couplets	alliteration
meter	simile	dark
rhythm	quatrain	imagery
rhyme scheme	Edgar Allan Poe	scary
haiku	quintet	ominous
cinquain	limerick	acrostic

Groupings (with labels):

Poets	Forms	Emotions/Moods	Poetic Devices
Shel Silverstein	cinquain	love	metaphor
Shakespeare	couplets	laughter	simile
Robert Frost	acrostic	sorrow	assonance
Emily Dickinson	quatrain	dark	alliteration
Maya Angelou	quintet	scary	imagery
Edgar Allan Poe	haiku	ominous	rhythm
Carl Sandburg	limerick	goofy	onomatopoeia
	ballad		meter
	sonnet		rhyme scheme
			personification

Note: Students generated additional words after completing their groupings.

Figure S35.3   List-Group-Label for a High School English Unit on Poetry

TROUBLESHOOTING

1. If you intend to have students List-Group-Label in small groups, be sure to provide enough modeling of the process to the whole class to ensure small-group success. It may be that you lead one or two whole-class List-Group-Label sessions before asking small groups to engage. Or, you may begin the listing process as a whole class and then move to small groups to complete the session.

2. Because List-Group-Label is an inductive strategy (one that requires students to form concepts or generalizations from specific data or terms), you must provide just enough direction to keep students engaged productively in the process. They cannot form concepts or connections for *themselves* if *you* state the groupings and labels.

STRATEGY 36 Content Links

LANGUAGE DEMANDS	LITERACY DEMANDS
Appropriate for:	Appropriate for:
Early English Learners	Emerging Readers/Writers
✔ Intermediate English Learners	✔ Intermediate Readers/Writers
✔ Advanced English Learners	✔ Proficient Readers/Writers

One way to deepen understandings about concepts is to explore the relationships or connections among them (Vaughn, Bos, & Schumm, 2003). Content Links allows learners to identify and articulate how major lesson or course topics fit together. In this strategy, each student is given a card with a word or short phrase written on it. Students hold up their cards for peers to see as they circulate around the room and try to find someone with a card that fits with theirs. This strategy provides an excellent opportunity for students to think about lesson content, to talk with peers about lesson content, and to be physically active. Additionally, the teacher is able to conduct a quick assessment of the students' understandings of concepts and linkages among them.

PREPARATION

1. Identify important concepts that will be discussed in the lesson.
2. Record the concepts on large cards or pieces of paper so they will be visible to the entire group. Write one concept per card. We usually use large index cards or 8½ × 11-inch paper folded in half.
3. Prepare enough cards so that every student receives one. Ensure that each concept has at least one related concept written on another card.

IMPLEMENTATION

1. Randomly distribute the cards to the students.
2. Explain that the students' task is to find a partner in the room. The partnership must be based on a relationship between the concepts on the cards the students are holding, and the students must be able to explain to the group how the concepts are related.
3. Allow sufficient time for all students to identify a partner. Support those who may be having difficulty, perhaps by providing multiple examples of how their concepts might link with others. As students become paired, move them into a large circle so they are all facing each other.
4. Whip around the circle, asking each pair to explain the concepts and their relationship(s).
5. An optional additional step entails asking each pair to now partner with another pair and explain the interconnections among all concepts represented in the new groups (a Concept Chain!). Or, ask students to find a new individual partner.

ALTERNATIVES

1. Extend by allowing students to write a group sentence or two about the content using the words in their partnership or group.

2. Do a Content Link after generating Important Words (p. 69).

3. Instead of writing words on the cards, write symbols or draw pictures. Although appropriate for any level, these cards will be especially useful with students who are emerging readers.

4. For students with learning disabilities or who need more support or time to process ideas, discuss their cards with them before turning the class loose to find partners. Prompts such as, "What do you remember about this term?" and "Let's think about some ideas related to your term" may prove helpful in scaffolding for success.

TIME ALLOTMENT

This strategy works well with large groups of students and usually takes about 15 to 20 minutes.

EXAMPLES

Figure S36.1 gives content words used in a first-grade earth and space science unit, and Figure S36.2 displays concepts discussed in a sixth-grade earth science class.

day
earth
ice
land
light
moon
night
rain
rocks
season
soil
sky
snow
steam
sun
temperature
water
weather

Figure S36.1   Words for Content Links Used in a First-grade Unit on Space

plate tectonics	normal fault
magnetic reversal	reverse fault
sea-floor spreading	San Andreas Fault
Mid-Atlantic Ridge	folded mountains
Pangaea	strike-slip faults
lithosphere	fault-block mountains
Alfred Wegener	transform boundaries
North American Plate	volcanic mountains
continental drift	Ring of Fire
asthenosphere	mantle
fossils	
magma	
crust	
convection	
stress	
subduction zone	
convergent boundaries	
mesosphere	
tension	
divergent boundaries	
GPS	
core	

Figure S36.2   Words for Content Links Used in a Sixth-grade Earth Science Class

TROUBLESHOOTING

1. Content Links calls for divergent thinking as there are numerous accurate linkings, and almost any pairing can be justified if the students are able to think deeply about the concepts. This is difficult for some students, and you may need to assist them in thinking about how concepts are connected in many ways.

2. If you have an uneven number of students, allow for one threesome. To avoid many threesomes, assign one person at the beginning to be the third member of a matching. Choose that person's card carefully.

STRATEGY 37 Give One, Get One

LANGUAGE DEMANDS	LITERACY DEMANDS
Appropriate for:	Appropriate for:
✔ Early English Learners	Emerging Readers/Writers
✔ Intermediate English Learners	✔ Intermediate Readers/Writers
✔ Advanced English Learners	✔ Proficient Readers/Writers

In this strategy, learners move around the room sharing an idea and collecting ideas from peers. Ideas are generated in response to a prompt, such as "What is one thing you learned about musical instruments?" or "Identify one type of information you would expect to see on a globe." After recording an idea, students "give" their idea to others in the room and then "get" ideas from those with whom they share. This strategy not only helps students reflect on information or experiences and learn from their peers, but also promotes discussion among learners and acknowledges the expertise of those in the room.

PREPARATION

1. Develop a prompt based on the immediate experiences of the group (e.g., after learning new information in the lesson or from a chapter they just read). Alternatively, use a relevant life experience as your prompt.

⊙ You can find these templates on the accompanying Teacher Resources CD and at the back of the book.

2. Develop a format for recording and collecting information. We have most frequently seen the information collected on a paper with boxes displayed in a grid (e.g., three or four boxes across and four boxes down). The grid can be distributed via handouts (such as the two Give One, Get One grids found in the Teacher Resources CD) or, more simply, learners can be asked to fold a piece of paper into the desired number of boxes.

IMPLEMENTATION

1. Request that students write an idea related to the prompt in one box of the grid. Allow a couple of minutes for them to think and record their idea.

2. Ask students to circulate around the room, find a partner, and share their idea. Each records the partner's idea in a box on the grid. Students find a new partner and repeat the sharing, again recording the new idea.

3. When it appears that most students are close to completing their grid, alert them that after the next sharing they should return to their seats.

4. Conclude the activity by allowing a few students to share with the entire group one interesting idea.

ALTERNATIVES

1. Instead of a single prompt, three or four prompts might be used—one for each column of the grid, although all would be related to the same general topic. Students record one idea in each column before sharing.

2. Instead of sharing only their own response, students might give ideas obtained from others.

3. Instead of recording ideas on a grid, try alternative formats. For example, we conducted a lesson with fourth graders on Latin roots. Learners constructed fold-up books (Yopp & Yopp, 2006). They gave the book a title (e.g., *My Little Latin Root Book*) on the cover page. On the first page, they wrote a Latin root and several examples (e.g., "rupt" followed by "erupt," "disrupt," and "interrupt"), and recorded classmates' roots and examples on the remaining six pages. They were excited not only to share their knowledge of Latin roots in this way but to learn a bookmaking technique that they could use for other purposes. See the accompanying Teacher Resources CD for directions on making fold-up books.

4. This strategy can be modified for use with young children. Allow students to share single-word responses or drawings. For instance, first graders may be asked to "draw a shape with corners" or "write a word with the long e sound."

You can find these directions on the accompanying Teacher Resources CD and at the back of the book.

TIME ALLOTMENT

This strategy generally takes 15 minutes and provides a good physical break for students as they get up and move around the room.

EXAMPLES

Figure S37.1 provides an example of a Give One, Get One grid used by sixth graders sharing information about three civilizations. Figure S37.2 shares a mathematics example conducted with secondary students.

What do you know about early Mesopotamian cultures?

Sumerians	Assyrians	Babylonians
They invented the cuneiform system of writing.	Assyria developed around the city of Ashur on the Tigris River.	The Code of Hammurabi was a set of laws written by King Hammurabi.
Ur was an important city.	Farmers grew wheat and barley and owned cattle, sheep, goats, and pigs.	Babylonian society was divided into classes.
They built canals and had a good system of irrigation.	Houses were built of clay.	The capital of Babylonia was Babylon.
Sumerians were skilled in the use of metals, including copper, gold, and silver.	The people worshipped a god called Ashur.	Slaves were mostly prisoners of war but were sometimes people being punished for crimes.

Figure S37.1   Give One, Get One Grid Completed by Sixth-grade Students Studying Mesopotamia

Different branches of mathematics have been used all over the world and throughout history in the games people play. In the first box, list one or two (or more!) games that use mathematics. Would you like some hints to get you started? Think probability, geometry, logic, operations with number, and measurement. Think *inside* (board games?) and *outside* (sports?). You will write ideas from your peers in the other boxes later. (All the ideas from one peer go in the same box.)

Monopoly football	marathons
basketball	Chess
Dominoes	Life
card games—Spades, 21, Hearts	shuffleboard
golf	building with Legos building with blocks
Bridge	Racko Yahtzee
baseball tennis	Cribbage
track and field events	bowling

Figure S37.2   Give One, Get One Grid Completed by High School Mathematics Students

TROUBLESHOOTING

1. The number of spaces to record ideas depends on the size of the group. A grid with 16 boxes works well with large groups, but the little book with seven pages (plus a title page) was perfect for our small group of fewer than 20 students.

2. Be sure to allow ample, but not too much, time for students to generate an idea for their own grids. Two or 3 minutes are usually sufficient because the strategy should be based on students' experiences and knowledge.

3. Develop a prompt that is broad enough to allow for a variety of responses, otherwise students' responses will converge and they will not hear new ideas.

4. Encourage wide sharing by requesting that students give and get ideas from peers not at their table. The variety of responses is enriched if students talk to others with whom they have not shared ideas all morning or afternoon. We have found that it is best to make this request before releasing students to the sharing because some will remain at their tables and just talk to those with whom they are most comfortable if not prompted to move to another table.

5. If you are concerned that students may share erroneous information, devise a plan for confirming the accuracy of responses either before students circulate (e.g., ask students to check their responses with a peer). This should not be a concern when the prompt is related to students' experiences or ideas. However, if the prompt calls for factual information, it may be an issue. You will want to support all learners in providing accurate information for both the sake of their peers who will be learning from them and the sake of the learner who needs to know if he is wrong and who will not want to be embarrassed by sharing inaccurate information.

STRATEGY 38 Sticker Selection

LANGUAGE DEMANDS	LITERACY DEMANDS
Appropriate for:	Appropriate for:
Early English Learners	Emerging Readers/Writers
✔ Intermediate English Learners	✔ Intermediate Readers/Writers
✔ Advanced English Learners	✔ Proficient Readers/Writers

Sticker Selection provides a novel way for students to reflect on their learning and make connections between their current learning and other knowledge or experiences. Students deepen their understanding of the content as they thoughtfully examine the concepts or generalizations under study and look for similarities with other concepts or generalizations, thus building association networks that support learning and retention (Gage & Berliner, 1975). Students select from among a variety of stickers the two that best connect to the content—but in different ways. Students write about their choices before sharing their thinking with their peers. Sticker Selection demands that students stretch their thinking, interpret the content, and make connections.

PREPARATION

1. Collect stickers so that you have quite a variety available. Connections may be abstract, so do not worry about matching the stickers to the content at the physical appearance level. Stickers may be obtained at discount, craft, teacher supply, and other stores or online (search for "stickers for children" and look for the best deals). Also, stickers are often sent as part of magazine or organization promotions so be sure to check your junk mail.

2. Most stickers come on rolls or sheets. You will need to cut these apart so that you have individual stickers.

3. Put approximately 10 different stickers in an envelope. Prepare enough envelopes so that each student in your classroom has one. Each envelope may have its own unique set of stickers or there may be duplication across envelopes.

4. Provide writing paper and instruments. You may wish to duplicate the Sticker Selection template found in the Teacher Resources CD to be used in place of writing paper.

You can find this template on the accompanying Teacher Resources CD and at the back of the book.

IMPLEMENTATION

1. Provide each student with an envelope of stickers.

2. Ask students to look carefully at each of the stickers in their envelopes and consider the stickers' relationships to the content.

3. After a few minutes ask students to select one sticker that is most related to the content and affix it to a paper, a page in their journal, or a copy of the template found in the Teacher Resources CD.

4. Have students write about their selections. What meaning did they assign the sticker they selected? How is it related to the content? Some students may make concrete connections, and others may make abstract connections. Accept both.

5. Ask students to select a second sticker that has a different connection to the subject matter. Why was this sticker selected out of all of those remaining? Have students affix this sticker to their paper, journal page, or Sticker Selection template.

6. Ask students to write about their second sticker selection, explaining their decision.

7. Have students show all their stickers to a peer and discuss the reasons for their two selections.

8. Engage in a whole-class discussion about students' connections.

ALTERNATIVES

1. If preparation time is short, do not place the stickers in individual envelopes. Instead, provide a stack to each table group.

2. The strategy will take less time if students are not asked to write about their selections. Further, you may wish to skip the writing aspect of this strategy if you choose to use it with younger students or early English learners. Have students make their selections and talk about their choices in small groups.

3. Ensure that each student has exactly the same stickers. The resulting conversations will be very interesting because students likely will make different selections. If all students have the same stickers, you may wish to have students place their stickers on a Group Graph (p. 58). How many students selected the same sticker? Why?

4. Have students make a connection between each sticker and the content.

5. Have students select a single sticker and brainstorm in list form as many connections between the sticker and the content as they can.

6. You may ask students to place their stickers on an Interactive Journal entry (p. 201) or to do an Idea Share (p. 53) with them.

7. If stickers are not available, use printed clip art, other duplicated images, or other readily available materials.

8. If students are working on the computer, allow them to select a piece of clip art and compose their reactions to it using a word processing program. Students might use a drawing program to create an image that best captures their reaction to the content. Save students' electronic selections and drawings as part of your collection for future use.

TIME ALLOTMENT

This strategy may take from 5 to 15 minutes, depending on the amount of sharing.

EXAMPLES

Figure S38.1 shows the stickers one third-grade student discovered in an envelope during a unit on oceanography and the explanation of her selections. Figure S38.2 shows the stickers considered by high school students enrolled in a health class and the selections of one student.

TROUBLESHOOTING

1. If stickers have no obvious relationship with the content, some students may not readily make connections between stickers and the content. You may wish to

demonstrate the strategy by engaging in a think-aloud: "I selected the sticker of the butterfly because we were studying chaos and sensitive dependence on initial conditions. Sometimes this is referred to as the 'butterfly effect,' meaning that the flap of a butterfly's wings can have a significant effect on a system such as the weather. I also thought about selecting the sticker of the wolf because the behavior of wolves can be difficult to predict." Alternatively, you may wish to begin with very concrete connections. For example, after studying mammals you may have stickers of different animals, only one of which is a mammal.

2. Some students will assume there is a correct selection. Be sure to honor each student's selections and make it clear that there is no single correct selection. You are looking for students' explanations of their choices, and you may hear many excellent explanations. Students will, hopefully, appreciate all the connections their peers make.

Student 1's selections and explanations:

I chose the sticker of the whale because it is an ocean animal. We learned that the blue whale is the largest animal in the ocean and on the earth.

My second choice is the STOP sign because we need to stop polluting the ocean. Human beings are destroying this important part of our planet. Not only is ocean life being harmed, but all life will be harmed.

Figure S38.1   Stickers Provided to Third Graders Studying Ocean Life

Student 1's selections and explanations:

The multicolored dots represent the complexity of the human body and the variety of nutrients—carbohydrates, proteins, fats, vitamins, minerals, and water—that are needed to keep it healthy and strong.

My second choice is the soccer ball because it stands for activity that humans must engage in so our bodies stay in shape. Eating well is important, but it is not enough to maintain good health. We also need to be physically active.

Figure S38.2   Stickers Provided to High School Health Students Studying Nutrition

STRATEGY 39 Treasure Hunts

LANGUAGE DEMANDS	LITERACY DEMANDS
Appropriate for:	Appropriate for:
✔ Early English Learners	✔ Emerging Readers/Writers
✔ Intermediate English Learners	✔ Intermediate Readers/Writers
✔ Advanced English Learners	✔ Proficient Readers/Writers

Students who are information literate know how to locate information in a variety of sources, evaluate information critically, and use that information accurately and creatively (American Association of School Librarians & Association for Educational Communications and Technology, 1998). Treasure Hunts provide students with opportunities to search for information related to the content at hand in an enjoyable team format. Treasure Hunts support students in making connections between major ideas and related examples, and between the content and its real-world applications. They can also support team-building efforts and can assist students in building a store of knowledge related to the content.

PREPARATION

1. Develop search items related to the content. A list of four to five items is appropriate for younger students; older students may search for 10 to 15 items. Be careful that the Treasure Hunt is not so long that it becomes tedious to students. Prepare a list to be distributed to the students.

2. Decide on students' data recording strategy and prepare materials. In some cases, students may gather the actual items on the list (such as brochures or business cards). In other cases, they will instead record some type of evidence that they have found the items. Instant, digital, or disposable cameras are one way for students to prove that they have collected items on the list. Video cameras are another. Or, you may simply ask students to gather a signature or to write or sketch their evidence on a worksheet or in a journal.

3. Ensure that the items (or answers) are accessible to the students. If the search requires moving students to another location, for example, ensure that the answers or items are in place. For instance, if students will do a Treasure Hunt in the community, check that the information they need can in fact be found on the city streets. If students are searching the World Wide Web for a Virtual Treasure Hunt, as in Alternative 3 below, check that relevant URLs are accessible. Verify that it is acceptable for your students to collect items (such as brochures) if that is part of your plan.

4. Trips away from the classroom may entail additional supervision. Gather and prepare assistants as necessary. Ensure that students' safety is protected by enlisting adults to help monitor groups.

5. Decide on team size and devise student teams.

6. We do not emphasize the competitive aspect of Treasure Hunts as competition can detract from the focus on searching for information and building connections. If you decide to emphasize competition, devise a criterion so that many teams can "win." For instance, "winning" can be defined as completing the list accurately and within the specified time limit.

IMPLEMENTATION

1. Present the students' task. State the major questions they will investigate, explain the list, and give the rules for the search. Distribute data collection devices (e.g., worksheets and cameras) and review rules of effective teamwork.

2. Monitor students as they conduct their Treasure Hunt.

3. After the hunt, review students' answers and the connections they were able to draw. Also discuss their search strategies, focusing on building efficient search techniques for the future. Consider displaying students' results in a bulletin board or using the information in some other way, such as in writing "I Didn't Know That . . ." Response Frames (p. 218).

ALTERNATIVES

1. Rather than preparing the list of items students are to hunt, allow students to generate the list. For example, many students ask a plethora of "why" questions ("Why do giraffes have long necks?" "Why do we hiccough?" "Why do all societies form governments?"). Collect those questions on cards, perhaps posting them on a bulletin board. When time for the hunt arrives, allow groups of students to select questions that intrigue them and explore a variety of information sources to determine the answers.

2. Conduct Treasure Hunts where the answers lie within the students themselves. As a team builder, some teachers begin the school year with a Treasure Hunt designed to help students get to know each other and their strengths. Sample prompts include, "Find someone who . . . is left-handed; . . . knows someone who met someone famous; and . . . has been outside this state." A sample Treasure Hunt for this purpose is found in the Teacher Resources CD.

   Students can also serve as the source of content knowledge to help their peers make connections. Sample prompts from such a hunt are presented in Figure S39.1. This alternative can be used to help students review content before a test as well.

> You can find this template on the accompanying Teacher Resources CD and at the back of the book.

3. Treasure Hunts are a popular way to help students find relevant information within the vast stores found on the Internet. The Internet is powerful for Treasure Hunts because it allows students to travel the world without leaving their seats. Figure S39.2 gives a few sample questions from an Internet-based Treasure Hunt for American Inventors. In fact, a Treasure Hunt may have already been written for your purpose. Conduct an Internet search using the terms *scavenger hunt* or *treasure hunt* along with your topic (such as *Grapes of Wrath*) to discover whether a Treasure Hunt already exists for your content. Devising your own questions for an Internet Treasure Hunt does not take long if you examine your lesson objectives and review major Web sites related to those objectives. Include a "big question" that requires students to synthesize what they have discovered from many sources.

4. Heighten the suspense—and allow students to sharpen specific skills—by giving hints along the way during the Treasure Hunt. Provide each team with a starting clue that, when solved, takes them to the next clue. One cross-country coach we know sharpens students' understanding of the city's layout as well as students' speed and endurance by holding a citywide cross-country Treasure Hunt to celebrate the end of every season.

5. Allow students to write their own Treasure Hunts as a culminating activity or as independent research. (See Self-directed Learning, p. 145.)

TIME ALLOTMENT

Simple Treasure Hunts conducted within the classroom can be completed in 15 minutes. More involved hunts, conducted outside the classroom, can take an hour or more. Keep the time limit fairly brief so that students experience a sense of urgency but can still experience success.

EXAMPLES

Figure S39.1 gives sample prompts for a Treasure Hunt for a fourth-grade theater unit. Figure S39.2 gives prompts for a middle school Treasure Hunt on American Inventors. Figure S39.3 gives a Shape Hunt for kindergartners studying geometry. Figure S39.4 gives a second-grade Treasure Hunt for students studying their community. Figure S39.5 gives a Dictionary Treasure Hunt for high school students studying Spanish 1.

Find someone who . . .

1. Can give an example of a *stock character*.
2. Can say the sentence, "I want you to go," two different ways to change its meaning.
3. Can summarize the *plot* of a favorite movie or play.
4. Has seen or been in a play outside of school.
5. Can give one of the *motives* of Cinderella in the play we recently saw.
6. Can use a facial expression to convey an emotion that you can identify.
7. Can explain how *resolution* and *conflict* go together.

Figure S39.1   Sample Prompts from a "Find Someone Who . . ." Treasure Hunt for a Fourth-grade Theater Unit

---

1. What did George Washington Carver do for southern farmers?
   URL Hint:
   http://www.150.si.edu/150trav/remember/r813.htm
2. Which Virginian invented the windshield wiper? When?
   URL Hint:
   http://www.enchantedlearning.com/inventors/women.shtml
3. Morrison's plastic Frisbee replaced which earlier version of the flying disk?
   URL Hint:
   http://inventors.about.com/library/weekly/aa980218.htm
4. Why did Garrett A. Morgan, who invented the gas mask and the traffic signal, hire a white man to impersonate him?
   URL Hint:
   http://ctct.essortment.com/augustusgarrett_ols.htm

Figure S39.2   Sample Prompts from a Middle School Virtual Treasure Hunt on American Inventors

---

1. Each student receives a shape cut from construction paper. Examples include circles, ovals, squares, and rectangles. Some students choose to wear their shapes on long yarn necklaces. The teacher suggests that students with the same shape pair up, if they like, to hunt together.
2. Students find examples of their shapes on the playground and around the school.
3. They draw pictures of their shapes on their clipboards. Many students choose to write words as well.

Figure S39.3   A Kindergarten Treasure Hunt for Shapes

1. Students are arranged in teams of four, each with an adult volunteer. Teams meet to discuss the list and their hunting strategy.

2. Each team is given an instant camera and instructions to have the members' pictures taken with things from the list. They write captions on the photos. Photos without accurate and convincing captions do not count.

3. The class walks downtown for a 45-minute trip.

4. The list contains items such as the following:
   ✔ Take a picture of something (not someone) **very old**.
   ✔ Take a picture of one team member with a **map**.
   ✔ Take a picture of one team member with a **rule** that helps people get along safely in the community.
   ✔ Take a picture of one team member with a **consumer** and a **producer** of goods or services.
   ✔ Collect three interesting business cards, and be ready to explain why your team finds them interesting.

Figure S39.4   A Second-grade Treasure Hunt for a Class Studying the Local Community

Question	Answer	Dictionary Page Number
1. *Alligator* is taken from which Spanish word for *lizard*?	el lagarto	36
2. A *comrade* is a friend. The related French word is *comarade*. What is the Spanish connection?	camarada	277
3. *Dried flesh* is a high protein, low-fat snack. Why do we call it *jerky*?	charqui = dried flesh in Spanish	718
4. The English *mosquito* is taken directly from the Spanish *mosquito*. What does it mean?	little fly	
5. What does *salsa* mean in Spanish?		
6. A *savvy* person knows things. What is the Spanish origin?	sabe	
7. *Sweet potato* comes from which Spanish word?		
BIG QUESTION: What is one thing you can conclude about the relationship between the English and Spanish languages?		

Figure S39.5   Sample Items from a Dictionary Treasure Hunt for Students Studying Spanish 1

TROUBLESHOOTING

1. Build teams carefully to support students who may need special consideration to succeed in a team setting. Consider using some device to maintain student accountability for all. For instance, each student (or pair of students) might be required to turn in individual worksheets.

2. Ensure that someone in each group has a watch; teach them to monitor their time well if you have created a Treasure Hunt with much student freedom.

3. Ensure that students are carefully supervised at all times.

STRATEGIES FOR FACILITATING REHEARSAL AND CONSOLIDATION OF CONTENT

Active teachers provide students with opportunities to rehearse, deeply process, and elaborate on information. They know that learning and remembering increase with practice: The more students engage with information, the better they will remember it. Likewise, the deeper the processing of the information—that is, the more details the students add to the information—and the greater the elaboration—the more associations they make with the information—the more likely they will remember it.

Chapter 7 provides 11 strategies that ask students to rehearse, process, or elaborate on the material. The strategies prompt students to review content through talking with others, writing, graphically representing the material, or dramatizing it. Individually, with partners, or in small groups, students consider the importance and relevance of information they are learning, identify key ideas, summarize the content, design ways to share what they know, and engage with classmates. The strategies encourage students to reflect on what they have learned.

When students participate in strategies for rehearsal and consolidation of content, they

✔ Attend to the information.

✔ Revisit and review information.

✔ Increase their depth of processing of the content.

✔ Summarize the content.

✔ Increase associations among key ideas and among other content and the content under study.

✔ Increase the likelihood of long-term retention of the content and its retrieval.

You may wish to review Chapter 2, especially Figures 2.1 through 2.3, for suggestions on using active teaching strategies with students who are not independent readers and writers, students who are learning English, and students who have specific learning needs. You may also wish to review Figure 1.4 for typical cognitive, physical, social, and emotional needs and interests of students of various ages.

STRATEGY 40 Geniuses and Super Inteligentes

LANGUAGE DEMANDS	LITERACY DEMANDS
Appropriate for:	Appropriate for:
Early English Learners	✔ Emerging Readers/Writers
✔ Intermediate English Learners	✔ Intermediate Readers/Writers
✔ Advanced English Learners	✔ Proficient Readers/Writers

"Docendo discimus," "We learn by teaching," said Seneca 2,000 years ago. Peer tutoring—having students teach each other—benefits both the tutor and the tutee in terms of content knowledge, attitudes toward the subject matter, and self-concept (Cohen, Kulick, & Kulick, 1982). Recent research suggests that peer tutoring has a number of positive effects for a wide range of students, including those placed at risk (Barley et al., 2002) and those with learning disabilities or behavior disorders at the elementary (Falk & Wehby, 2001), middle school (Spencer, Scruggs, & Mastropieri, 2003), and high school (Mastropieri, Scruggs, Spencer, & Fontana, 2003) levels. Geniuses and Super Inteligentes is a short-term, highly controlled peer-tutoring strategy in which students are paired and, after hearing information from the teacher, take turns teaching each other. This strategy allows students to hear the information more than once, it helps them comprehend the content as they work to explain it to a peer, and it provides lower-risk opportunities for clarification from the teacher.

PREPARATION

1. Divide information into chunks that your students can manage. Just a few minutes' worth of information is sufficient.

2. Decide which pairings will be best and then pair students. You may, for instance, consider factors such as English proficiency, performance level, and student preference as you choose pairings. Random pairings may also be effective.

3. If students will need objects or visual aids for their teaching, gather them.

IMPLEMENTATION

1. At the beginning of the lesson, determine which student in each pair is the Genius, and which is the Super Inteligente. You can decide or you can allow the students to pick. A game of rock-paper-scissors might decide.

2. Explain the strategy to students: You will present information in front of the entire class, but you will be speaking to just one of the partners, the Genius. The Super Inteligentes may all relax as you address the Geniuses. Then each Genius will teach his or her Super Inteligente partner that information. In a few minutes, the Super Inteligentes will hear the next chunk of information while the Geniuses relax. Then the Super Inteligentes teach the Geniuses. In our experience, the partner who is "relaxing" also attends to the information, but with a lower level of concern and attention. This allows partners to hear the information twice, which facilitates comprehension.

3. Use this alternating partner strategy to present information. Before releasing students to teach their peers, check their understanding of the content and allow them to ask clarifying questions as necessary. Provide objects or visual aids, as appropriate, for them to use in teaching their partners.

4. Monitor so that you can answer questions that arise from the peer tutors as they teach.

ALTERNATIVES

1. Many students like being called "Genius" or "Super Inteligente," but you can use silly names as well. Bird names—Dodos and Blue-Footed Boobies—are catchy, for instance.

2. In Three Person Teach, the teacher (who counts as Teacher 1) explains a concept or point to the entire class rather than to just one partner, and then paired students (who count as Teachers 2 and 3), teach it to each other. In this alternative, all students are responsible for each chunk of information the teacher shares, and they share the peer teaching time after each information chunk.

3. Students who are very new to English can be assigned to a trio and take a third role, that of Mastermind. Masterminds listen to both the teacher's information and to their peers' information rather than teaching any themselves. Their job is to oversee instruction, inserting additional points and asking for clarification as they see fit.

4. If you like, teach each group out of earshot of the other group. Make sure the group that is not with you is productively engaged in some other content-related activity.

TIME ALLOTMENT

It will take students longer to present a chunk of information than it takes you because the content is newer for them, they are using their own words, and they are interacting with another person. For each 2-minute information chunk you present, plan on a 3- to 4-minute peer teaching session.

EXAMPLES

Chapter 2's U.S. history lesson (Figure 2.7) uses Geniuses and Super Inteligentes. Figure S40.1 provides examples of information chunks that might be presented through Geniuses and Super Inteligentes at different grade levels.

TROUBLESHOOTING

1. Because it requires high student accountability and careful attention to the presentation, this strategy can be intense. Require just a small number of partner teachings; two may be adequate.

2. Giving students an actual task to check for understanding can help them ensure that their partner has comprehended the information. Can their partner, for instance, find an equivalent fraction for 2/3?

3. Occasionally a "relaxing" partner may have attended to the information you were sharing with one group and may feel eager to "share." Ask students to allow their partners the opportunity to teach rather than to interrupt to demonstrate their knowledge.

4. Debrief after the lesson to help students improve their teaching skills: What did their partners do that helped them learn the information? What can they do differently next time?

	Genius	Super Inteligente

First-grade geography lesson on locating some of Earth's major features	Locating oceans:
	  Atlantic
	  Pacific
		Locating continents:
		  North America
		  South America

Third-grade vocabulary lesson on prefixes	Using:
	  bi-
	  pre-
		Using:
		  un-
		  mis-

Seventh-grade lesson on statistics	Explaining and calculating:
	  minimum & maximum
	  median
		Explaining and calculating:
		  lower & upper quartiles
		  mean

High school lesson on theater vocabulary	Using:
	  style
	  genre
	  theme
		Using:
		  acting values
		  design
		  motivation

Figure S40.1   Sample Information Chunks for Genius and Super Inteligentes

STRATEGY 41 Jigsaw

LANGUAGE DEMANDS	LITERACY DEMANDS
Appropriate for:	Appropriate for:
Early English Learners	Emerging Readers/Writers
Intermediate English Learners	✔ Intermediate Readers/Writers
✔ Advanced English Learners	✔ Proficient Readers/Writers

In the Jigsaw strategy (Aronson, Stephen, Sikes, Blaney, & Snapp, 1978), students become experts in a small body of information by reading a selection and then discussing what they have read with peers who read the same selection. Then they share what they have learned with others who became experts in different, but related, material. Small groups benefit from the expertise of each of their members, and every member of the group plays an important role because each has a unique contribution to make the group's learning.

PREPARATION

1. Select reading materials that will enhance the students' understanding of your topic. A book chapter or short related articles are ideal. If you select a single document such as a book chapter, divide it into self-contained parts so that each member of a group can be assigned a different part of the reading material that can stand alone. In other words, each section should not rely on the other sections to make sense.

2. Determine in advance the number of students you will assign to each group so that you can provide enough materials for each member of the group to read something different. For example, if you have groups of four, you need four selections. If you have groups of five, you need five selections.

3. Gather or make enough copies of the reading selections so that each group has one copy.

4. Give each selection a label: A, B, C, or D (or A, B, or C if you have three selections; A, B, C, D, or E if you have five selections). Ensure that all copies of the same selection have the same label.

IMPLEMENTATION

1. Begin by assigning students to small groups of a predetermined size based on the number of selections to be read. Or, allow students to select their own groups. These are the "original" groups.

2. Provide one copy of each selection to each group. Have each group distribute the selections among the group members and tell students that their task is to study the materials independently.

3. Provide the students with sufficient time to read and take notes on their selection.

4. Ask all students who read selection A to meet at a designated table to form an "expert" group. The students discuss what they learned from reading their selection. Ask all students reading selection B to meet together at another table, and so forth. If there are more than six students at the tables, you may want to divide these groups into smaller groups to promote participation from everyone.

5. Tell students to share in their expert groups their understandings, questions, or comments about the reading selection. Alert them that they will be asked to share with their original groups the expertise acquired through their reading and discussion.

6. After the students have discussed their readings, have them return to their original small groups to teach and learn from their peers.

7. Close the strategy by asking each group to share something interesting the group learned. Or, increase accountability by testing students on their knowledge.

ALTERNATIVES

1. Rather than taking notes on the reading selections, have students identify the Important Words (p. 69) in their selections and share these with their groups. They must be prepared to talk about why these words were critical to the reading selection. Or, students in expert groups may develop Graphic Organizers (p. 204) to share with their original groups.

2. This strategy is most commonly used with reading materials such as textbooks or multiple articles on related topics. However, you may choose to have students gain expertise in important class content through means other than reading. For instance, some junior high school students might gain expertise in the use of a classroom set of microscopes, others might become expert at metric conversions, and still others might become expert at setting up data charts. Students then share their knowledge with their peers, following the Jigsaw structure. Third-grade students studying weather phenomena might meet in expert groups to study photographs, pictures, charts, and diagrams of hurricanes, blizzards, lightning storms, and floods. Once each expert group has worked together to identify important information and concepts, students return to their original groups to share their knowledge.

3. If you have students with a wide range of literacy and language levels in your classroom, have a broad array of materials that each expert group may peruse. For instance, provide picture books, photographs, maps, physical objects—items that do not require reading.

TIME ALLOTMENT

This strategy often takes about 1 hour. The amount of time you allot to the strategy, however, will be determined by the length and density of the study materials as well as by the size of the original groups. Four is a very comfortable size. If you have three students per group (because, for example, you had only three selections you wanted to share), the strategy will take less time because only three people will need to teach their material in the small-group meeting (step 6 above). If you have five students per group, the strategy will take longer.

EXAMPLE

See Figure S41.1 for examples of groupings.

TROUBLESHOOTING

1. If the numbers are not a perfect fit (and they usually are not), simply assign more than one reader to a selection in one or more original groups. For example, if you have four selections and do not have a multiple of four students—say, you have 33 students—you will need to assign two people in one of the original groups to read selection A (or B or C or D). In this case, two students in a group will become experts

Three Readings (A, B, and C)

1. Sort students, or have students sort themselves, into groups of three.

2. Distribute one copy of selection A, one copy of selection B, and one copy of selection C to each group.

3. Students assign a selection to each group member and members independently read and take notes on their assigned selection.

4. All students with selection A meet to discuss the selection.
   All students with selection B meet to discuss the selection.
   All students with selection C meet to discuss the selection.

5. Students return to their original groups of three and teach each other the content of their selections.

Four Readings (A, B, C, and D)

1. Sort students, or have students sort themselves, into groups of four.

2. Distribute one copy of selection A, one copy of selection B, one copy of selection C, and one copy of selection D to each group.

3. Students assign a selection to each group member and members independently read and take notes on their assigned selection.

4. All students with selection A meet to discuss the selection.
   All students with selection B meet to discuss the selection.
   All students with selection C meet to discuss the selection.
   All students with selection D meet to discuss the selection.

5. Students return to their original groups of four and teach each other the content of their selections.

Five Readings (A, B, C, D, and E)

1. Sort students, or have students sort themselves, into groups of five.

2. Distribute one copy of selection A, one copy of selection B, one copy of selection C, one copy of selection D, and one copy of selection E to each group.

3. Students assign a selection to each group member and members independently read and take notes on their assigned selection.

4. All students with selection A meet to discuss the selection.
   All students with selection B meet to discuss the selection.
   All students with selection C meet to discuss the selection.
   All students with selection D meet to discuss the selection.
   All students with selection E meet to discuss the selection.

5. Students return to their original groups of five and teach each other the content of their selections.

Figure S41.1   Sample Groupings for Different Numbers of Readings

on the same information and both will share information about selection A when they return to their original group. If you have 34 students, assign an extra A in two groups. You may wish to be selective about which material you choose to double assign. If one reading is more complex or a bit longer than the others, you will probably want to select that reading for the double reader.

2. We do not recommend distributing more than five different readings. The groups become too large and, because of concerns about time, conversations become less thoughtful as the number of group members increases.

3. To ensure that the original groups finish sharing at roughly the same time, consider using a timer that helps each expert know how much time has elapsed. An overhead timer is effective for this purpose.

STRATEGY 42 Note Checking Pairs

LANGUAGE DEMANDS	LITERACY DEMANDS
Appropriate for:	Appropriate for:
Early English Learners	Emerging Readers/Writers
✔ Intermediate English Learners	✔ Intermediate Readers/Writers
✔ Advanced English Learners	✔ Proficient Readers/Writers

Note Checking Pairs provides an opportunity for students to review the content of a lesson or unit of study and identify the most important ideas. In this strategy, students work in pairs to review their notes (Ruhl, Hughes, & Schloss, 1987) and then select the most important ideas to share with peers. This strategy provides a structure for students to support each other with the content as they articulate their understandings based on their notes. Questions or misconceptions are addressed by their partner. The strategy also encourages students to discriminate among more and less important ideas and negotiate meaning with a peer as they discuss the relative importance of ideas.

PREPARATION

1. Identify places in your lesson or unit that are logical opportunities for students to review together.

IMPLEMENTATION

1. At the conclusion of a segment of the lesson or unit of study, provide a short time for students to review their notes in pairs. Depending on the length of the segment and the density of material, you might allow as few as 3 minutes or as many as 10 minutes. Tell students that once they have reviewed their notes, they are to select the most important idea or ideas from the segment to share with the rest of the group.

2. After the designated length of time, have pairs share their important ideas by conducting a Whip around the room.

3. Important ideas will vary because importance is determined not only by the content but by relevant experiences of the students. Invite a few students to share the reasons for their selection, if you have time.

4. Note the consensus or lack of consensus in the room and convey respect for all ideas. All contributions have value because importance of ideas will depend on each individual's background experiences and prior knowledge of the topic. Clarify any misunderstandings that are revealed by their sharing.

ALTERNATIVES

1. You can simplify this strategy by merely pausing at strategic points and asking students to consolidate their notes. As they look over their notes, they can check for holes and misunderstandings. This simplification saves time and is an important variation, but it loses the richness of partner talk.

2. If you do not have time for sharing, ask students to record a single important idea on an index card and then collect the cards. Later, you can quickly skim the cards to determine students' understandings of the content as well as determine what is important to your students. When you have a few moments read aloud some (or all) of the cards to the class and clarify misunderstandings, extend certain points, and generally share your appreciation of students' thinking.

TIME ALLOTMENT

The entire strategy generally takes between 10 and 20 minutes. You can complete it more quickly if smaller chunks of material are addressed before note checking.

TROUBLESHOOTING

1. Any time you pair students, you run the risk that one member of a pair may be a hesistant participant. As students share their notes, you should observe their conversations to determine whether you will allow these same pairings on subsequent use of Note Checking Pairs, whether you will ask students to select a new partner each time, or whether you will need to provide support to a pair that does not seem to be working well together.

2. Be sensitive that some students will feel uncomfortable sharing their notes with others for a number of reasons. One reason may be that they are unsure of the quality of the content of their notes. Reinforce the expectation that note checking time is a great chance for students to revise their notes as a result of their partner's input. Others may be concerned about their spelling, mechanics, or handwriting. Allow students to talk about their understanding of the content without demanding explicit attention to their notes.

STRATEGY 43 Q & A Match

LANGUAGE DEMANDS	LITERACY DEMANDS
Appropriate for:	Appropriate for:
Early English Learners	✔ Emerging Readers/Writers
✔ Intermediate English Learners	✔ Intermediate Readers/Writers
✔ Advanced English Learners	✔ Proficient Readers/Writers

Goodlad (1984) found "frontal practices" prevalent in American classrooms: Many teachers stand in front of their classes and quiz students at length on factual information. Q & A Match can help teachers move away from such "frontal practices" and toward more interactive opportunities for students to rehearse information. This strategy is similar to Content Links (p. 173) in that students each receive a card with information and find a match with one of their peers. In this case, half of the students receive questions, and half receive answers. Q & A Match requires students to talk to each other about lesson or unit content as they attempt to determine whether they belong together as a match of question and answer. It also allows the teacher to assess students' understanding of the material and provides a review for the whole group.

PREPARATION

You can find this template on the accompanying Teacher Resources CD and at the back of the book.

1. Prepare questions and answers related to lesson or unit content and record them on large cards or pieces of paper. Prepare enough for each student to receive a unique card. If there is an odd number of participants, prepare one question that has two answers (e.g., "What are two properties of iron?"). Use the template found in the Teacher Resources CD to record questions and answers if you like.

2. Think about "questions" and "answers" broadly as you prepare. You might have students match pictures with the words that name them, for example, or chemical symbols with their names.

IMPLEMENTATION

1. Randomly distribute the cards to students.

2. Explain that half the students received cards with questions and the other half received cards with answers. Tell the students that their task is to find a partner in the room. The partnership must be based on a match between question and answer, and the students must be able to explain their question-answer match to the group.

3. Allow sufficient time for all students to identify a partner and support those who may be having difficulty. As students become paired, move them into a large circle so they are all facing each other.

4. Ask each pair to share their question and answer with the group.

ALTERNATIVES

1. Include more answers than questions, with the extra answers being incorrect. Thus, students cannot simply "default" to an answer once everyone else has been matched. Students holding answers for which there is no matching question stand together. When sharing as a group, ask students to generate a question that would be an appropriate match for these answers.

2. Include multiple correct answers to questions. Tell students that some questions have more than one correct response so they must continue searching even after finding an initial match. Thus, in a class of 30 students, you may have 10 questions and 20 answers.

3. Students can devise sets of Q & A cards. You might hand them a copy of the Q & A template found in the Teacher Resources CD. Developing Q & A cards is an invigorating alternative for homework, and it is often a good choice for early finishers. Many students find it motivating to see their work "performed" by the class. Further, question generating is a powerful way for students to identify and integrate main ideas and to improve their memory of the information (Trabasso & Bouchard, 2002).

4. For English learners who are just gaining comfort with reading and speaking in English, you may choose to assign two people to a card so that one can support the other during the matching phase.

TIME ALLOTMENT

Depending on the number of students and the complexity of the questions, this strategy takes from 5 to 15 minutes.

EXAMPLES

Figure S43.1 displays questions and answers from a middle school physical education class that is learning the rules of soccer. Figure S43.2 presents questions and answers for high school students learning the properties of triangles.

TROUBLESHOOTING

1. Even though students may form defensible matches, you may need to support them in finding different matches so students with more restrictive questions and answers can form pairs.

2. Keep one set of matched cards as the key, perhaps duplicating them as in Figures S43.1 and S43.2 or as shown in the Q & A template in the Teacher Resources CD. Also, be sure to check the cards carefully before distributing them to students. It can be difficult to sort out an error during the strategy, and it wastes instructional time.

Questions	Answers
What is a direct kick?	free kick given after fouls such as hitting or kicking another player
When is the goalkeeper not permitted to use his or her hands?	on a teammate's pass
Who alone can drop kick the ball?	goalkeeper
How many of the player's feet must be on the ground during a throw-in?	2
What happens when a player gets a red card?	The player is ejected from the game.

Figure S43.1   Questions and Answers Prepared for a Middle School Physical Education Class Participating in Soccer

Questions	Answers
What must happen on an indirect kick before the ball may go into the goal?	It must be touched by another player.
Can a player who throws in the ball from the sideline kick it before another player has contact?	no
Is a player who receives a yellow card allowed to continue playing?	yes
How many people on a team play at one time?	11
What constitutes a hand ball?	when the player uses any part of the body from the fingers to the shoulder
"Off side" does not happen in what side of the field?	on the offensive half
How far must the ball go into the goal box in order to count as a goal?	completely over the line
What is the Golden Goal?	the first goal scored in overtime

Figure S43.1   *Continued*

Questions	Answers
What do you call two triangles whose corresponding sides are the same and corresponding angles are the same?	congruent
What is the sum of the measures of the interior angles of a triangle?	180°
What is the sum of the measures of the interior angles of a quadrilateral?	360°
An equilateral triangle is also what?	an acute triangle
An isosceles triangle has at least how many congruent sides?	2
A scalene triangle has how many congruent sides?	none
What do you know about the side opposite the largest interior angle of a triangle?	it is longest
What is the balancing point of a triangle?	centroid
What is the measure of one of the angles in a right triangle?	90°
Why are triangles used in structural supports for buildings?	They are rigid because a triangle with given side lengths has only one possible size and shape.
In what fields does knowledge of the properties of triangles help you solve problems?	art, architecture, engineering
The angle bisectors of a triangle intersect at what point?	incenter

Figure S43.2   Questions and Answers Prepared for High School Geometry Students

STRATEGY 44 Interactive Journals

LANGUAGE DEMANDS	LITERACY DEMANDS
Appropriate for:	Appropriate for:
Early English Learners	Emerging Readers/Writers
✔ Intermediate English Learners	✔ Intermediate Readers/Writers
✔ Advanced English Learners	✔ Proficient Readers/Writers

Writing is often thought of as a process by which students report what they have learned, yet writing can also be a powerful means for students to discover, clarify, and consolidate knowledge (Elbow, 1994; Emig, 1977). In short, students can *learn as they write*. When students reflect on, grapple with, and articulate their understanding of or reactions to content through writing, they mediate their knowledge and make personal connections with the subject matter. When students work to put their thinking in writing, they examine and refine their understandings, build relationships among ideas, and make decisions about ideas' meaning and value. Writing demands active engagement with the content (Fulwiler, 1980) and has been shown to result in greater retention of information (Reaves, Flowers, & Jewell, 1993).

Interactive Journals provide the students with important quiet time to reflect on, reconstruct, and become personally involved with the content of a lesson or unit of study; share their thoughts, discoveries, or reactions with a peer; and respond to and learn from a peer. Pairs of students record their thoughts in journals at specified points and then trade journals with one another for feedback.

PREPARATION

1. Prepare journals for student use. These may be composition books, pieces of paper stapled together, or blank pages at the end of a handout.

2. Determine points in the lesson or unit of study at which reflection and communication with peers might support student learning. Develop prompts based on the content. Prompts may be specific or general and may tap cognitive or affective domains.

3. Make decisions about how partnerships will be established. You may wish to assign partners, or you may wish to allow students to select their own partners. If students are to choose their own partners, you can simplify the exchange by asking students to identify their partners before writing: "Make eye contact with the person who will be your partner," for example.

IMPLEMENTATION

1. Stop at predetermined points and ask students to record their thoughts in their journals. Advise the students that their writing will be read by a peer in the room, but note that you will not collect and read the journals. Allow 3 or 4 minutes for writing.

2. Ask students to trade their journal with a partner, read their partner's journal, and then respond in writing to the comments. Allow 3 or 4 minutes for this response before asking the students to return journals to their owners.

3. Provide journal owners with a minute or two to read the comments of their partners, but do not allow them to respond at this time.

4. At subsequent points in the lesson, allow additional written exchanges. Students' thinking and concerns or insights will evolve over the course of the lesson or unit and will be reflected in their comments in the journals.

5. At the end of the lesson or unit of study, invite students to share observations they may have about the interactive journaling experience.

ALTERNATIVES

1. In the format discussed above, students keep the same journal partner throughout the process. As an alternative, journals might be rotated around a table. Each student writes and then receives responses from a variety of peers as the journal moves around the table at several points during the lesson or unit. Although this might be an effective strategy for allowing feedback from more than one person and for promoting community, it does not allow for the more personal and ongoing discussion between two students that the original format allows.

2. Invite students to record ideas in pictures instead of—or in addition to—words.

3. Consider using "intra-active" journals occasionally as well, where the author is the sole audience of the journal.

4. Pick up the entire set of journals (or a subset of them) and read to check students' comprehension of and reactions to the content. Advise students in advance that you may read their journals.

5. As increasing numbers of students have discovered through their own blogs, or weblogs, electronic journals provide a popular opportunity for writers to post their thoughts and gain reactions from readers. You can ask students to create interactive electronic journals by instructing them to compose word processing documents and use the "track changes" function of the program, or they can e-mail each other and submit printed copies of their exchanges to you (if you desire). Threaded discussions on an electronic bulletin board allow all students to contribute to a line of thought. Be sure that students understand the rules of "netiquette" for polite and appropriate electronic conversations. Review your expectations before encouraging electronic Interactive Journals. Additionally, review your school's safety policies for Internet usage.

TIME ALLOTMENT

Plan for each interactive writing experience to last no more than 10 minutes. Schedule as many writing opportunities as seem appropriate for your group.

EXAMPLES

Figure S44.1 shares a sample journal prompt and entry from a junior high music class. Figure S44.2 gives a prompt and entry from a high school world history class.

TROUBLESHOOTING

1. Some groups may require that ground rules be established prior to engaging them in this strategy. Students need to feel safe sharing their understandings and reactions in writing. Discuss confidentiality and respect for the ideas or concerns of others. Note

that no idea or reaction is "stupid," that all have merit if they represent the genuine responses of the student.

2. Some students may be self-conscious about their writing skills. You may wish to provide an option of allowing students to read aloud or paraphrase their entries to a partner rather than show their writing. Hopefully, you have established an atmosphere of trust in your classroom and built a community of students who respect one another, but you must know your students. If some would be embarrassed to share their writing, consider allowing students to write in pairs with one of the students recording the pair's thinking in a single journal. Then pairs of students exchange journals.

3. Avoid very narrow prompts, as they will limit conversations.

We have just listened to a recording of Mussorgsky's "Night on Bald Mountain." Choose Prompt One or Prompt Two for your journal entry.

Prompt One: List at least five words or phrases that come to your mind as you listened to the piece.

Student response:

thunderous	*excited*
dark	*well composed*
villainous	*brassy*
sad	*chase*

Partner response:

I like the words you picked! I didn't think of the word "villainous," but I think it captures the mood! Have you ever heard this composition before?

Prompt Two: Draw a picture or some doodles that somehow capture the music and the emotions it evoked.

Figure S44.1   Interactive Journal Prompts and an Entry from a Junior High Music Class

---

Prompt: Napoleon Bonaparte left a lasting imprint on the world. In what ways, if any, are you similar to Napoleon?

Student One

First of all, I'm mostly different from Napoleon. He was short, but not as short as people typically think. Also, people say his ulcer was a real pain. My stomach never hurts! In some important ways, I'm similar to him, though. He was bored of school, and I'm sometimes bored. He was faithful to the woman he loved, and that's my plan. He could be ruthless, and if I had a really good reason (like if someone hurt my family), I might be ruthless too.

Student Two's Response to Student One's Entry

You didn't need to convince me: You are SO NOT Napoleon! Neither am I. I have no French accent, and my parents were not Italian. I'm like him in a couple ways too, though. I know what you mean about being bored once in a while. Also, Napoleon was an average student, and lately I feel average. Here's the big thing: Napoleon left a huge mark on the world. I hope that I leave a mark on the world, even though it will probably be smaller than Napoleon's influence.

Figure S44.2   Interactive Journal Prompt from a World History Class and Two Students' Exchange

STRATEGY 45 Graphic Organizers

LANGUAGE DEMANDS	LITERACY DEMANDS
Appropriate for:	Appropriate for:
✔ Early English Learners	✔ Emerging Readers/Writers
✔ Intermediate English Learners	✔ Intermediate Readers/Writers
✔ Advanced English Learners	✔ Proficient Readers/Writers

After participating in a learning experience, students in small groups create Graphic Organizers that display their understanding of the topic. This strategy requires students to discuss and organize their understandings and make decisions about how to share information with peers. Talking and planning with peers in small groups, translating the information from one form (verbal) into another (graphic), and explaining their graphic will deepen students' understanding of the topic (Marzano, Pickering, & Pollock, 2001) and will support English learners' interactions with the content (Echevarria & Graves, 1998). And, like many of the other strategies in this book, Graphic Organizers allow the teacher to assess students' understanding of the topic.

PREPARATION

1. Identify the concepts or information that will be depicted in the Graphic Organizers (e.g., characteristics of mammals or causes of the American Revolution). You might identify the same content for all groups or assign different content to each group.

2. Select the reading materials or other information sources that students will use to develop their Graphic Organizers. Other sources might include pictures, class notes, and hands-on materials.

3. Gather charting materials—colored markers, chart paper, and tape or tacks for hanging the charts.

4. Plan how groups will be determined. Early English learners may need to be grouped with students who can provide translation so that they can be included in the conversations about and organization of the content. Emerging readers and writers may need to be grouped with students who are more skilled readers and who can support the group's efforts at recording their ideas.

IMPLEMENTATION

1. Organize the students into groups, considering the suggestions in number 4 above.

2. Provide each group with appropriate resources and charting tools.

3. Instruct the students that their job is to ensure they understand the material by discussing it in their small groups and then depicting the information graphically on chart paper. Inform the students that they will be asked to share their Graphic Organizers with the rest of the class.

4. Allow time for groups to work.

5. Have the groups post their Graphic Organizers around the room and ask a representative or two from each group to explain their Graphic Organizer to the class.

ALTERNATIVES

1. Instead of developing Graphic Organizers in small groups, you might ask students to work in pairs or individually and then share their Graphic Organizers in small groups or with the whole class.

2. Allow students to use computer software such as Inspiration or Kidspiration to create their Graphic Organizers.

TIME ALLOTMENT

This strategy generally takes 30 to 45 minutes, including reviewing resources, discussing the information, planning and creating the Graphic Organizer, and sharing it with the entire class.

EXAMPLES

Figure S45.1 displays a Graphic Organizer developed by a group of third-grade students studying habitats. In this class, each group of students studied and depicted information about a different habitat. The example shares the work of the group that studied tropical rainforests. Note that the Graphic Organizer includes words and drawings. Figure S45.2 shows a Graphic Organizer developed by eighth-grade students studying the causes of the American Revolution. Note its cause-and-effect structure.

TROUBLESHOOTING

1. Groups should be small enough so that all members feel ownership of the task and have an opportunity to contribute. Our personal experiences lead us to limit group size to six, and four is even better.

2. If the students have had little exposure to Graphic Organizers, you may need to provide instruction in their use and development for several days before you use this strategy. For example, you might utilize Graphic Organizers in your presentation of information and assist students in interpreting them. You might model the development of Graphic Organizers and provide guided practice as you create an organizer as a class. Be sure to provide examples that depict hierarchical information, cause-and-effect information, descriptive information, and sequential information, as appropriate for the content.

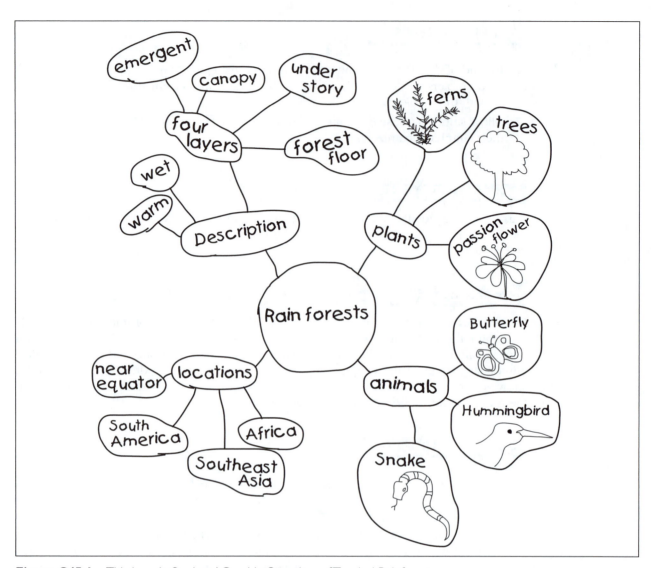

Figure S45.1 Third-grade Students' Graphic Organizer of Tropical Rainforests

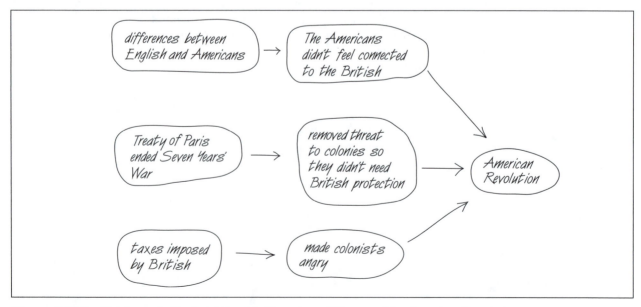

Figure S45.2 Eighth-grade Students' Graphic Organizer of Causes of the American Revolution

STRATEGY 46 Word Journal

LANGUAGE DEMANDS	LITERACY DEMANDS
Appropriate for:	Appropriate for:
Early English Learners	Emerging Readers/Writers
✔ Intermediate English Learners	✔ Intermediate Readers/Writers
✔ Advanced English Learners	✔ Proficient Readers/Writers

Providing learners with opportunities to review information, process it deeply, and elaborate on it are important for supporting retention of information (Marzano, 2004). Word Journal (Angelo & Cross, 1993) requires students to revisit information, analyze it, summarize it in a single word, and provide an explanation for the selection of the word. Thus, students think about and engage with the content in a way that will support their memory of it. In Word Journal, students first participate in a learning experience, such as listening to a lecture, reading a text, or participating in a discussion or hands-on activity. Then they review and reflect on the information and select a single word that summarizes the material. They record their word in a Word Journal and compose an explanation of their word choice. Finally, they share their selections and explanations with classmates.

PREPARATION

1. Determine the point or points in the learning experience when summarization of content is appropriate. For younger students, you will probably wish to address less material before asking them to reflect on it and select a word. Older students may be able to summarize information learned over the course of several days in a single word.

2. Prepare Word Journal booklets for use throughout a lesson or unit of study, or simply ask students to record their words and explanations on a piece of paper. Have the booklets or paper available. You may choose to duplicate the Word Journal template found in the Teacher Resources CD for this purpose. If students will post their work electronically, prepare your electronic bulletin board or journals.

You can find this template on the accompanying Teacher Resources CD and at the back of the book.

IMPLEMENTATION

1. Provide input as you normally would.

2. At an appropriate stopping point, ask the students to review their notes, the text, or other materials and to generate a single word that best summarizes the material. Tell them that after selecting a word, they are to record it in their Word Journal, on blank paper, on a copy of the Word Journal template, or on the electronic bulletin board and write an explanation of why they selected that particular word. Explain that there is no one correct answer and that their explanation of their selection is more important than the word they selected.

3. After the students have chosen their words and written their explanations, ask volunteers to share their selections. You might want to do this as a whole class and write their word choices on the board, perhaps tallying the number of times a word is chosen, or you might ask students to share their selections and reasons in small groups or pairs.

4. Ask students to complete a Word Journal at several points in the lesson or unit. Later, have them use the words recorded in their Word Journals to write a summary paragraph of their learning. You may or may not require them to use every word recorded in their journal. Requiring the use of all words increases the difficulty of the task and calls for students to explain the connections among the words.

ALTERNATIVES

1. Allow students, especially English learners, to work with a partner to review material, select a word, and write an explanation for the choice.

2. Ask students to share other words they considered but rejected in favor of their final choice. Ask them to explain why they rejected these words.

3. Invite students to record word choices and brief explanations on Graffiti Boards (p. 81) at various points in the lesson or unit.

4. Use Word Journal with very young students by asking them to share words and explanations orally, rather than in writing.

5. Collect students' words, which is particularly easy if they are stored electronically, and make them available for all students to review and use.

6. Have students circulate among their peers after they have selected a word and recorded it on a paper. Students show their words to one another and talk about them, and they may exchange words if they so desire, as in Idea Share (p. 53). Then students return to their seats to write explanations for their word choices.

7. Direct students to www.tenbyten.org for a fascinating Word Journal of world events.

8. Use Word Journal as an opportunity to informally assess students' understanding of the material.

TIME ALLOTMENT

You should allot adequate time for students to review materials and thoughtfully consider their word selections. Depending on the students and the amount of material they are reviewing, 10 to 15 minutes may be sufficient. In other instances, you may need to give the students more time, perhaps allowing them to complete their Word Journal before the next class meeting so they may thoroughly review their notes or a text at home if they choose. This may be especially true if a great deal of material has been addressed or if it is the first time you are using a Word Journal. Discussions about Word Journal selections may be as brief or as extended as you choose. Fifteen minutes is usually enough time to explore students' choices in some depth.

EXAMPLES

Figure S46.1 shows several sample Word Journal entries.

TROUBLESHOOTING

1. Some students may be concerned about the "correctness" of their word choice. Assure them that the choice of the word is not as important as the explanation for the choice. Be accepting of word choices, as long as the students provide reasonable explanations for their words. Allow the students to change their words after engaging in a class or group discussion.

2. Some students may need support the first time or two you use a Word Journal. Consider completing class Word Journals as a means of modeling the process and providing guided practice. Select a word as a group and compose a group explanation using a projection system.

3. Encourage students to use online dictionaries and thesauruses to identify a word that best reflects their understanding of the material. Although words often will come directly from students' notes or learning materials, it is not essential that they do.

4. Some students will plead to use more than one word, such as a brief phrase. Hold firm. Using just one word requires most students to think longer and more deeply about the content rather than merely selecting a prevalent phrase.

Second-grade Language Arts: After listening to the story *Chrysanthemum* by Kevin Henkes (1991), students select a single word that summarizes the story. One student records the word *name* and writes, *"The book is all about a mouse named Chrysanthemum and how she likes her name and then doesn't like her name and then likes her name again."*

Another student picks the word *flower*. He writes, *"The girl is named after a flower and so is her teacher. Other kids tease the girl but then decide they want to be named after flowers too."*

Middle School Science: After discussing the scientific method and watching the teacher demonstrate an experiment, students review their notes and select a word that summarizes their learning. One student selects *steps*. She writes, *"The scientific method involves several steps. They are (1) ask a question, (2) form a hypothesis, (3) test the hypothesis, (4) analyze the results, (5) draw conclusions, and (6) communicate results. Each of these steps is important, even if scientists don't use them in that exact order. If I can remember the six steps, I can behave like a scientist and answer questions or solve problems."*

Another student selects *observation*. He writes, *"I picked observation because it seems really important to the whole process. When people observe something interesting, they start asking questions and might want to study it. Studying it involves developing a hypothesis based on observations. Then you observe some more when you test the hypothesis. Analyzing the results involves organizing the data into charts and graphs and looking at it carefully. You draw conclusions from the data you observed and share everything with other scientists. Careful and systematic observation seems to be what the scientific method is all about."*

High School U.S. Government: The teacher lectures on the three branches of government established by the U.S. Constitution. One student selects the word *power* and writes, *"The main idea behind the establishment of the three branches of government is to make sure nobody got too much power. I selected the word* power *because the reason for the three branches was to spread out the power. The executive branch has some power, the legislative branch has some power, and the judicial branch has some power. Also, this system limits new attempts to seize power, like when a governor recently tried to pass a bill to give himself more power and the courts said, 'no.'"*

Another student chooses *balance* and writes, *"I think the word that best summarizes the topic is* balance *because the three parts of government balance each other's responsibilities. The executive branch can veto bills and can nominate judges for federal courts. The legislative branch can override vetoes and can approve judges for federal courts. The judicial branch can rule acts and laws unconstitutional. The branches each have jobs, but the branches can influence what the other branches do. This balance has been important as our country has had growing pains throughout its history. For instance, the courts have had to continue to interpret the Constitution (legislation) in cases like* Marbury v. Madison *and* United States v. Nixon. *Balance has made democracy possible."*

Figure S46.1 Sample Word Journal Entries

STRATEGY 47 Invented Dialogs

LANGUAGE DEMANDS	LITERACY DEMANDS
Appropriate for:	Appropriate for:
Early English Learners	Emerging Readers/Writers
✔ Intermediate English Learners	✔ Intermediate Readers/Writers
✔ Advanced English Learners	✔ Proficient Readers/Writers

Pairs or small groups of students work together to script dialogs that might take place between two or more people they are studying or who might have knowledge of the content they are studying. This strategy requires students to take the perspective of others and to synthesize their knowledge of the subject to generate conversations and present arguments or information in an organized manner (Angelo & Cross, 1993; Davis, 1981).

PREPARATION

1. Make decisions about the dialog or dialogs you want the students to invent.
2. If you want students to invent dialogs based on different topics, record the dialog directions on index cards.

IMPLEMENTATION

1. Organize students in pairs or small groups.
2. Tell students that their job is to write a conversation that might have taken place (or might take place) between two or more people who would have knowledge of the topic you are studying. If you have planned for several topics of dialog, provide written directions to the groups.
3. Allow time for students to create their dialogs—generally 10 to 20 minutes is sufficient, unless you expect an extended conversation. You might provide suggestions for the length of the conversation, which will vary depending on the age of the students. Elementary-aged children might develop dialogs that are 5 lines per speaker. Older students might compose 10 or more lines per speaker. Encourage students to record their dialog in writing—either verbatim or in detailed notes—and inform them they will be allowed to use their written record during their presentations.
4. Have students perform their dialogs.
5. Applaud each group, and invite feedback on the presentation from the whole group.

ALTERNATIVES

1. Require students to weave actual quotes into their dialogs if they are studying historical figures (Angelo & Cross, 1993).
2. Perform the dialogs as a radio program, with students seated out of sight, perhaps blocked by a screen or curtain.

3. Present photocopied images of people or characters with speech bubbles above their heads. Ask students to fill in dialog that integrates and displays their knowledge of the time period, event, or characters. What might, for instance, a woman dressed in colonial garb be saying to the man beside her?

TIME ALLOTMENT

We usually allow participants from 10 to 20 minutes to prepare their dialogs. The time required for the presentations and comments depends on the number of groups you will have sharing Invented Dialogs. This entire strategy could take 45 to 60 minutes.

EXAMPLES

Figure S47.1 presents several sample prompts for Invented Dialogs.

TROUBLESHOOTING

1. You will probably want to impose a time limit on the presentations. Tell students beforehand that they will be allowed no more than 2 minutes (or whatever time you select) for their presentations. You do not want the dialogs to be too long if you have more than a few groups because interest will wane by the time you get to your last group. We have found that short presentations and a quick pace maintain student interest and still yield the positive opportunities provided by this strategy: taking different perspectives, synthesizing information, organizing thoughts, and sharing knowledge.

Fourth-grade Students Studying the Westward Movement:

Write a dialog for three family members who are planning their move to California. (What will they take? What route will they travel? How long will the trip take?)

Eighth-grade Students Studying U.S. History:

Write a dialog between two brothers living in the American colonies during the mid-1700s who disagree about whether to be loyal to the king of England or to fight for freedom. (What are the reasons for their choices?)

Write a dialog between John Adams and Thomas Jefferson about the writing of the Declaration of Independence.

High School Students Studying Art History:

Write a dialog between two artists explaining their techniques to each other.

Figure S47.1   Sample Invented Dialog Prompts

STRATEGY 48 Dramatizations and Tableaux

LANGUAGE DEMANDS	LITERACY DEMANDS
Appropriate for:	Appropriate for:
✔ Early English Learners	✔ Emerging Readers/Writers
✔ Intermediate English Learners	✔ Intermediate Readers/Writers
✔ Advanced English Learners	✔ Proficient Readers/Writers

Dramatization and the creation of tableaux facilitate students' understanding of content because they require students to synthesize, summarize, and represent content in a new way. Their use is advocated by many (Rose, Androes, Parks, & McMahon, 2000; McMaster, 1998; Tortello, 2004). In small groups, students make decisions about what they will represent and how they will represent it so that it communicates to an audience. In a dramatization, students create and perform a scene related to the topic. In a tableau, they position themselves in a manner that represents their understandings and then hold the pose for a moment or two. They may choose to have a narrator explain the pose or ask the audience to tell what the pose represents. These activities support community building, allow students to assess their understanding of the content, and introduce a performance aspect to the content study that is enjoyable for many students.

PREPARATION

1. You may wish to prepare several prompts and allow groups to draw one from a hat (or bag), or you may allow students to choose a learning to dramatize or represent in a tableau. If you decide on the former, write each idea on a piece of paper, fold it, and put it in a hat.

2. Although not necessary, you may wish to have a collection of possible props available for students.

IMPLEMENTATION

1. We like to engage students in Dramatizations and Tableaux at the end of a lesson or unit of study. Explain that the students will be asked to work in small groups to express an important learning.

2. Determine groups or let students select their own groups.

3. Invite a representative from each group to draw the group's task out of a hat, or let each group decide what important learning it wishes to represent.

4. Provide sufficient time and space for students to prepare their dramatization or tableau.

5. Have each group perform, and show appreciation for each production.

6. Provide a few moments for participants and observers to comment on each dramatization or tableau. If students need assistance in providing substantive comments, use prompts such as, "Which aspect of the performance really helped you understand the idea?" or "Which part surprised you?"

ALTERNATIVES

1. Introduce musical instruments. You may use traditional instruments, or you may invite students to use materials around them to add a musical element to their performance.

2. Allow student groups to videotape their dramatizations outside of class hours. Later, all students in the class enjoy watching the tapes together.

3. Students can conduct their dramatization or tableau in front of a projected image that provides a backdrop for the scene.

4. Some teachers we know expand this strategy into major productions, such as a Pageant of Historical Moments, and invite the community to participate.

TIME ALLOTMENT

Unless you select one of the extended alternatives, Dramatizations and Tableaux may take 15 to 30 minutes. Factors such as the number of groups, the complexity of the material, and the choice of dramatizations instead of tableaux can add to the time required.

EXAMPLES

Figure S48.1 shares sample ideas for Dramatizations and Tableaux across the grade levels and curriculum.

TROUBLESHOOTING

1. Many students have limited experience with the performing arts. Prepare students for success by teaching them basic rules that enhance a performance. Examples may include:
   - In dramatizations, face the audience when speaking.
   - Speak slowly, and articulate.
   - Especially in tableaux, emphasize body language and facial expression to convey your meaning.

Present one important learning from today's lesson.

—OR—

Kindergarteners after a Math Unit:

  Present some geometric figures.

Third Graders after a Music Unit:

  Present the families of orchestral instruments.

Middle School Health Students:

  Present the basic components of physical fitness.

High School Physics Students:

  Present Newton's laws of motion.

High School English Students:

  Present a scene that depicts an important theme in Golding's *Lord of the Flies*.

Figure S48.1 Sample Ideas for Dramatizations and Tableaux

2. If you ask students to draw their task from a hat, you are assured variety. However, you do limit the freedom of the students to identify their own important learning. You also do not allow yourself to discover what students found most important, as you would by providing a prompt such as "Represent one important learning from this unit of study."

3. Gauging the perfect amount of time to allow groups to work is always difficult. You will find that some groups complete the task more quickly than others. If this happens, and you cannot comfortably hasten the other groups, you may wish to challenge those who finished earlier than the others to prepare a second dramatization or tableau representing their important learning. They might also prepare some materials to accompany their dramatization, such as an overhead transparency that announces their work.

4. You will probably want to assign either a dramatization or a tableau to all groups. If you let groups choose, you may face the time issue discussed in number 3 above. A dramatization often takes longer to create than a tableau because tableaux are nonverbal and are limited to one scene.

5. You must establish a safe environment before asking students to perform in front of one another. Reinforce expectations for positive behaviors throughout the performances as well.

STRATEGY 49 Found Poems

LANGUAGE DEMANDS	LITERACY DEMANDS
Appropriate for:	Appropriate for:
✔ Early English Learners	Emerging Readers/Writers
✔ Intermediate English Learners	✔ Intermediate Readers/Writers
✔ Advanced English Learners	✔ Proficient Readers/Writers

After reading or studying a topic, students return to their texts or notes to identify words and phrases they believe capture the key ideas in the content. They record these words verbatim and arrange them to form a poem (Dunning & Stafford, 1992). Thus, their work is a poem *found* in the text of their notes or a reading selection.

PREPARATION

1. Identify the reading selection, notes, or other text source that you wish students to revisit.
2. Ensure that students have highlighters (in the case of students' written notes) or pencils to identify and record significant words or phrases.
3. Cut heavy paper, such as index cards, into small strips.
4. Decide whether you wish to have students create poems independently, in pairs, or in small groups.
5. Duplicate the Found Poem template found in the Teacher Resources CD, if you wish, to structure students' writing.

You can find this template on the accompanying Teacher Resources CD and at the back of the book.

IMPLEMENTATION

1. Organize students into pairs or small groups if desired.
2. Ask students to review the text materials and highlight, underline, or copy words or phrases that they consider key to the content.
3. Have students record their selections on the small sheets of heavy paper, one word or phrase per strip. There is space on the Found Poems template for students to record their selections as well.
4. Ask students to examine their selections, order them in a way that poetically communicates their understanding, and arrange them into a visually appealing or content-related display.
5. Glue the strips onto a piece of paper, perhaps the Found Poems template.
6. Prepare an opportunity for students to share their poems. Poems may be mounted on a bulletin board to form a wall book or bound together into a traditional book.

ALTERNATIVES

1. If you have time, you may wish to encourage students to construct three-dimensional poems. Students glue their strips onto paper in such a way as to make the strips pop up from the paper. For instance, mathematics students might develop a Found Poem

from a chapter on shapes in a geometry text by manipulating the strips on which they write words or phrases to form various shapes.

2. Allow students to reuse a phrase or word if they wish in order to contribute to the message, rhythm, or power of their poem.

TIME ALLOTMENT

Depending on the amount of text, it could take 20 to 30 minutes to create and share poems.

EXAMPLES

Figure S49.1 shares a Found Poem developed by a pair of second graders after reading Laurie Krasny Brown's *Dinosaurs Alive and Well! A Guide to Good Health.* Figures S49.2 and S49.3 share Found Poems developed by fourth graders studying state history and eighth graders studying matter.

Take care of yourself
Body
Mind
Spirit
Exercise your body
   Exercise your mind
      Believe in yourself
         Be a good friend.
Take care of yourself!

Figure S49.1   Found Poem Developed by a Pair of Second Graders after Reading a Book about Health

---

The Texas Constitution of 1876
Sets rules for
   State
      County
         Schools
            Public land
               Taxes
                  Railroads
Protects freedoms and rights of people.
Articles
   First, the Bill of Rights
   Second, three branches of government
   Legislative branch makes state laws
   Executive branch makes sure laws are carried out
Judicial branch makes sure laws are fair, decides cases

Figure S49.2   Found Poem Developed by Fourth-grade Students Studying a Selection on Texan State Government

An important breakthrough!
The atom is not
    In–di–vis–i–ble
Subatomic particles
Nucleus (contains almost all the mass of an atom)
Positively-charged protons
Neutral neutrons
    Negatively-charged electrons (lightweights!)
Balance the charge
A more complete model of the atom.

Figure S49.3   Found Poem Developed by Eighth-grade Students Studying Matter

TROUBLESHOOTING

1. If poems lack cohesion or students create poems that leap from topic to topic, you have likely asked students to revisit text that is too lengthy or addresses too many topics. Found Poems are best developed from text that addresses in some depth a single topic.

2. Some students may simply record key terms without demonstrating any conceptual understanding of the content. You may need to encourage students to use more complete phrases and thoughts, as in the examples.

3. Some students may need to hear a few examples of poetry before writing their own to remind them that powerful poetry often distills language down to its most meaningful or evocative words and phrases.

STRATEGY 50 "I Didn't Know That . . ." Response Frames

LANGUAGE DEMANDS	LITERACY DEMANDS
Appropriate for:	Appropriate for:
✔ Early English Learners	✔ Emerging Readers/Writers
✔ Intermediate English Learners	✔ Intermediate Readers/Writers
✔ Advanced English Learners	✔ Proficient Readers/Writers

The "I Didn't Know That . . ." Response Frame provides a structure for summarizing important information from a lesson or unit of study. Students engage in literary borrowing (Lancia, 1997) as they use the phrase "I didn't know that . . ."—drawn from a series of informational books published by Copper Beech—to precede each concept or fact they have learned. Other frames, original or borrowed from literature, are similarly helpful in assisting students to compose coherent thoughts and expressions in response to new learnings.

PREPARATION

1. Ideally, expose students to one or more of the Copper Beech Publishers' "I didn't know that . . ." books so they are familiar with the authors' page-by-page use of the introductory phrase, "I didn't know that. . . ." Examples of the Copper Beech books include *I Didn't Know That Crocodiles Yawn to Keep Cool* (Oliver, Field, Moore, & Petty, 1988) and *I Didn't Know That Mountains Gush Lava and Ash* (Oliver, Thompson, Moore, & Roberts, 1998).

2. Decide what size paper to use and what direction the information will be displayed (horizontally or vertically). For example, each student may use a 12" × 18" construction paper and the papers may be mounted to the wall to develop a wall book similar to a mural. Also decide whether you wish all students to use the same medium. For instance, should all students use marking pens, pencils, or water color? If you are compiling a book, you may wish to encourage uniformity. Have the materials ready.

3. Decide whether each student will develop a single page or more than one page.

IMPLEMENTATION

1. At the conclusion of a lesson or unit of study, ask students to reflect on their learning. You may lead a discussion or suggest that students talk in pairs about information they found interesting, surprising, or new.

2. Introduce or remind students that some books use the phrase "I didn't know that . . ." to share information with readers or listeners. Have students select ideas from the lesson or unit of study that they will contribute to a class book on the topic.

3. Have older students record and illustrate their ideas. Younger children may dictate their sentence to an adult who records it for them. They illustrate their idea.

4. After all pages have been completed, talk about ordering them in ways that make the most sense conceptually.

5. Compile the pages and bind them together in a traditional class book, or display them on a wall, as a wall book.

6. Invite students to reread the book frequently.

ALTERNATIVES

1. Allow each student to identify several learnings from the lesson or unit of study and develop his or her own multipage book.

2. Have students generate in small groups as many statements as they wish. Groups may share their statements with the entire class and each student selects one to illustrate.

3. Use a different pattern (or "frame") as a model. Kingfisher Publications has an "I Wonder Why" series. Each page of *I Wonder Why Snakes Shed Their Skin and Other Questions about Reptiles* (O'Neill, 1998), for example, has one or two questions ("Why do lizards lose their tails?" "Why do snakes stare?") followed by a paragraph answer. Have students think about their learning after a lesson or unit of study, generate questions that they are capable of answering, and write an "I Wonder Why" book.

4. Frames that are original, rather than found in literature, can also serve as the foundation for effective student writings. One sixth grader, for example, used the frame, "I didn't see . . ." "but I did see . . ." to structure his PowerPoint presentation on ancient Sumer. The text of some of its slides is found in Figure S50.1.

TIME ALLOTMENT

Depending on how elaborate you wish the final product to be, this strategy may take from 15 or 20 minutes to more than an hour.

EXAMPLES

Chapter 2's sample fifth-grade science lesson (Figure 2.6) uses "I Didn't Know That . . ." Response Frames. Figure S50.1 shows some text from a student's PowerPoint presentation on ancient Sumer. Figures S50.2 and S50.3 share "I didn't know that . . ." statements generated by kindergarteners after a field trip to an aquarium and fifth graders after listening to a book on sleep, both of which students subsequently illustrated.

My Journey Back In Time or Things I Didn't (and Did) See in Sumer

I didn't see . . . a car.

But I did see . . . a chariot.

Sumerians invented the first wheel. Early wheels were made out of solid wood. Later they were made out of the hub, the spokes, and the felloes (or bent wooden pieces). Sumerians used wheels on the chariot. The chariot was a box-type car on top of four wheels dragged by onagers (wild horse-like creatures).

I didn't see . . . cursive.

But I did see . . . cuneiforms.

Cuneiforms were a wedge-shaped system of writing. They have idea symbols, picture symbols, and sound symbols. Later, cuneiforms evolved to only sound symbols.

I didn't see . . . a church.

But I did see . . . a ziggurat.

A ziggurat was a tall building that had many different uses. It was used as a place of government, a working place, a gathering place, and a temple. Most importantly, it was a shrine. The ziggurat was placed in the middle of the city so the gods would not punish the city.

Figure S50.1   Sample Text from a Sixth-grade Student's PowerPoint Presentation on Ancient Sumer

- I didn't know that most sharks aren't dangerous to humans.
- I didn't know that sea life is so colorful.
- I didn't know that sea turtles are endangered.
- I didn't know that some species of jellies are very small and some are very big.
- I didn't know that sea otters have the densest fur of all mammals.
- I didn't know that kelp is used in ice cream.
- I didn't know that the sunflower sea star can get up to 39 inches from tip to tip.
- I didn't know that some crabs look like rocks.
- I didn't know that seahorses are dried and used as medicine in some Asian countries.
- I didn't know that the red octopus can change to white in less than one second.

Figure S50.2 "I Didn't Know That . . ." Responses Developed by Kindergarteners after a Trip to an Aquarium

I didn't know that . . .

- losing sleep might cause you to have difficulty with language, memory, concentration, and making decisions the next day.
- when you need to heal from something, your body makes you feel sleepy.
- scientists aren't sure why people yawn.
- some foods (like milk and turkey) contain tryptophan that makes you sleepy.
- plants have a daily schedule.
- during REM sleep, most people are paralyzed.
- deep sleep occurs before 2 A.M. for most people.
- dreams may be a type of exercise that helps the brain develop.
- if you are prevented from dreaming somehow, your brain makes up for it by giving you extra dream sleep as soon as it can.
- snoring may have been a way our bodies protected us from predators at night.
- about 15% of kids sleepwalk at least once.
- giraffes and elephants sleep only about 3 hours a day; cats sleep about 16 hours and bats sleep 20 hours.

Figure S50.3 "I Didn't Know That . . ." Responses Developed by Fifth-grade Students after Reading a Book on Sleep by Romanek (2002)

TROUBLESHOOTING

1. If you wish to compile the pages into a book, ensure that students all turn their papers the same direction, unless you do not mind that readers must rotate the book occasionally.

2. If the pages of the book will be displayed on a wall, text and illustrations must be large and vivid enough to be seen from across the classroom.

3. Students may wish to examine the original materials in order to develop accurate illustrations. If the lesson or unit drew from a textbook, students may refer to their text. If it drew from materials that only you have, consider making multiple copies available. For instance, in Figure S50.3, one of the authors shared an informational trade book with students. She borrowed several copies from the local library so that students could use them as they began their work.

TEACHER RESOURCES: TEMPLATES FOR SELECTED STRATEGIES

Appointment Clock

Appointment Log

Time	Appointment (Record name in this column.)
Spring	
Summer	
Fall	
Winter	

STRATEGY 1 Quick Scans

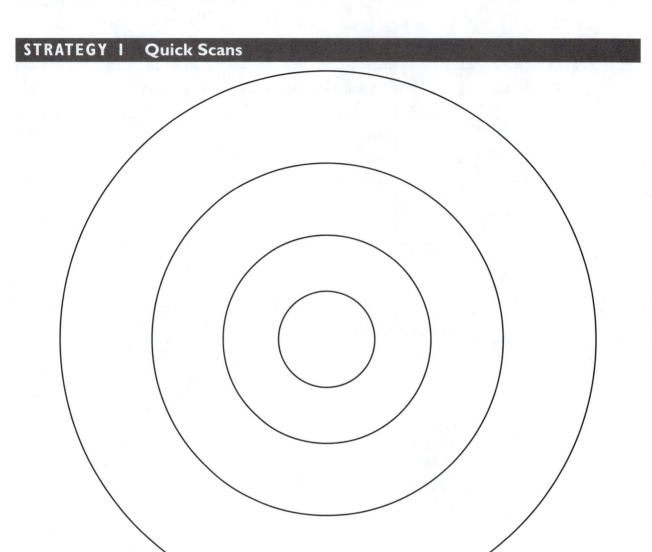

STRATEGY 4   Idea Share

My Idea

Idea I Received in a Trade

Reason I Traded

STRATEGY 5 Partner Share

| Partner A |
| Partner B |
| Partner A |
| Partner B |
| Partner A |
| Partner B |
| Partner A |
| Partner B |

STRATEGY 5   Partner Share

Partner A	Partner B
Partner A	Partner B
Partner A	Partner B
Partner A	Partner B
Partner A	Partner B
Partner A	Partner B
Partner A	Partner B

STRATEGY 6 **Group Graphs**

STRATEGY 6   Group Graphs

STRATEGY 7   Overheard Quotes

My Quote
Initial Impressions
Impressions after Hearing Other Quotes
Patterns Noted in Group Sharing

STRATEGY 9   Important Words

STRATEGY 9   Important Words

1.	6.
2.	7.
3.	8.
4.	9.
5.	10.

Paragraph

STRATEGY 11   Think-Pair-Share

Think (Record your ideas.)

Pair (Record one or more ideas you and your partner discussed.)

Share (Record something interesting you heard during the group sharing.)

STRATEGY 14   Make the Point

Resize and color these images to suit your purposes. Either print them on transparencies and cut them out for pointers that are transparent or translucent, or print them on paper for opaque pointers. Use them on the overhead projector or, if you print them very large, on the board to highlight key terms and ideas.

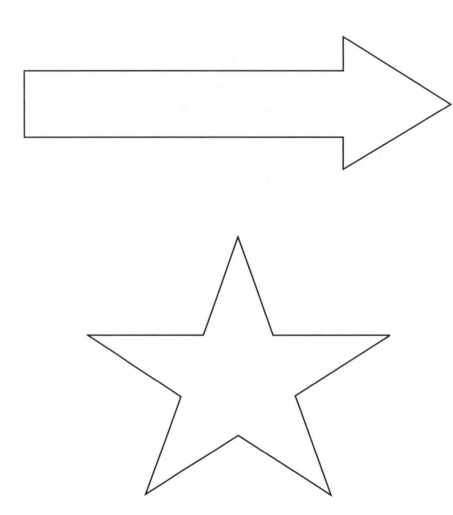

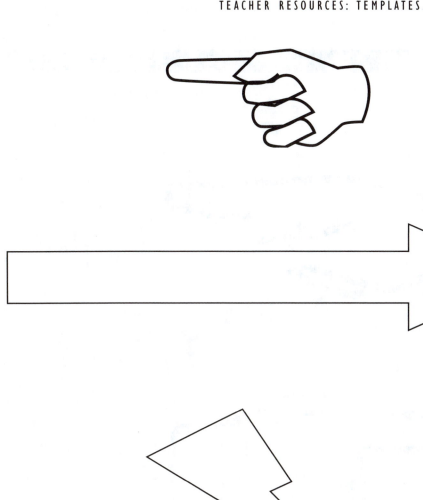

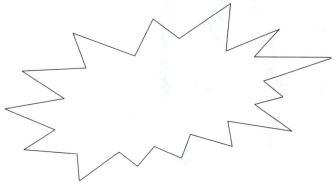

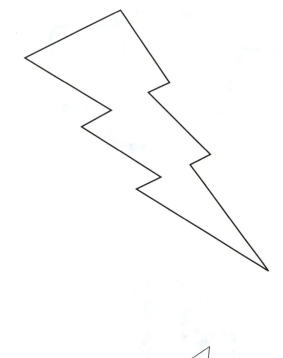

STRATEGY 19 Four Corners

	SA	A	D	SD
1.	SA	A	D	SD
2.	SA	A	D	SD
3.	SA	A	D	SD
4.	SA	A	D	SD
5.	SA	A	D	SD
6.	SA	A	D	SD
7.	SA	A	D	SD
8.	SA	A	D	SD
9.	SA	A	D	SD
10.	SA	A	D	SD

STRATEGY 23 Question Only

Who?

What?

When?

Where?

Why?

How?

STRATEGY 23 Question Only

Initial Questions	Subsequent Questions
Who?	Who?
What?	What?
When?	When?
Where?	Where?
Why?	Why?
How?	How?

STRATEGY 23   Question Only

Know-Want-Learn (KWL) Chart		
What We Know	What We Want to Learn	What We Learned

STRATEGY 25   Object-based Inquiry

Observations

What I Wonder

What I Found Out

Conclusions

STRATEGY 26 Problem-based Learning

What Do We *Know*?	What Do We *Need* to Find Out?	What Do We Have to *Do*?

STRATEGY 28   Photo Analysis

Historical or Factual Analysis

What is your overall impression of the photograph?	
Who or what is in the photograph?	What is happening in the photograph?
When was the photograph taken?	Where was it taken?
What do you know about the subject of the photograph?	
What can you conclude about the subject, events, or time period in the photograph?	
Why was the photograph taken?	
How might the photograph have been used originally?	
What is the message, idea, or thought suggested by the photograph?	

Is the photograph a valid historical document?
What questions has the photograph raised?
What sources might you use to learn more?

STRATEGY 28   Photo Analysis

Artistic Analysis

What is your overall impression of the photo?

What decisions did the photographer make regarding the arrangement of things in this photo?

What do you know about how this photo was created?

What are the important visual features of this photo?

What is the message of this photo?

STRATEGY 29   Structured Decision Making

Weighted Sum Chart

Decision to be made

	Criterion 1 _____	Criterion 2 _____	Criterion 3 _____	Total Rating for Each Option
Option 1 _____ _____				
Option 2 _____ _____				
Option 3 _____ _____				

Rate each option for each criterion. Optional: Weight the criteria and then multiply each rating by the weight for a final rating in each cell. Add the ratings across each row to find a total rating for each option.

STRATEGY 29   **Structured Decision Making**

PMI Chart

Plus	Minus	Interesting

STRATEGY 29   Structured Decision Making

Six Thinking Hats Mat

(Color the hats and use on overhead transparency or at desks.)

White Hat

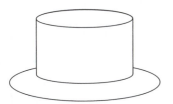

What are the facts?

Green Hat

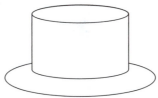

What are the possibilities?

Yellow Hat

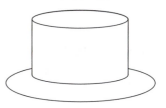

What are the benefits?

Black Hat

What are the drawbacks?

Red Hat

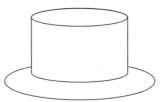

What are our feelings?

Blue Hat

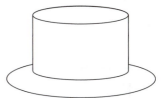

How can we organize
and summarize?

STRATEGY 37 Give One, Get One

STRATEGY 37   Give One, Get One

STRATEGY 37 Give One, Get One

Directions for Fold-up Book

1. Fold paper into eighths. Crease all folds very well. Unfold.

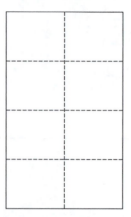

2. Refold the paper in half as shown below, with the folded edge at the top and the open edge at the bottom. Starting at the top, cut the paper along the vertical fold until you reach the horizontal fold.

Cut along the vertical fold. Stop at the intersection of the folds.

Folded edge

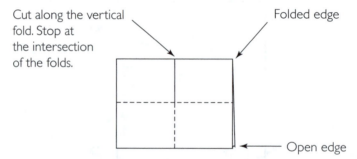

Open edge

3. Hold the folded paper up. Grasp the paper on both sides of the cut and gently pull the two sides away from each other. Separate the bottom edges as you do so. You will create a star shape. Each section of the star is a page of your book. Press the pages together.

Top view

Source: Yopp, H. K., & Yopp, R. H. (2006). *Literature-based reading activities*. 4th ed. Boston: Allyn & Bacon.

STRATEGY 38   Sticker Selection

Sticker	Meaning

STRATEGY 39 Treasure Hunts

Team Builder

Find someone who

Is left-handed who has met someone famous	Knows someone one language	Speaks more than	Has more than two pets
Has traveled outside the state	Has traveled outside the country	Knows how to water ski	Has known you for three or more years
Has the same hobby as you	Has recently read a really good book	Is new to the school	Has the same color of hair or eyes as you
Has visited the Grand Canyon	Has a birthday in the same month as you	Has recently seen the same movie as you name as you	Has the same number of letters in his or her first

STRATEGY 43   Q & A Match

Question	Answer
Question	Answer
Question	Answer
Question	Answer
Question	Answer
Question	Answer
Question	Answer
Question	Answer
Question	Answer
Question	Answer
Question	Answer
Question	Answer
Question	Answer
Question	Answer

STRATEGY 46 Word Journal

Word One	Word Two	Word Three
Word	Word	Word
Reason	Reason	Reason

STRATEGY 49   Found Poems

Words or Phrases I Found

The Poem I Found

REFERENCES

Afflerbach, P. (2002). Teaching reading self-assessment strategies. In C. C. Block & M. Pressley (Eds.), *Comprehension instruction: Research-based best practices* (pp. 96–111). New York: Guilford.

Alderfer, C. (1972). *Existence, relatedness, & growth.* New York: Free Press.

Alvarado A. E., & Herr, P. R. (2003). *Inquiry-based learning using everyday objects.* Thousand Oaks, CA: Corwin.

Amato, M. (2000). *The word eater.* New York: Holiday House.

American Association of School Librarians & Association for Educational Communications and Technology. (1998). *Information literacy standards for student learning: Standards and indicators.* Retrieved March 27, 2006, from http://www.ala.org/aaslTemplate.cfm?Section=Information_Power&Template=/ContentManagement/ContentDisplay.cfm&ContentID=19937

Ames, C. A. (1990). Motivation: What teachers need to know. *Teachers College Record, 91*(3), 409–21.

Anderson, R. (1984). Role of reader's schema in comprehension, learning, and memory. In R. Anderson, J. Osborn, & R. Tierney (Eds.), *Learning to read in American schools: Basal readers and content texts.* Hillsdale, NJ: Erlbaum.

Anderson, T. H., & Armbruster, B. B. (1984). Studying. In P. D. Pearson, R. Barr, M. L. Kamil, & P. Mosenthal (Eds.), *Handbook of reading research.* New York: Longman.

Angelo, T. A., & Cross, K. P. (1993). *Classroom assessment techniques: A handbook for college teachers* (2nd ed.). San Francisco: Jossey Bass.

Apel, S. B. (1995, Spring). Kinetic classroom. *The Law Teacher.* Gonzaga University School of Law. Retrieved March 26, 2006, from http://www.law.gonzaga.edu/Programs/Institute+for+Law+School+Teaching/The+Law+Teacher+-+Newsletter/Past+Issues+of+The+Law+Teacher/Spring+1995/default.htm (www.law.gonzaga.edu/The+Law+Teacher+.+Newsletter/)

Aronson, E., Stephen, C., Sikes, J., Blaney, N., & Snapp, M. (1978). *The jigsaw classroom.* Beverly Hills, CA: Sage.

Babbitt, N. (1975). *Tuck everlasting.* New York: Farrar, Straus and Giroux.

Barley, Z., Lauer, P. A., Arens, S. A., Apthorp, H. A., Englert, K. S., Snow, D., & Akiba, M. (2002). Helping at-risk students meet standards: A synthesis of evidence-based classroom practices. Mid-Continent Research for Education and Learning, Aurora, CO. Retrieved March 26, 2006, from http://www.eric.ed.gov/contentdelivery/servlet/ERICServlet?accno=ED475904

Blachowicz, C. L. (1986). Making connections: Alternatives to the vocabulary notebook. *Journal of Reading, 29,* 643–649.

Bloom, B. (1956). *Taxonomy of educational objectives: Handbook I cognitive domain.* New York: David McKay Co.

Bower, B., & Lobdell, J. (2003). *Social studies alive: Engaging diverse learners in the elementary classroom.* Palo Alto, CA: Teachers' Curriculum Institute.

Brophy, J. (1987). Synthesis of research for motivating students to learn. *Educational Leadership, 45*(2), 40–48.

Brophy, J. (1997). Effective instruction. In H. J. Walberg & G. D. Haertel (Eds.), *Psychology and educational practice* (pp. 212–232). Berkeley: McCutchan.

Brophy, J. (2004). *Motivating students to learn* (2nd ed.). Mahwah, NJ: Lawrence Erlbaum.

Brophy, J., & Good, T. (1986). Teacher behavior and student achievement. In M. Wittrock (Ed.), *Handbook of research on teaching* (3rd ed., pp. 328–375). New York: Macmillan.

Brown, L. K., & Brown, M. (1990). *Dinosaurs alive and well! A guide to good health.* New York: Little, Brown.

Bruner, J. (1986). *Actual minds, possible worlds.* Cambridge, MA: Harvard University Press.

Bruner, J., Goodnow, J., & Austin, A. (1956). *A study of thinking.* New York: Wiley.

California Department of Education. (1999). *Reading/language arts framework for California public schools, kindergarten through grade twelve.* Sacramento, CA: California Department of Education.

California Department of Education. (2003). *Health framework for California public schools, kindergarten through grade twelve.* Sacramento, CA: California Department of Education.

Cazden, C. (1986). Classroom discourse. In M. Wittrock (Ed.), *Handbook of research on teaching* (3rd ed., pp. 432–462). New York: Macmillan.

Chaillé, C., & Britain, L. (2003). *The young child as scientist: A constructivist approach to early childhood science education* (3rd ed.). Boston: Allyn & Bacon.

Charles, C. M., & Senter, G. W. (1995). *Elementary classroom management* (2nd ed.). White Plains, NY: Longman.

Chin, C., Brown, D. E., & Bruce, B. C. (2002). Student-generated questions: A meaningful aspect of learning in science. *International Journal of Science Education, 24,* 521–549.

Coates, G. D., & Stenmark, J. K. (1997). *Family math for young children.* Berkeley, CA: The Regents of the University of California.

Cohen, P. A., Kulik, J. A., & Kulik, C. C. (1982). Educational outcomes of tutoring: A meta-analysis of findings. *American Educational Research Journal, 19,* 237–248.

Corno, L. (1992). Encouraging students to take responsibility for learning and performance. *Elementary School Journal, 93*(1), 69–83.

Cotton, K. (1991). Teaching thinking skills. *School Improvement Research Series*. Northwest Regional Laboratory. Retrieved March 26, 2006, from http://www.nwrel.org/scpd/sirs/6/cu11.html

Cummins, J. (1981). The role of primary language development in promoting educational success for language minority students. In California State Department of Education (Ed.), *Schooling and language minority students: A theoretical framework* (pp. 3–49). Los Angeles: National Dissemination and Assessment Center. (ERIC Document Reproduction Service No. 249 773)

Davis, R. (1981). A plea for the use of student dialogs. *Improving College and University Teaching, 29*(4), 155–161.

De Bono, E. (1985). *Six thinking hats*. Toronto: Key Porter Books Limited.

De Bono, E. (1994). *De Bono's thinking course*. New York: Facts on File.

Dewey, J. (1909). *How we think*. Boston: DC Heath.

Dillon, J. T. (1988a). *Questioning and teaching: A manual of practice*. London: Croom Helm.

Dillon, J. T. (1988b). The remedial status of student questioning. *Journal of Curriculum Studies, 20*, 197–210.

Dochy, F., Segers, M., & Buehl, M. M. (1999). The relation between assessment practices and outcomes of studies: The case of research on prior knowledge. *Review of Educational Research, 69*(2), 145–186.

Dunning, S., & Stafford, W. (1992). *Getting the knack: 20 poetry writing exercises*. Urbana, IL: National Council for Teachers of English.

Echevarria, J., & Graves, A. (1998). *Sheltered content instruction: Teaching English-language learners with diverse abilities*. Boston: Allyn & Bacon.

Edwards, J., & Fraser, K. (1983). Concept maps as reflectors of conceptual understanding. *Research in Science Education, 13*, 19–26.

Elbow, P. (1973). *Writing without teachers*. New York: Oxford University Press.

Elbow, P. (1994). *Writing for learning—not just for demonstrating learning*. Retrieved March 26, 2006, from www.ntlf.com/html/lib/bib/writing.htm

Elias, M. J. (2003). *Academic and social-emotional learning*. Brussels: International Academy of Education and Geneva: International Bureau of Education.

Emig, J. (1977). Writing as a mode of learning. *College Composition and Communication, 28*, 122–127.

Falk, K. B., & Wehby, J. H. (2001). The effects of peer-assisted learning strategies on the beginning reading skills of young children with emotional or behavioral disorders. *Behavioral Disorders, 26*, 344–359.

Findley, M. J., & Cooper, H. M. (1983). Locus of control and academic achievement: A literature review. *Journal of Personality and Social Psychology, 44*, 419–427.

Fletcher, R. (1998). *Flying solo*. New York: Clarion.

Florida Grade Level Expectations. (1999). Retrieved April 27, 2005, from www.statestandards.com

Forbes, E. H. (1943). *Johnny Tremain*. New York: Houghton Mifflin.

Frohardt, D. C. (1999). *Teaching art with books kids love: Teaching art appreciation, elements of art, and principles of design with award-winning children's books*. Golden, CO: Fulcrum.

Fulwiler, T. (1980). Journals across the disciplines. *English Journal, 69*(12), 14.

Gage, N. L., & Berliner, D. C. (1975). *Educational psychology*. Chicago: Rand McNally.

Gagne, R. M. (1965). *The conditions of learning*. New York: Holt, Rinehart and Winston.

Glasser, W. (1986). *Control theory in the classroom*. New York: Harper & Row.

Goldhaber, D. D., & Brewer, D. (2000). Does teacher certification matter? High school teacher certification status and student achievement. *Educational Evaluation and Policy Analysis, 22*, 129–145.

Good, T., & Brophy, J. (2000). *Looking in classrooms* (8th ed.). New York: Longman.

Goodlad, J. (1984). *A place called school*. New York: McGraw-Hill.

Gregory, G. G., & Chapman, C. (2002). *Differentiated instructional strategies: One size doesn't fit all*. Thousand Oaks, CA: Corwin.

Guillaume, A. M. (1997). Oohs and icks. *Science and Children, 34*(7), 20–23.

Guillaume, A. M. (2005). *Classroom mathematics inventory*. Boston: Allyn & Bacon.

Haddix, M. (2000). *Among the hidden*. New York: Aladdin.

Hart, L. (1983). *Human brain, human learning*. New York: Longman.

Henkes, K. (1991). *Chrysanthemum*. New York: Greenwillow.

Hibbing, A. N., & Rankin-Erickson, J. L. (2003). A picture is worth a thousand words: Using visual images to improve comprehension for middle school struggling readers. *The Reading Teacher, 56*, 758–770.

Hobbs, W. (1997). *Far north*. New York: HarperCollins.

Horak, V. M., & Horak, W. J. (1983). Let's do it: Take a chance. *Arithmetic Teacher, 30*(9), 8–13.

Horton, P. B., McConney, A. A., Gallo, M., Woods, A. L., Senn, G. J., & Hamelin, D. (1993). An investigation of the effectiveness of concept mapping as an instructional tool. *Science Education, 77*(1), 95–111.

Hunter, M. (1969). *Motivation theory for teachers*. Thousand Oaks, CA: Corwin.

Johnson, D. D., & Pearson, P. D. (1984). *Teaching reading vocabulary* (2nd ed.). New York: Holt, Rinehart and Winston.

Jones, F. (2000). *Tools for teaching*. Santa Cruz, CA: Fredric H. Jones & Associates.

Kagan, S. (1994). *Cooperative learning*. San Clemente, CA: Kagan.

Keller, J. M. (1987). Development and use of the ARCS model of motivational design. *Journal of Instructional Development, 10*(3), 2–10.

Kellner, D. (2002). Critical perspectives on visual imagery in media and cyberculture. *Journal of Visual Literacy, 22*(1), 81–90.

Koch, J. (2005). *Science stories: Science methods for elementary and middle school teachers* (3rd ed.). Boston: Houghton Mifflin.

Kohn, A. (1993). *Punished by rewards*. Boston: Houghton Mifflin.

Krashen, S. D. (1981). *Second language acquisition and second language learning*. Pergamon Press. Retrieved October 30, 2005, from http://www.sdkrashen.com/SL_Acquisition_and_Learning/index.html

Lancia, P. J. (1997). Literary borrowing: The effects of literature on children's writing. *The Reading Teacher, 50*, 470–475.

Leal, D. J. (1993). The power of literary peer-group discussions: How children collaboratively negotiate meaning. *The Reading Teacher, 47*(2), 114–120.

Linksman, R. (2005). The fine line between ADHD and kinesthetic learners. *Latitudes, 1*(6). Retrieved March 26, 2006, from http://www.latitudes.org/articles/learn01.html

Lyman, F. (1981). The responsive classroom discussion. In A. S. Anderson (Ed.), *Mainstreaming digest* (pp. 109–113). College Park, MD: University of Maryland College of Education.

Many, J. E., Fyfe, R., Lewis, G., & Mitchell, E. (1996). Traversing the topical landscape: Exploring students' self-directed reading-writing-research processes. *Reading Research Quarterly, 31*(1), 12–35.

Manzo, A. V., & Manzo, U. (1997). *Content area literacy: Interactive teaching for active learning*. Upper Saddle River, NJ: Prentice-Hall.

Marzano, R. J. (2004). *Building background knowledge for academic achievement*. Alexandria, VA: Association for Supervision and Curriculum Development.

Marzano, R. J., Pickering, D. J., & Pollock, J. E. (2001). *Classroom instruction that works: Research-based strategies for increasing student achievement*. Alexandria, VA: Association for Supervision and Curriculum Development.

Maslow, A. (1954). *Motivation and personality*. New York: Harper.

Mastropieri, M. A., Scruggs, T. E., Spencer, V., & Fontana, J. (2003). Promoting success in high school world history: Peer tutoring versus guided notes. *Learning Disabilities: Research & Practice, 18*(1), 52–65.

McClelland, D. (1987). *Human motivation*. New York: Scott, Foresman.

McKendree, J., Small, C., Stenning, K., & Conlon, T. (2002). The role of representation in teaching and learning in critical thinking. *Educational Review, 54*, 57–67.

McMaster, J. C. (1998). "Doing" literature: Using drama to build literacy classrooms: The segue for a few struggling readers. *The Reading Teacher, 51*, 574–584.

Middendorf, J., & Kalish, A. (1996). The "change-up" in lectures. *TRC Newsletter, 8*(1). Retrieved March 26, 2006, from www.iub.edu/~teaching/changeups.shtml

Miller, G. A. (1956). The magical number seven, plus or minus two: Some limits on our capacity for processing information. *Psychological Review, 63*, 81–97.

Miller, G. A., Galanter, E., & Pribram, K. H. (1960). *Plans and the structure of behavior*. New York: Holt, Rinehart & Winston.

Mintzes, J., Wandersee, J., & Novak, J. D. (2000). *Assessing science understanding*. San Diego: Academic Press.

Morris, R. (2000). *New management handbook*. San Diego: New Management.

National Center for Education Statistics. (2001a). *Average mathematics scores by teachers' reports of undergraduate major, grade 8: 2000*. Retrieved March 26, 2006, from http://nces.ed.gov/nationsreportcard/mathematics/results/preparation.asp

National Center for Education Statistics. (2001b). *Average science scale scores by teacher's undergraduate major, grades 4 and 8 (public and nonpublic schools combined): 2000*. Retrieved March 26, 2006, from http://nces.ed.gov/nationsreportcard/science/results/preparation.asp

National Center for Education Statistics. (2003). *Highlights from the TIMMS 1999 video study of eighth-grade mathematics teaching*. Retrieved March 26, 2006, from http://nces.ed.gov/pubs2003/timssvideo/

National Reading Panel. (2000). *Teaching children to read: An evidence-based assessment of scientific research literature on reading and its implications for reading instruction* (NIH Publication No. 00-4769). Washington, DC: U.S. Government Printing Office.

National Research Council. (1996). *National science education standards*. Washington, DC: National Academy Press.

No Child Left Behind Act of 2001, Pub. L. No. 107–110, 20 U.S. C. § 6301, *et. seq.*

Northwest Regional Educational Laboratory. (2003). *Strategies and resources for mainstream teachers of English language learners*. Portland, OR: Northwest Regional Educational Laboratory. Retrieved March 26, 2006, from http://www.nwrel.org/request/2003may/overview.html

Northwest Regional Educational Laboratory. (2004). *Developing self-directed learners*. Topical summary from the Office of Planning and Service Coordination. Portland, OR: Northwest Regional Educational Laboratory. Retrieved March 26, 2006, from http:// www.nwrel.org/planning/reports/self-direct/

Novak, J. D. (1990). Concept maps and Vee diagrams: Two metacognitive tools for science and mathematics education. *Instructional Science, 19*, 29–52.

Novak, J. D. (1991). Clarify with concept maps: A tool for students and teachers alike. *The Science Teacher, 58*(7), 45–49.

Novak, J. D., & Gowin, D. B. (1984). *Learning how to learn*. New York & Cambridge, UK: Cambridge University Press.

Ogle, D. (1986). K-W-L: A teaching model that develops active reading of expository text. *The Reading Teacher, 39*, 564–570.

Oliver, C. (1998). *I didn't know that mountains gush lava and ash*. Brookfield, CT: Copper Beech.

O'Neill, A. O. (1998). *I wonder why snakes shed their skin and other questions about reptiles.* New York: Kingfisher.

Orem, R. F. (1998). *Biology: Living systems.* New York: Glencoe.

Osborn, A. (1953). *Applied imagination: Principles and procedures of creative thinking.* New York: Charles Scribner's Sons.

Paivio, A. (1971). *Imagery and verbal processes.* New York: Holt, Rinehart and Winston.

Paivio, A. (1986). *Mental representations: A dual coding approach.* New York: Oxford University Press.

Paulsen, G. (1987). *Hatchet.* New York: The Trumpet Club.

Petty, K. (1998). *I didn't know that crocodiles yawn to keep cool and other amazing facts about crocodiles and alligators.* Brookfield, CT: Copper Beech.

Piaget, J. (1929). *The child's conception of the world.* New York: Harcourt, Brace Jovanovich.

Pressley, M. (2002). Comprehension strategies instruction: A turn-of-the-century status report. In C. C. Block & M. Pressley (Eds.), *Comprehension instruction: Research-based best practices* (pp. 11–27). New York: Guilford.

Pressley, M., Johnson, C. J., Symons, S., McGoldrick, J. A., & Kurita, J. A. (1989). Strategies that improve children's memory and comprehension of text. *The Elementary School Journal, 90*(1), 3–32.

Reaves, R. R., Flowers, J. L., & Jewell, L. R. (1993). Effects of writing-to-learn activities on the content knowledge, retention, and attitudes of secondary vocational agriculture students. *Journal of Agricultural Education, 34*(3), 34–40.

Rhem, J. (1998). Problem-based learning: An introduction. *The National Teaching and Learning Forum 8*(1), 1–4. Retrieved March 26, 2006, from http://www.ntlf.com/html/pi/9812/v8n1smpl.pdf

Romanek, T. (2002). *Zzz . . . The most interesting book you'll ever read about sleep.* Toronto: Kids Can Press.

Rose, D. S., Androes, K., Parks, M., & McMahon, S. D. (2000). Imagery-based learning: Improving elementary students' reading comprehension with drama techniques. *The Journal of Educational Research, 94*(1), 55–63.

Rosenshine, B., Meister, C., & Chapman, S. (1996). Teaching students to generate questions: A review of the intervention studies. *Review of Educational Research, 66,* 181–221.

Rowe, M. B. (1972). *Wait-time and rewards as instructional variables, their influence in language, logic, and fate control.* Paper presented at the National Association for Research in Science Teaching, Chicago, IL. ED061103.

Rowe, M. B. (1986). Wait time: Slowing down may be a way of speeding up. *Journal of Teacher Education, 37*(1), 43–50.

Ruhl, K. L., Hughes, C. A., & Schloss, P. J. (1987). Using the pause procedure to enhance lecture recall. *Teacher Education and Special Education, 10,* 14–18.

Sarquis, J. L., Sarquis, M., & Williams, J. P. (1995). *Teaching chemistry with toys: Activities for Grades K–9.* Middletown, OH: Terrific Science Press.

Short, K. G., Harste, J. C., & Burke, C. (1996). Sketch to stretch, sketch me a story, interwoven texts and song maps. In J. C. Harste, K. Short, & C. Burke (Eds.), *Creating classrooms for authors and inquirers* (pp. 528–535). Portsmouth, NH: Heinemann.

Showers, B., Joyce, B., & Bennett, B. (1987). Synthesis of research on staff development: A framework for future study and a state-of-the-art analysis. *Educational Leadership, 45*(3), 77–87.

Silberman, M. (1996). *Active learning: 101 strategies to teach any subject.* Boston: Allyn & Bacon.

Singer, H. (1978). Active comprehension: From answering to asking questions. *The Reading Teacher, 31,* 901–908.

Spencer, V. G., Scruggs, T. E., & Mastropieri, M. A. (2003). Content area learning in middle school social studies classrooms and students with emotional or behavioral disorders: A comparison of strategies. *Behavioral Disorders, 28*(2), 77–93.

Spurlin, Q. (1995). Put science in a bag. *Science and Children, 32*(4), 19–22.

Stahl, R. J. (1994). Using "think-time" and "wait-time" skillfully in the classroom. ERIC Digest. ERIC Clearinghouse for Social Studies/Social Science Education, Bloomington, IN. ED370885.

Stephens, E. C., & Brown, J. E. (2000). *A handbook of content literacy strategies: 75 practical reading and writing ideas.* Norwood, MA: Christopher Gordon.

Strangman, N., & Hall, T. (2004). *Background knowledge.* Curriculum Enhancement Report for the National Center on Accessing the General Curriculum. Retrieved March 26, 2006, from http://www.cast.org/publications/ncac/ncac_backknowledge.html

Stronge, J. H. (2002). *Qualities of effective teachers.* Alexandria, VA: Association for Supervision and Curriculum Development.

Suchman, J. R. (1962). *The elementary school training program in scientific inquiry.* Urbana, IL: Illinois Press.

Suchman, J. R. (1964). *Studies in inquiry training.* In R. Ripple & V. Bookcastle (Eds.), *Piaget reconsidered.* Ithaca, NY: Cornell University Press.

Swain, M. (1985). Communicative competence: Some roles of comprehensible input and comprehensible output in its development. In S. Gass & C. Madden (Eds.), *Input in second language acquisition.* Rowley, MA: Newbury House.

Taba, H. (1967). *Teachers handbook for elementary social studies.* Reading, MA: Addison-Wesley.

Thomas, W. P., & Collier, V. P. (2002). *A National Study of School Effectiveness for Language Minority Students' Long-Term Academic Achievement Final Report: Project 1.1.* Center for Research on Education, Diversity & Excellence. Retrieved March 26, 2006, from http://www.crede.org/research/llaa/1.1_es.html

Torp, L., & Sage, S. (2002). *Problems as possibilities: Problem-based learning for K–16 education* (2nd ed.). Alexandria, VA: Association of Supervision and Curriculum Development.

Tortello, R. (2004). Tableaux vivants in the literature classroom. *The Reading Teacher, 58,* 206–208.

Trabasso, T., & Bouchard, E. (2002). Teaching readers how to comprehend text strategically. In C. C. Block & M. Pressley (Eds.), *Comprehension instruction: Research-based best practices* (pp. 176–200). New York: Guilford.

Tyler, B., Marcus, R., Flatter, C., & Hunt, J. (1975). *Developmental characteristics of children and youth.* Washington, DC: Association for Supervision and Curriculum Development.

United States Department of Education. (2003). *Meeting the highly qualified teachers challenge: The secretary's second annual report of teacher quality.* Retrieved March 26, 2006, from http://www.ed.gov/about/reports/annual/teachprep/2003title-ii-report.pdf

Valencia, R. R., & Villarreal, B. J. (2003). Improving students' reading performance via standards-based school reform: A critique. *The Reading Teacher, 56,* 612–631.

Vaughn, S., Bos, C. S., & Schumm, J. S. (2003). *Teaching exceptional, diverse, and at-risk students in the general education classroom.* Boston: Allyn & Bacon.

Visual Understanding in Education (VUE). (1998). *Guidelines for Image Selection for Beginning Viewers.* New York: Visual Understanding in Education. Retrieved March 26, 2006, from http://www.vue.org/download/Guidelines_for_Image_Select.pdf

Vroom, V. (1964). *Work and motivation.* New York: John Wiley and Sons.

Vygotsky, L. S. (1978). *Mind in society.* Cambridge, MA: Harvard University Press.

Wilson, P. S. (Ed.). (1993). *Research ideas for the classroom: High school mathematics.* New York: Macmillan.

Wingfield, A. (1979). *Human learning and memory.* New York: Harper & Row.

Wong, B. Y. L. (1985). Self-questioning instructional research: A review. *Review of Educational Research, 55,* 227–268.

Yenawine, P. (1997). Thoughts on visual literacy. In J. Flood, S. B. Heath, & D. Lapp (Eds.), *Handbook of research on teaching literacy through the communicative and visual arts* (pp. 845–846). New York: Prentice-Hall.

Yopp, H. K., & Yopp, R. H. (2002). Ten important words: Identifying the big ideas in informational text. *Journal of Content Area Reading, 2,* 7–13.

Yopp, H. K., & Yopp, R. H. (2006). *Literature-based reading activities* (4th ed.). Boston: Allyn & Bacon.

Yopp, R. H. (1988). Questioning and active comprehension. *Questioning Exchange: A Multidisciplinary Review, 3*(2), 231–238.